The
RAPTURE

TIM LaHAYE

Ms. Joye Spears
323 W Fifth St.
Pawnee, OK 74058

HARVEST HOUSE PUBLISHERS
Eugene, Oregon 97402

Cover by Terry Dugan Design, Minneapolis, Minnesota

Published in association with the literary agency of Alive Communications, Inc., 7680 Goddard Street, Suite 200, Colorado Springs, CO 80920.

THE RAPTURE
Copyright © 2002 by Tim LaHaye
Published by Harvest House Publishers
Eugene, Oregon 97402

Library of Congress Cataloging-in-Publication Data
LaHaye, Tim F.
    [Rapture under attack]
    The rapture / Tim LaHaye.
        p. cm. — (The LaHaye prophecy library series)
    Includes bibliographical references.
    ISBN 0-7369-0952-4
    1. Rapture (Christian eschatology) I. Title.

BT887 .L345 2002
236'.9—dc21   2001051581

Printed in the United States of America.

02 03 04 05 06 07 08 / DC-MS / 10 9 8 7 6 5 4 3 2 1

Dedicated to the members of the Pre-Trib Research Center, a group of dedicated prophecy scholars, authors, teachers, and preachers of various denominations who are committed to rightly dividing the biblical teachings about Christ's often-promised second coming. Their careful scholarship, teaching, and writing is returning the "blessed hope" aspect of His coming to the body of Christ, providing scriptural answers to their sincere questions, and inspiring many to renewed dedication to holiness, evangelism, and missions.

About the Pre-Trib Research Center

In 1991, Dr. Tim LaHaye became concerned about the growing number of Bible teachers and Christians who were attacking the pre-Tribulational view of the Rapture as well as the literal interpretation of Bible prophecy. In response, he wrote this book, *The Rapture*. In the process of writing this book, Tim was impressed by the Christian leaders who, in Great Britain during the 1820s and 1830s, set up conferences for the purpose of discussing Bible prophecy. In 1992, Tim contacted Thomas Ice about the possibility of setting up similar meetings, which led to the first gathering of what is now known as the Pre-Trib Study Group in December 1992.

In 1993, Dr. LaHaye and Dr. Ice founded the Pre-Trib Research Center (PTRC) for the purpose of encouraging the research, teaching, propagation, and defense of the pre-Tribulational Rapture and related Bible prophecy doctrines. It is the PTRC that has sponsored the annual study group meetings since that time, and there are now over 200 members comprised of top prophecy scholars, authors, Bible teachers, and prophecy students.

LaHaye and Ice, along with other members of the PTRC, have since produced an impressive array of literature in support of the pre-Tribulational view of the Rapture as well as the literal interpretation of Bible prophecy. Members of the PTRC are available to speak at prophecy conferences and churches, and the organization has a monthly publication titled *Pre-Trib Perspectives*.

To find out more about the PTRC
and its publications, write to:

Pre-Trib Research Center
P.O. Box 14111
Arlington, TX 76094

You can also get information through the Web site:
www.timlahaye.com

Contents

Acknowledgments

No author is a creative island unto himself. We are all influenced by others, sometimes consciously and at other times unknowingly. The following are individuals and groups that I know influenced me in the writing of this book, to whom I wish to express my heartfelt gratitude.

The authors I quote and those in the bibliography

Most of all, my wife, Beverly, who graciously endured my mental preoccupation during the writing of this book

The many who corresponded with me on the subject and sent material:

Dr. James Combs, Springfield, Missouri

Dr. Thomas Ice, Arlington, Texas

Dr. David Allen Lewis, Springfield, Missouri

Dr. Richard Mayhue, Sun Valley, California

Dr. Ray Stedman, Palo Alto, California

Dr. Robert Sumner, Murfreesboro, Tennessee

Tricia Tillin, Derbyshire, England

And finally, Harvest House Publishers, for publishing the book and making it available to the Christian community

Introduction

The amazing response to our Left Behind® series of prophetic novels (coauthored with Jerry Jenkins and still enjoying top bestseller status in sales in both hardback and paperback for all the books) proves that laymen who take the Bible literally want to believe what it says—that Jesus Christ will "descend from heaven with a shout....the dead in Christ will rise first. Then we who are alive and remain shall be caught up [raptured] with them in the clouds to meet the Lord in the air. And thus we shall always be with the Lord" (1 Thessalonians 4:16-18). They also believe, or want to believe, that this will occur before the awful times of tribulation which our Lord said "will try the whole earth," calling it the "great tribulation, such as has not been since the beginning of the world until this time, no, nor ever shall be" (Matthew 24:21).

And why shouldn't they believe it? It is what the New Testament clearly teaches if you consider all the prophecy passages about the Second Coming and take them literally (unless the immediate context indicates otherwise). When Jesus promised to come again and take His followers to be with Him in His Father's house (John 14:1-3), He meant it. Believing that the Rapture takes place before the Tribulation allows plenty of time for us to enjoy the Father's house, which He has been preparing for almost 2,000 years, before returning with Him to this earth when He sets up His 1,000-year kingdom age of peace.

This concept is not new; it has been held by many for centuries. In fact, I shall show that it was clearly taught in the ancient world as early as A.D. 376 and in America as early as 1784, long before John Darby was born. Mr. Darby may rightly be accused of popularizing the concept in England, America, and Canada during the nineteenth century, but he certainly did not invent it.

Yet for some reason this concept, which has brought so much hope and comfort to millions of Christians throughout church history, has been under savage attack during the last 60 years by those who refuse to take prophecy as literally as they do other Scriptures. Some of these attacks have taken the form of vicious personal assaults on those who held the position, others have involved gross distortions of the facts. Unfortunately, those who have a vendetta against the pre-Trib Rapture have been amazingly successful in causing many innocent victims to abandon their expectation of rapture in their lifetime and in the process have not only stolen their hope but, in some cases, their zeal for service.

In fact, the original publication of this book was ignited by a letter I received from an old friend that contained a vicious and frenzied attack on the pre-Tribulation rapture theory. Obviously, my friend had changed his views! We had corresponded at some length over my concern that he was working too closely with Reconstructionists who refused to accept the plain teachings of the Bible on the nature of the kingdom of God.

In one of his letters, this graduate of Dallas Theological Seminary (he had been "steeped in dispensational teachings, including the pre-Trib rapture of the church") suddenly took off on a tangent to condemn this "false teaching" in terms I had never heard used in that context. I was flabbergasted and concerned.

Some weeks later a pastor friend wanted to make sure that when I held an upcoming family seminar in his church I wouldn't inject any of my prophetical views. The reason was that he no longer believed the church would be raptured before the Tribulation. Apparently he was looking forward to going through it.

About that time I received in the mail a booklet on the Rapture by an evangelist who claimed he was reared in a funda-mentalist background and trained in a dispensational school. He attacked the pre-Tribulation position with a vehemence I am used to hearing only from Christians who attack heretics who deliberately deceive people about the deity of our Lord. He made claims and accusations against some of my theological heroes that could not be ignored.

Then while jogging one morning I was listening to a cassette tape by a minister friend I deeply admire and love, only to find he had moved to a mid-Tribulation view of our Lord's return. A short time later, a nationally known TV evangelist friend sent me his new book on the kingdom, in which he teaches the post-Tribulation position.

That started me on the greatest research project of my life. Now, after 10,000 pages of reading, visits to both congressional and Christian college and university libraries, computer book research, a canvas of used bookstores, reading hundreds of letters, many conversations both in this country and the British Isles, and after the careful examination of every Bible verse related to the subject, I can honestly say I am more convinced than ever of the pre-Tribulation rapture position.

This book is the result of my research. It is my prayer that it will reaffirm the faith of all its readers in the fact that the Bible teaches that Jesus Christ is coming soon, and that He will rapture His church to be with Him in the Father's house—at least seven years before He descends in "power and great glory" to set up His 1,000-year kingdom of peace on earth. This truth should both comfort God's people in times of chaos and challenge us to faithful service until He comes.

After the publication of this book in 1992, I invited a number of the leading prophecy scholars, writers, and teachers of the pre-Trib view of end-time events to meet me for three days in Dallas, Texas, for in-depth discussions on prophecy. Dr. John Walvoord was there (the dean of all living prophecy scholars and authors), as were Drs. Charles Ryrie, Dwight Pentecost, Stanley Toussaint, Gerald Stanton, Hal Lindsey, Dr. Thomas Ice, and many others. We all agreed that a permanent group was needed, so we formed the Pre-Trib Research Center (PTRC). Since then, almost 200 prophecy scholars have joined from many Christian colleges, seminaries, Bible schools, churches, and related ministries.

For ten years this group has met faithfully for three days annually to consider all the attacks on our position, to study its scriptural basis, and to provide biblical answers to the questions against it. It has since been thrilling to see the plethora of good books, videos, and cassettes on the end times that have come out of the pens of our members. Some have gone out to start whole ministries about the end times.

In March of 1998, we held our first regional prophecy conference in the Washington, D.C., suburbs. It was a smashing success. Now we are contacting pastors of megachurches throughout the country in an attempt to hold such conferences in every region in the nation. We are convinced that such concentrated times of study under some of the leading prophecy experts of our day can energize the whole body of Christ to greater heights of consecration, evangelism, and missions in these last days. Hopefully, the reading of this book will not only stir your heart, but answer any questions you may have about the pre-Tribulation position. If it doesn't, you may write to Pre-Trib Research Center at P.O. Box 14111, Arlington, TX 76094-4111, and we will try to address your questions. We will also acquaint you with the regional prophecy conference nearest you and send you a sample copy of the *Pre-Trib Perspective,* the bimonthly magazine edited by the Center's executive director, author, and prophecy scholar, Dr. Thomas Ice.

After attending all of the three-day sessions of the Pre-Trib Research Center, listening to the cassettes one or more times, and considering all the current questions and attacks on the pre-Trib position, I am not only more convinced than ever in the rightness of this biblical position, but I see a trend in the body of Christ in that direction, not only in believing it, but also in defending it from Scripture. I think by the time you finish reading this book you will agree that one day soon Jesus is coming in the air to rapture His church and take her back to His Father's house *before the greatest time of tribulation in all of history,* called by the Hebrew prophets "the time of Jacob's trouble." The reason the prophets gave it that title is because it is meant for Israel, not the church. Then after that seven-year period of tribulation, which will be governed by the Antichrist or "man of sin" (2 Thessalonians 2:3) that the elite planners of the one-world government are working tirelessly to prepare for, Jesus our Lord will finish His second coming by descending in the midst of the Battle of Armageddon to conquer the world and usher in His wonderful 1,000-year kingdom of peace.

The marvelous plan that God has for the future of His children is the most inspiring challenge in the world. Don't let anyone steal it from you! May reading this book make that "blessed hope" (Titus 2:13) real in your life.

Part One

THE "BLESSED HOPE"
OF CHRIST'S RETURN

Chapter One

Great
Expectation

Down through the centuries millions of Christians have lived out their hours and days and years...an Expectation.

Not always in the forefront of their thoughts, it was yet never out of their thoughts.

It hovered just over the horizon of their daily responsibilities and cares, like the first pale light of a rising sun.

It walked with them down lonely, sorrowful, sometimes torturous pathways. A silent companion. A comforting presence.

Through dry years and bleak landscapes and withered hopes, it bubbled up from deep within them. A hidden fountain. A secret well of refreshment and joy. A hope beyond all hope.

And the Expectation was that in the next breath,
the next blink of the eye,
the next tick of the clock,
the next beat of the heart,
the next rustle of the leaves,
the next sigh,
the Lord Jesus Christ could descend from heaven with a shout and call them home.

Prisoners have looked expectantly through dungeon windows. Slaves have looked up from the fields. Children have wondered at a slant of sunlight through a sudden break in the clouds. Jesus is coming. Soon! Maybe today. Maybe tonight. Maybe before I draw my next breath.

And yet that comforting belief is under greater attack today more than at any time in recent history. Christian mothers now worry that their precious sons and daughters will be forced to undergo the horrors of the Great Tribulation. Christian fathers fret about the impossible task of keeping their families alive through the most gruesome period the world has ever known.

It Makes Me Wonder...

Are you able to look at your children playing in the sunlight and believe firmly in your heart that they will not have to endure the monstrous horrors of the Tribulation?

Are you able to sit at the deathbed of a believing loved one and cling to the hope that before your own life has ended—in an instant of time—you may meet again in the clouds?

Are you able to impress on your teenagers the need to live pure lives in the constant expectation of the Lord's sudden return?

Are you able to look up from your consuming labors, at home or in a career, and draw sustaining energy and joy from the conviction that the Lord Jesus could call you to Himself that very day?

If once you could, but are no longer sure, you're not alone. Recent assaults on the pre-Tribulation rapture view have left many Christians confused and in some cases disillusioned. Some have even abandoned this blessed hope, discarding their belief that the Lord could return at any moment. Why do they give up such a reassuring and biblical hope? It's because many of these attacks at first sight do seem plausible—but further examination reveals their profound bankruptcy.

The promise that our Lord could appear at any moment to take His church up to His Father's house was delivered by the Lord Himself (see John 14:1-3). Details of that rapture were supplied by the apostle Paul in 1 Thessalonians 4:16-18:

> For the Lord Himself will descend from heaven with a shout, with the voice of an archangel, and with the trumpet of God. And the dead in Christ will rise first.

> Then we who are alive and remain shall be caught up
> together with them in the clouds to meet the Lord in the
> air. And thus we shall always be with the Lord. There-
> fore comfort one another with these words.

For more than nineteen centuries, Bible-believing Christians have gained much comfort from this passage. But the relentless attacks of recent years (including some vicious distortions of the facts) have prompted many to question its truth. This has led to confusion for some and complacency for others, causing both to redirect their affections to "things on the earth" instead of "on things above" (Colossians 3:2).

Some of the attacks on the pre-Tribulation (or pre-Trib) rapture view are merely revivals of old and discredited theories. These are easily dismissed. Others, new and at first glance convincing, need to be answered. The rest are so bizarre I am amazed anyone accepts them.

One well-publicized attack on this treasured theory insists that it originated in a vision given to a 15-year-old girl back in 1830. Another suggests that the Jesuit theologian Lacunza was the first to propose it. Still another maintains that it was all part of the Illuminati's conspiracy to put Christians to sleep politically so humanists could advance their cause. Recent books such as *The Pre-Wrath Rapture* (1990) dogmatically purport still another pre-Tribulation theory.

Those who challenge the truth of the pre-Trib rapture view often cite its short history (175 years out of an almost 2,000-year-old church) and ask, "Why did God wait so long to reveal it to us?" In addition, a number of Christian leaders have embraced the mid-Tribulation and post-Tribulation theories in recent days. All of these matters will be dealt with carefully.

This book proposes first to show clearly what the Bible teaches about the subject. Then we will examine the major criticisms of the theory and provide some convincing answers so that you can be reassured in your belief that at any moment our Lord could "descend from heaven with a shout" to rapture His church. Last, we will look briefly at the doctrinal options and explain why the pre-Trib rapture position is still the most trustworthy.

After carefully studying scores of books, articles, and letters on both sides of this issue, I am convinced there is no reason to abandon this comforting view. The new attacks, much like the old ones, are simply unconvincing. After weighing the evidence, I am more persuaded than ever that we can still confidently believe in the pre-Tribulation rapture of the church.

We have not followed "cunningly devised fables" (2 Peter 1:16), visions and prophecies by a teenage girl, or faulty Bible study, but instead can point to scriptural, historical, and logical reasons for believing that our Lord could return at any moment—the view that has rightly predominated in the evangelical, Bible-believing church for much of the last two centuries.

Why This Issue Is So Crucial

It's not hard to name the two most evangelistic periods of church history. The early church "turned the world upside down" (Acts 17:6) in the first three centuries; in the last two centuries, the gospel has spread to every continent on the globe. What do these two great soul-winning periods share in common?

1. A belief in an authoritative, Holy Spirit-inspired, inerrant Bible.
2. The anticipation that Christ could come for His church at any time.

Confidence in both of these teachings is recurring in these last days. After a century of skepticism, criticism, and secularism, many are returning to belief in the second coming as the last, best hope for a world in turmoil. During the past decade, the largest Protestant denomination in the United States (Southern Baptist) has won the so-called battle for the Bible against those who would take it figuratively or as an allegory. Those who believe in an inspired, inerrant, and authoritative Bible have wrestled control of their denomination from those who do not. This is the first time in church history that any such feat has been accomplished.

Other churches, too, are moving in the direction of accepting the Bible literally and authoritatively. Interestingly enough, those who preach an authoritative Bible that offers practical answers for today's problems seem to produce growing churches. Most of the superchurches of this country are Bible-teaching churches, and regardless of their denomination, I know of no liberal church anywhere that is growing explosively. In fact, the mainline churches that largely accepted "higher criticism" back in the thirties and forties are dying today. They provide no message for the guilt-ridden and empty-hearted victims of our secular society, so their members either look to Bible-teaching churches that offer biblical answers to life or are swept into the deceptions of the cults. Lost souls rarely seek out liberal churches that play fast and loose with the Bible. Somehow, even the man on the street knows that church leaders who do not accept an authoritative Bible have nothing to offer.

Consequently, we are seeing and will continue to see a resurgence of belief in the imminent return of Christ for His church. Whenever we accept the Bible literally, we automatically witness a renewed interest in the study of Bible prophecy. When Bible students interpret the Scriptures literally, they naturally conclude that our Lord has promised to return to this earth someday to establish His kingdom. Further study reveals that before that event a tribulation period will test the inhabitants of this earth. Consequently, those who accept the Bible literally usually adopt the pre-Tribulation view of His return and expect Him at any moment.

Historically, belief in the any-moment-coming of Christ has three vital effects on Christians and their churches.

1. It produces holy living in an unholy society. John said, "Everyone who has this hope in Him [the return of Christ] purifies himself, just as He is pure" (1 John 3:3).

2. It produces an evangelistic church of soul-winning Christians. When we believe Christ could appear at any moment, we seek to share Him with our friends lest they be left behind at His coming.

An interesting statistic came to light in one of George Gallup's polls on religion. He found that 62 percent of Americans believe Jesus Christ literally will return to this earth, yet according to another poll by the same organization, just under 40 percent of the population describes itself as born again. In other words, some 22 percent of those who believe in His coming are not ready for it. That means that two out of every ten people we meet today have enough faith to believe in His return, but have not received

Him personally as their Savior. I hope that reading this book will inspire you to be on the lookout for them so you can explain to them the good news of the gospel.

3. Belief in the imminent return of Christ impels Christians and churches to develop a worldwide missionary vision of reaching the lost for Christ. And we have more reason to believe that Christ will come in our lifetime than any generation since He ascended into heaven and promised to return. Naturally, we should eagerly desire to reach our friends with His good news.

Believing in the soon coming of Christ for His church will have a profound effect on the way we live. It's much easier to "set your affections on things above, not on the things of this earth" (Colossians 3:2 KJV) if we believe that Christ could come at any moment.

I know a Christian businessman who recently pledged $5,000 to help publish a soul-winning book in the Polish language. "I'm 66 years old," he declared. "My wife and I believe that Jesus is coming very soon, and the last thing we want Him to find is a lot of money in our bank account. We want to use it now for the winning of the lost." Such a decision naturally issues from a firm belief that Christ's return is imminent.

It is a conviction that cannot help but change the way you live. Firmly believing that at any instant you could find yourself hurtling through the skies to meet your Lord face to face makes a difference in how you conduct your life. You're a little more careful. A little more aware. A little more guarded. A little more thoughtful. A little more prepared.

It is as our Lord told His disciples:

> Be dressed ready for service and keep your lamps burning, like men waiting for their master to return from a wedding banquet, so that when he comes and knocks they can immediately open the door for him. It will be good for those servants whose master finds them watching when he comes....You also must be ready, because the Son of Man will come at an hour when you do not expect him (Luke 12:35-37,40 NIV).

The pre-Tribulation rapture view expounded in this book is the only one that provides Christians with an at-any-moment expectancy. As we shall see, all other views leave something more to be accomplished before Jesus can return.

The Millennial Fever Factor

In the decades leading up to the Persian Gulf War, many Christians lost their interest in the study of prophecy. But when the war in the Persian Gulf flared, suddenly apocalyptic literature became one of the hottest genres in Christian bookstores. Even *Time* magazine featured a two-page article on the last days. One woman who for years had not attended services called a Bible-believing church in her neighborhood during the war to ask, "Is *this* the Battle of Armageddon?" Obviously it was not, but just as the thoughts of people gravitated to second-coming teachings after the French Revolution and the subsequent turmoil in Europe, people today identify the focus on the Middle East as "a sign of the times." And they aren't far wrong. In fact, the terrorist attacks on the World Trade Center and the Pentagon on September 11, 2001 found people turning to the Bible for answers. Bible sales went up, and sales of the books in the Left Behind® series went up 50 percent. The attacks and subsequent events have made it much easier for Christians to share their faith as people's fear of the future has reached new heights. The Hebrew prophets predicted that in the last days, world events would focus on the Middle East, Babylon, the Arab nations, Israel, and Russia—the very nations that make front-page headlines in today's newspapers.

What does all this mean? It suggests that God's prophetic clock is moving forward and people are showing a renewed interest in Bible prophecy. And that doesn't include the "millennial fever" that arose as we approached the twenty-first century. Such a phenomenon occurred at the close of the first millennium, featuring wild speculations that Christ would reappear between A.D. 990 and the year 1000, and the same happened again as we drew near to the year 2000. Millennial fever aside, the interest people today are showing in Bible prophecy is real and growing. And there is far more evidence that Christ could come in our lifetime than at any time before in history.

The Oldest Theory of Christ's Return

The oldest theory relating to Christ's return predates Christianity. Some Jews believe that the Messiah would come to fulfill His kingdom promises in the seventh millennium from creation. This conjecture was based on combining the seven days of creation and the biblical statement that, with God, "one day is as a thousand years" (2 Peter 3:8; see Psalm 90:4). Since He created the earth in six days and then rested, and since "One day is as a thousand years," the 4,000 years of Old Testament history that had already passed suggested that Messiah would come in 2,000 years. That would be followed by the kingdom age, which would correspond to the seventh day of creation. These Jews assumed that Israel would enjoy kingdom rest for 1,000 years after the Messiah came. When some in the early church noted in Revelation 20 that the kingdom would last 1,000 years, they assumed that Christ would return for His church around the year 2000.

Suffice it to say that such ideas, even without scriptural backing, were used to create an enormous interest in the return of Christ and other prophetic teachings as the year 2000 drew near. The cults took advantage of this as well. Now that millennial fever has died down, it's only a matter of time before we see the next fad that will deceive many. We need to know the truth about future events so that we will not be victimized by unscrupulous teachers. Remember, when the disciples asked about "the sign...of the end of the age" (Matthew 24:3), Christ quickly warned them, "Take heed that no one deceives you. For many will come in My name, saying, 'I am the Christ,' and will deceive many" (verses 4-5). The best antidote to deception is truth—to satisfy our own curiosity and to provide a ready answer for those who are confused.

Jesus' Last Day Warning to His Church

There must be some significant reason our Lord warned His disciples in the Olivet Discourse (Matthew 24–25), which is the most important outline of future events in the Bible, to beware of false teachers. Thirteen times He warned or challenged His end-times followers to beware or to not be deceived or to watch and be ready. If we are indeed those end-times believers—that is, those who see the signs of the times of the glorious appearing of Christ to this earth—then we have reason to beware of deception, both from without and within. Satan, the master deceiver, does not want us to get excited about the fact that there are more signs of Christ's return today than at any time in church history. Consequently, we can expect him to send all kinds of deceivers into the church to rob us of the keen consciousness of living every day in the light of Christ's possible coming.

My prophetic studies have convinced me that we Christians living today have more evidence to believe we are the generation of His coming than any generation before us. So I am not surprised by the increase of confusion by deceived attackers of the spiritually inspiring pre-Tribulation position of end-time events.

This book, in addition to answering critical questions about the pre-Tribulation rapture, will help prepare you for what very well could be the last days before Christ shouts from heaven to rapture His church.

Chapter Two

Translated—
Snatched—
Raptured!

The idea of God translating people from earth to heaven is not limited to the Rapture; such translation took place in the Old Testament, too. The first and most remarkable incident involves Enoch. In Genesis 5:18-24, we learn of a pre-Flood man who was so righteous in his lifestyle that he "walked with God three hundred years....and he was not, for God took him" (verses 23-24). Obviously he was translated into the presence of God.

Elijah, the great Hebrew prophet, was also translated by God directly from this earth into heaven, and his disciple Elisha saw him go. Again we have a human being translated, or as the apostle Paul would later describe it, "when this corruptible [body] has put on incorruption, and this mortal has put on immortality, then shall be brought to pass the saying that is written: 'Death is swallowed up in victory' " (1 Corinthians 15:54). As we shall see in this chapter, that moment of translation for dead Christians will be when Christ descends from heaven with the shout that shall rapture His church. The remnants or ashes of their bodies (or their bodily elements, wherever they are) will be translated into new and heavenly bodies and taken up to meet the Lord. All living Christians will also be translated immediately with them to meet in the "clouds" and together they will "meet the Lord in the air" (1 Thessalonians 4:17).

In Hebrews 11:5 the apostle Paul made it clear that even in the Old Testament this translation (or resurrection) experience was dependent on faith:

> By faith Enoch was translated so that he did not see death, "and was not found because God had *translated* him"; for before his translation he had this testimony, that he pleased God (emphasis added).

Enoch was in one place in space and time, in one form of existence, when God simply and suddenly transferred him to another. God did something similar with Elijah. It will be no more difficult for Him to perform such a translation for every living believer in the space of a heartbeat.

Ever since our Lord promised the early Christians that He was returning to His Father's house to prepare a place for them and that He would "come again and receive you to Myself; that where I am, there you may be also" (John 14:3), believers have looked forward to being translated rather than seeing death.

Even the apostle Paul referred to the translation of Christians with the editorial *we*, for in 1 Corinthians 15, which some call the resurrection chapter, he explained, "We shall not all sleep [referring to death for the Christian], but we shall all be *changed*—in a moment, in the twinkling of an eye" (verses 51-52, emphasis added). For centuries Christians have eagerly anticipated the day when our Lord would translate His church so that they would not see death but instead be taken by Him to His Father's house. As we shall see, this is called a "mystery," the Rapture, or "the blessed hope" (Titus 2:13) of the church.

The apostles and the church of the first three centuries wholeheartedly expected that Christ would return for His church during their lifetime. The blessed hope that motivated the first-century church was the expectation of an imminent return of Christ—that is, the sudden, unexpected coming of Christ at any moment.

The little church at Thessalonica became upset because someone claimed the appointed day had already taken place and that the believers had been left behind. Paul's answer to them in 1 and 2 Thessalonians probably gave more impetus to the belief in the imminent return of Christ than any other single scripture. (It is, however, also taught in other passages.) Most first-century Christians believed so intensely in Christ's at-any-moment coming that they were driven with a passion to share their faith everywhere. That was true about the Thessalonian believers, to whom Paul wrote:

> You became followers of us and of the Lord, having received the word in much affliction, with joy of the Holy Spirit, so that you became examples to all in Macedonia and Achaia who believe. For from you the word of the Lord has sounded forth, not only in Macedonia and Achaia, but also in every place. Your faith toward God has gone out, so that we do not need to say anything. For they themselves declare concerning us what manner of entry we had to you, and how you turned to God from idols to serve the living and true God, and to wait for His Son from heaven, whom He raised from the dead, even Jesus who delivers us from the wrath to come (1 Thessalonians 1:6-10).

While the church of the first three centuries did not label this resurrection of dead believers and translation of living Christians *the Rapture,* it anticipated it. And even during the Dark Ages, when literal interpretation of the Bible was eclipsed, some still anticipated the imminent translation of the church.

Second-century churches were under such severe persecution that they considered themselves already in the Tribulation. Later Christian saints like Hugh Latimer (burned at the stake for his faith in 1555) expressed assurance of the Rapture: "peradventure it may come in my days, old as I am, or in my children's days...the saints *'shall be taken up to meet Christ in the air'* and so shall come down with Him again"[1] (emphasis added).

That's the essence of hope, isn't it?

"It may come in my days...or in my children's." Whether I am facing terrible trials or fiery persecution. Whether my days have been blessed with peace and beauty and golden sunlight or whether I've had to walk in paths of pain and loss and darkness.

It may come in my day. *He* may come in my day and deliver me. And if not in my day, then in my children's. But He *will* come.

Whatever may happen on this sometimes dark and blighted planet, He will come.

Since Latimer's time, the Bible has been translated into many languages. Wherever it has gone, this expectation of translation to be with Christ during their own lifetime quickly became the anticipation of the church. Anticipation of this event has had a tremendous influence on the church during the past two centuries as millions of Christians have accepted the literal message of our Lord's promise to come for His church.

Translation Equals Rapture

Modern Christians know this event as the Rapture, or that moment when, in the "twinkling of an eye," Christ will shout from heaven and "the dead in Christ will rise first. Then we who are alive and remain shall be caught up together with them in the clouds to meet the Lord in the air" (1 Thessalonians 4:16-17).

The Greek word here is *harpazo*, meaning "snatched up" to be with Christ. The familiar word *rapture* does not appear in the Greek New Testament, for it is a Latin word. Those who translated the Greek New Testament into Latin used *rapture* to describe "snatched up." Somehow that word caught on as the unofficial title of the event. Actually, it may be a better translation than "snatch up" or "caught away," because it suggests a joyous exaltation—which is not the case when a person is snatched away by a kidnapper or someone who plans to do him harm.

This is being snatched away to something better.

This is being caught up into Life.

This is stepping suddenly out of a dark and stuffy room into a brilliant morning.

This is looking out the window and suddenly spotting a loved one, smiling and beckoning you outside.

This is like a little child being suddenly swept into the arms of her laughing father.

In the Library of Congress, where I did research for this book, I typed the word *rapture* into the computer catalog. Many references to books about the second coming of Christ appeared, but scattered among them were several books of romances, love stories, and even erotica, all relating to a rapturous experience. Since the Rapture, a joyous catching away, saves Christians from death (the universal fear of all men), that term accurately describes the event.

Some Christians are disappointed when they learn that the word *rapture* does not appear in the New Testament. They shouldn't be, nor is that a very good argument against the pre-Tribulation concept of the Lord's return for His church. Actually, none of the words of our English Bible are found in the New Testament. It was written in Greek and then translated into Latin in the fourth century. It is from the Latin translation that we get the word *rapture*, which best describes that instant translating experience of resurrection which our Lord promised His church. There are other English words that are not found in the original Greek text yet are often used by the church to describe New Testament teachings. Another example is the word *trinity*. The Bible certainly teaches the Trinity, but the word did not begin to appear until sometime around the third century. As we shall see in the pages ahead, the Bible definitely teaches the rapture of the church.

Rapture Is a Mystery Revealed

Twelve mysteries revealed in the New Testament were not known to Old Testament saints. They were not given to make Christianity mysterious, but to reveal things that had never before been announced. That is what Paul explains to us in 1 Corinthians 2:7-10:

> We speak the wisdom of God in a mystery, the hidden wisdom which God ordained before the ages for our glory, which none of the rulers of this age knew....but God has revealed them to us through His Spirit.

The greatest of these mysteries, in my opinion, is the rapture of the saints. Paul refers to this mystery in 1 Corinthians 15:51,53, where he describes the resurrection of the human body and affirms, "We shall not all sleep, but we shall all be changed....For this corruptible [body] must put on incorruption." When? At the resurrection of dead believers.

Faith in the resurrection was common to all Jews in Paul's day. The New Testament account of the raising of Lazarus shows this clearly. Martha, a typical Jewess of her day, reflected her understanding of the coming resurrection of the dead when she answered our Lord's challenge to believe that He would raise her brother to life: "I know that he will rise again in the resurrection at the last day."[2] Paul builds upon that assurance with the teaching of the Rapture, which occurs when Christ comes, or more specifically, when He will "descend from heaven with a shout."

In 1 Corinthians 15 Paul provided greater detail than ever before by explaining that this old "corruptible" body could not enter God's eternal kingdom but would have to be made like our Lord's body after His resurrection. And then he revealed this awesomely important mystery of the Rapture:

> Behold, I tell you a mystery: We shall not all sleep, but we shall all be changed—[made incorruptible and translated] in a moment, in the twinkling of an eye, at the last trumpet. For the trumpet will sound, and the dead will be raised incorruptible, and we shall be changed. For this corruptible must put on incorruption, and this mortal must put on immortality (1 Corinthians 15:51-53).

This is the second time Paul presented the mystery in detail. Three years earlier he addressed it when he wrote his first epistle to the church at Thessalonica (see 4:13-18). In order to gain a complete picture of the Rapture, one must consider these two passages together, along with our Lord's promise of rapture in John 14:1-3, where He promises to take us to be with Him in His "Father's house."

When Paul wrote 1 Corinthians 15, it was probably the first time anyone had penned such a detailed account of how the dead bodies of believers would be raised and translated along with living people. Both groups would be changed and united with the Lord. We're going to look now at the specific details of all that happens during this translation. And as you read the following list, keep in mind that no other religion in the world offers such a sublime teaching about resurrection.

The Order of Rapture/Translation Events

When we combine 1 Corinthians 15:51-53, 1 Thessalonians 4:13-18, and John 14:1-3 and study them carefully, we can outline the sequence of events in the Rapture. They are totally different from what will happen during the coming of Christ to this earth in power and great glory, which we will examine in chapter 7. (Note: The numbers in this list each have a corresponding number on the accompanying chart to help you locate exactly when that event occurs.)

Rapture Events

1. The Lord Himself will descend from His Father's house, where He is preparing a place for us (John 14:1-3 and 1 Thessalonians 4:16).

2. He will come again to receive us to Himself (John 14:1-3).

3. He will resurrect those who have fallen asleep in Him (deceased believers whom we will not precede, 1 Thessalonians 4:14-15).

4. The Lord will shout as He descends ("loud command," 1 Thessalonians 4:16 NIV). All this takes place in the "twinkling of an eye" (1 Corinthians 15:52).

5. We will hear the voice of the archangel (perhaps to lead Israel during the seven years of Tribulation as he did in the Old Testament, 1 Thessalonians 4:16).

6. We will also hear the trumpet call of God (1 Thessalonians 4:16), His last trumpet for the church. (Don't confuse this with the seventh trumpet of Revelation 11:15.)

7. The dead in Christ will rise first. (The corruptible remnants and ashes of their dead bodies are made incorruptible and joined together with their spirit, which Jesus brings with Him, 1 Thessalonians 4:16-17).

8. Then we who are alive and remain will be changed (made incorruptible by having our bodies made "immortal," 1 Corinthians 15:51,53).

9. Then we will be caught up [raptured] together (1 Thessalonians 4:17).

10. With them in the clouds (where we assume the dead and living believers will have a monumental reunion, 1 Thessalonians 4:17).

11. To meet the Lord in the air (1 Thessalonians 4:17).

12. Jesus said He will do this to "receive you to Myself." Jesus will take us to the Father's house "that where I am, there you may be also" (John 14:3).

13. "And thus we shall always be with the Lord" (1 Thessalonians 4:17).

Additional Events

14. The judgment seat of Christ (2 Corinthians 5:10). This verse teaches that at the call of Christ for believers, He will judge all things. Christians will stand before the judgment seat of Christ (Romans 14:10; 2 Corinthians 5:10), which is described in detail in 1 Corinthians 3:11-15, and will evidently be in the "Father's house." This judgment prepares Christians for...

15. The Marriage Supper of the Lamb. Just prior to Christ's coming to earth in power and great glory, which we call the glorious appearing, Christ will meet with His Bride, the church, and the wedding and Marriage Supper will take place. In the meantime, after the church is raptured, the world will suffer the unprecedented time of the wrath of God which our Lord called the Great Tribulation (Matthew 24:21).

The Rapture and the Glorious Appearing— Not the Same Event

It is impossible to equate these 15 events and the rapture translation verses (including the resurrection of both the dead and living believers of the church age) with the coming of Christ

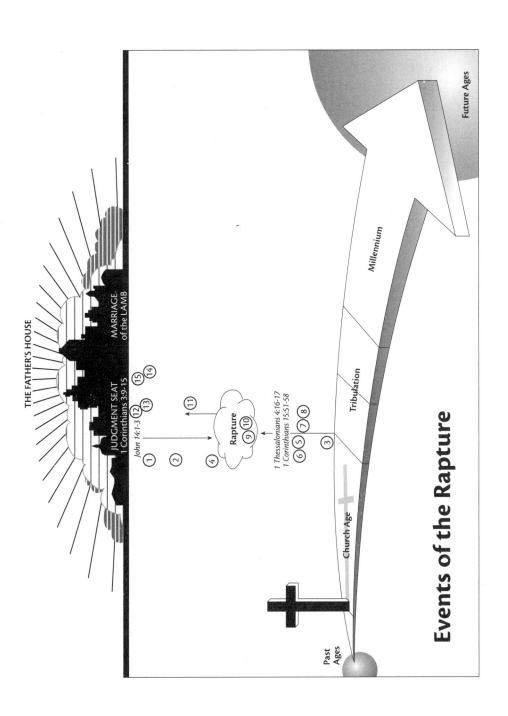

Events of the Rapture

THE FATHER'S HOUSE

MARRIAGE of the LAMB

JUDGMENT SEAT
1 Corinthians 3:9-15

John 14:1-3

Rapture

1 Thessalonians 4:16-17
1 Corinthians 15:51-58

Church Age

Past Ages

Tribulation

Millennium

Future Ages

in power and great glory to set up His earthly kingdom. They are obviously two separate events! And while some Christians may disagree as to the length of time between the two events, all must concur that they are distinctly different from one another.

Notice what is missing in the Rapture events. Christ does not come to the earth with power and the holy angels as He promised. Instead, He comes in the air, which is defined as "in the clouds" (1 Thessalonians 4:16-17). Nor does He set up His earthly kingdom, for He gathers His translated church into His Father's house. He does not deal with the Antichrist or bind Satan, nor does He destroy the kings of the earth who are gathered at Jerusalem to oppose Him. In the Rapture Christ leaves the Father's house yet does not come to the earth, but calls the "dead in Christ" and the living church to "be caught up," where they join with each other in the clouds and then proceed to meet Him in the air. He then will take them to live with Him in the Father's house, as He promised. Only by robbing these passages of their obvious meaning can we ignore the two comings of Christ, one for His church and another for the world.

We can also view these events as two stages of one coming. I see no contradiction in viewing the second coming as a single event in two phases. These two episodes, the Rapture and the second coming, are so different that it is impossible to combine them. One involves Jesus coming for His church; the other concerns His appearance in power and judgment to the earth. I realize some will accuse me of teaching two future comings of Christ, but that is untrue. The second coming is an end-time event that shows Christ culminating and fulfilling all end-time prophecies. Before He comes publicly and for the general popu-lation, He will rapture His church—which is certainly not the entire second coming, but only the first stage of it. The second phase is the one in which He is recognized as the King of kings and Lord of lords.

The different activities listed on the chart on page 37 clearly demonstrate that one cannot combine into a single event the two phases of Christ's coming: First for His church, and second to return to earth in great power and glory. For example, the follow-ing five points that describe the glorious appearing (on the chart) in no way resemble the first five events of the Rapture:

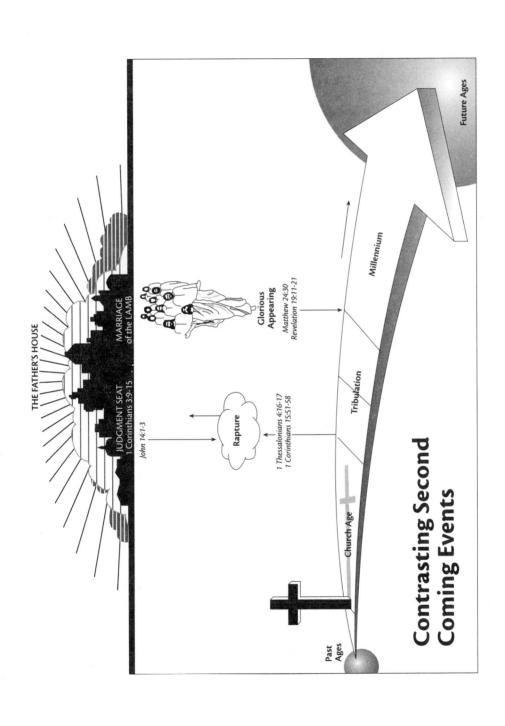

THE FATHER'S HOUSE

JUDGMENT SEAT
1 Corinthians 3:9-15

MARRIAGE
of the LAMB

John 14:1-3

Rapture

1 Thessalonians 4:16-17
1 Corinthians 15:51-58

Glorious
Appearing
Matthew 24:30
Revelation 19:11-21

Past
Ages

Church Age

Tribulation

Millennium

Future Ages

**Contrasting Second
Coming Events**

1. Christ descends with the hosts of heaven to earth riding on a white horse (Revelation 19:11-14)

2. He makes war with the inhabitants of earth (19:11)

3. The armies of the world gather against Him and He makes war with them (19:18-21)

4. The Beast and the False Prophet are thrown into the Lake of Fire (19:20)

5. Satan is bound in the bottomless pit for 1,000 years (20:2-3)

By studying the Rapture and glorious appearing from the Scriptures and by examining their locations on the chart, we are forced to conclude that they do not describe the same events. Whereas Christ's second coming is the predominant event in Scripture—the time when He comes in power and great glory to set up His kingdom on this earth for 1,000 years—the Bible also describes His coming in the air for His church. The Rapture and glorious appearing are not identical and cannot occur simultaneously without violently twisting several passages of Scripture.

Secret Rapture?

Through the years some have tried to discredit the pre-Tribulation rapture theory by calling it the *secret rapture.* Of course, nowhere in Scripture is the term *secret* applied to this event. However, anyone who does not participate in the Rapture will not actually see it, for it will occur in the "twinkling of an eye." The word "twinkling" has been defined as "a gleam in your eye," which is faster than the eye can see. The occurrence would much better be labeled the *sudden rapture.*

But how sudden is sudden?

It's no time at all. Scripture describes the translation of Enoch this way: "Enoch walked with God; and he was not, for God took him" (Genesis 5:24). He WAS NOT. One minute he was walking with God, feet on the warm dust of planet earth, sunshine warming his shoulders, the fragrance of the fields in his nostrils—and then *he was not.* With no warning, no buildup, no mysterious quivering of the air, he was simply gone. Just that fast. From here to there.

I expect the Rapture to be electrifyingly sudden but not secret, for when Christ calls His living saints to be with Him, millions of people will suddenly vanish from the earth. An unsaved person who happens to be in the company of a believer will know immediately that his friend has vanished. There will certainly be worldwide recognition of the fact, for when over one-half of a billion people suddenly depart this earth, leaving their earthly belongings behind, pandemonium and confusion will certainly reign for a time.

A million conversations will end midsentence.

A million phone receivers will suddenly go dead.

A woman will reach for a man's hand in the dark...and no one will be there.

A man will turn with a laugh to slap a colleague on the back and his hand will move through empty air.

A basketball player will make a length-of-the-floor pass to a teammate streaking downcourt and find there is no one there to receive it. And no referee to call it out-of-bounds.

A mother will pull back the covers in a bassinet, smelling the sweet baby smell one moment but suddenly kissing empty space and looking into empty blankets.

Think of the countless homes where, "in the twinkling of an eye," only clothes will remain in the chair where a believer sat moments before. Consider the passengers aboard airplanes with a Christian crew. Many believe that the Rapture will result in titanic chaos as Christian auto and bus drivers, train engineers, pilots, and others suddenly vanish. The Rapture just may create the greatest freeway gridlock in history!

The world will somehow have to come to terms with between 500 million to one billion missing Christians. The ensuing outcry of sorrow, loss, and confusion will make the Rapture a well-publicized event, dominating the media for weeks and weeks.

If I am right that all babies under the age of accountability will be considered innocent of personal sin through the blood of Christ (see Romans 5:13-21), then youngsters from age one minute to the age of personal accountability (only God knows that date) will vanish with the Christians. If that is true, unsaved mothers left behind will sorrow intensely over the sudden loss of their children. That alone would make the event anything but secret. Unexpected, yes! Unseen, yes! But not secret. The absence of millions of people will occupy the minds of those left behind until the events of the Tribulation begin and the revelation of the Antichrist, the man of sin, will crowd thoughts of the Rapture out of their minds.

The world will recognize the Rapture...but too late to prepare for it.

Rapture Is Not New

For God to rapture people to heaven is not new in biblical history. It has already occurred three times.

Enoch: "Enoch walked with God; and he was not, for God took him" (Genesis 5:24). The New Testament adds, "By faith Enoch was translated so that he did not see death, 'and was not found because God had translated him'; for before his translation he had this testimony, that he pleased God" (Hebrews 11:5).

Elijah: "Then it happened, as they continued on and talked, that suddenly a chariot of fire appeared with horses of fire, and separated the two of them; and Elijah went up by a whirlwind into heaven" (2 Kings 2:11).

Jesus Christ: After His resurrection, He, as "the firstfruits of those who have fallen asleep" (1 Corinthians 15:20), ascended into heaven. "Now when He had spoken these things, while they watched, He was taken up, and a cloud received Him out of their sight. And while they looked steadfastly toward heaven as He went up, behold, two men stood by them in white apparel, who also said, 'Men of Galilee, why do you stand gazing up into heaven? *This same Jesus,* who was taken up from you into heaven, will so *come* in like manner as you saw Him go into heaven' " (Acts 1:9-11, emphasis added).

All three events describe a natural body of flesh being changed and translated into the presence of God. In our finite body we cannot enter His presence, and thus a sudden translation becomes necessary.

No one saw Enoch's translation. He was walking on the earth one moment, and in the next he was translated. Elijah's rapture, however, had a witness: Elisha. And when our Lord was translated, He was seen by His apostles.

The Power of the Rapture

Those in Christ who will be snatched up in the Rapture do not have to generate their own power. As in all our dealings with God, He provides the impetus. He has not assigned our resurrection to an angel or specifically created being, for "the Lord *Himself* will descend from heaven *with a shout*" (emphasis added). In other words, He will do the raising. In John 5:21,28-29 He clearly claimed to possess resurrection power for Himself, using it as proof that He was God in human flesh.

Since so much is at stake here, including our eternal destiny, may I point to a most comforting truth? Christ has already demonstrated His power to raise the dead. Three times He did it during His brief ministry, the most dramatic of which was Lazarus in John 11:43 when He commanded, "Lazarus, come forth!" To the astonishment of the people of Bethany, a man dead four days was delivered from his tomb. When that same, experienced voice shouts from heaven at the Rapture, all those who are in Christ by faith will respond.

The Lord Jesus Himself declared, "I am the resurrection and the life. He who believes in Me, though he may die, he shall live. And whoever lives and believes in Me shall never die" (John 11:25-26). For almost 2,000 years all Christians who died immediately went in spirit to heaven to be with Christ. As Paul said, "To be absent from the body [is] to be present with the Lord" (2 Corinthians 5:8). When Christ comes for His church, He will resurrect the bodies of deceased saints, unite them with their soul and spirit in heaven, and translate all living believers to be with them and Him forever. No wonder the early Christians used to greet each other with "Maranatha!" (The Lord is coming!).

Yes, Christ is coming to resurrect and translate His church. We call that the Rapture.

The Argument that the Pre-Tribulation View Is of Recent Origin

One popular argument against the pre-Tribulation theory of the "blessed hope" phase of Christ's return is that it was invented by John Darby in the nineteenth century (1828) and was never seen or mentioned by the early Christian fathers or for almost 19 centuries of church history. That argument is simply not true! In fact, one post-Tribulation writer advertised an offer of 500 dollars to anyone who could prove it was seen before John Darby began to popularize it in Great Britain, the U.S., and Canada in the 1840s. Subsequently, he had to pay that 500-dollar challenge when it was discovered that the Reverend Morgan Edwards saw it back in 1742. Since then that minister has had to admit his error and has withdrawn his offer.

Reverend Morgan Edwards was a Baptist pastor in Philadelphia who included a discussion on the pre-Tribulation return of Christ for His church in his book *Millennium, Last Days Novelties,* written in 1788. Although he saw only a three-and-a-half-year Tribulation, he definitely saw the Rapture occur *before* the Tribulation. What is even more interesting is that he claimed he had written the same thing as early as 1742. He may have been influenced by John Gill before him or even others whose writings or teachings were available at that time but have not been preserved.

Historically, the Protestant Reformation resulted in a proliferation of Bibles being translated, printed, and made available to the common people for the first time in 1,700 years. As they began reading it, they were impressed with the many prophetical teachings it contained. I have a copy of a commentary on the book of Revelation written by Sir Isaac Newton in the mid-seventeenth century. He was an avid Bible scholar (as well as one of the greatest scientists in all of history) and was obviously influenced by other writers before him. So historically, the development of prophecy is understandable; it progressed parallel with the availability of the Bible and the study of it. By the nineteenth century, the Bible was available and being read by millions in the English-speaking world. It is said that "prophecy was in the air," particularly at Trinity College of Dublin, Ireland, where John Darby and other prophecy scholars attended between the years 1800 and 1830. Doubtless some of the Bible teachers on the faculty had a strong influence on his thinking, as perhaps did S.R. Maitland, who developed the case for futurism, which is the position that teaches that most of the book of Revelation and other Bible prophecies will be fulfilled sometime in the future. He wrote the first book on that subject in 1826.

John Darby claimed he got the inspiration for the pre-Tribulation rapture of Christ in 1828 after he saw the distinction between Israel and the church in his study of the book of Ephesians. Few scholars who do not make that distinction see a pre-Tribulation rapture of the church. In fact, separating Israel and the church is one of the major keys to rightly understanding Bible prophecy. The second key is taking the prophetic scriptures literally whenever possible.

Grant Jeffrey, a current prophecy scholar and speaker, has done extensive research of the writings of many eighteenth-century prophecy scholars. In his book *Apocalypse* (Toronto, ON: Frontier Research Publications, 1992), he quotes many who had a definite understanding of the difference between the two phases of our Lord's coming, particularly His coming for His own people prior to the Tribulation and the revealing of the man of sin (see pages 85-94).

Jeffrey's most important find was his discovery of a statement in an apocalyptic sermon from the fourth century. The author is designated "Pseudo-Ephrem" because there is some question whether or not it was really written by Ephrem of Nisibis (c. 306–373), a Syrian church father. Some prefer a later date for the sermon (attributed to him) called, "Sermon on the End of the World," suggesting it may have been written sometime between 565 and 627. For our purpose the real date is immaterial, for even allowing it to have been written as late as the seventh century proves that early Christians (1,100 years before John Darby) saw the Rapture happening *before* the Tribulation. Here is the statement in English, translated from its Greek and Latin versions that date to that period. Challenging Christians to holy living (always the purpose of rapture teaching), he wrote:

> Why therefore do we not reject every care of earthly actions and prepare ourselves for the meeting of the Lord Christ, so that he may draw us from the confusion, which overwhelms all the world?....*All the saints and elect of God are gathered together before the tribulation, which is to come, and are taken to the Lord,* in order that

they may not see at any time the confusion which over-
whelms the world because of our sins.[3]

—Pseudo-Ephrem, A.D. 372 (emphasis added)

There can be no doubt this fourth- (or at the latest seventh-)
century Bible scholar saw the saints gathered together by the
Lord before the Tribulation. His statement has all the marks of a
pre-Tribulation rapture of the saints as distinct from the glorious
appearing, which our Lord promised would occur "immediately
after the tribulation of those days" (Matthew 24:29). Admittedly,
Ephrem only saw the Tribulation lasting 42 months or three-and-
a-half years (as taught later in the sermon). The fact remains,
however, that he saw a pre-Tribulation rapture of the church long
before the nineteenth century, which some have erroneously
claimed to be the time when such a teaching first arose.
Considering that less than 10 percent of the ancient Christian
books ever written have been preserved to our day, we have no
doubt that even though the details of the pre-Tribulation rapture
were not widely recognized back in the fourth century, there
must have been other Bible students besides Ephrem who also
discovered the "blessed hope" teaching.

It should be evident to the reader that the timing of the
Rapture as taught in Scripture is scheduled before the
Tribulation, before the revelation of the "lawless one" (2 Thessalonians 2:8) and his desecration of the temple in the middle of
that period. It is not a new theory, for it was seen by Christians
down through church history. The failure to recognize this truth
has led some to teach that Christians will go through the
Tribulation, contrary to our Lord's promise to deliver us "from
[out of] the wrath to come" (1 Thessalonians 1:10).

The People of the Rapture

The Bible is clear: The coming of Christ for His church will be
selective. The Rapture is not for everyone. Only certain people
will be included. Some will be taken and others left. Two of the
primary passages on the Rapture call them "those who are
Christ's at His coming" (1 Corinthians 15:23) and "those who
sleep in Jesus" or "the dead in Christ" (1 Thessalonians 4:14,16).

The Rapture is for believers only (see 1 Thessalonians 4:14,17). The clarification "if we believe that Jesus died and rose again" (verse 14) clearly refers to those who have accepted the gospel message "that Christ died for our sins according to the Scriptures, and that He was buried, and that He rose again the third day" (1 Corinthians 15:3-4). Christ is not coming for the churches, implying church members, or merely for good people. He will rapture only those who are in Him through believing on Him and receiving Him as their Lord and Savior.

That makes me wonder: Have you put your faith in Christ by receiving Him into your life? Can you honestly say, "I am in Christ"? It is not difficult to be in Christ, if you wish to be. But the biblical word *believe* carries with it the concept of "trust" or "committing oneself to." If you have not committed yourself to Christ, may I urge you right now to prayerfully invite Him into your life?

Then you will be certain that the Rapture will include you.

Chapter Three

Kept from
the Hour

We "wait for His Son from heaven, whom He raised from the dead, even Jesus who delivers us from the wrath to come" (1 Thessalonians 1:10).

One of the most amazing aspects of the mystery revealed in 1 Thessalonians 4:13-18 and 1 Corinthians 15:51-54 is the promise that the church of Jesus Christ will not pass through the Tribulation. That is one reason why the Bible calls the Rapture "the blessed hope" (Titus 2:13), which we will discuss in a future chapter.

Most believers realize that becoming a Christian does not save them from the ordinary tribulations that plague all men from time to time. Church history is replete with martyrs who have suffered all kinds of persecution, particularly in the first three centuries of the church, during the inquisition, and in the last century (as well as today). Many of these were godly people who lived dedicated lives. Nonetheless, persecution led to their untimely deaths.

For that reason, many Christians, when they first discover that the Rapture of the church will occur prior to the Tribulation, often respond in one of two ways: 1) "It's too good to be true!" or 2) "I don't deserve to be saved from the wrath to come—I deserve to suffer. Did not the apostle Peter warn Christians they would suffer?" (see 1 Peter 4:12-13).

We often overlook, however, the principle that trials are a standard part of life in a fallen world. By contrast, our Lord specifically informed us that the Tribulation is a special judgment of God. The Lord Jesus said of that day, "For then there will be *great tribulation,* such as has not been since the beginning of the world until this time, no, nor ever shall be. And unless those days were shortened, no flesh would be saved; but for the elect's sake those days will be shortened" (Matthew 24:21-22, emphasis added).

We readily welcome the good news that Christians will be raptured before that period arrives. Admittedly, we do not deserve deliverance from the hour of wrath that will try the whole earth, but escape from wrath is not based on merit. It is founded solely on what the Bible says. God deals with us on the basis of grace when we turn to Him in faith, and this principle includes escape from the Tribulation. The contemporary church, with all her carnality, worldliness, and sin, does not warrant escape from the Tribulation; but typical of His mercy, God will save us from the wrath to come not because we deserve it but because of His mercy.

We didn't deserve Emmanuel, God in the flesh, born as a tiny baby in a dark stable in a backwater corner of the world. Nevertheless, He came.

We didn't deserve a Savior, the sinless Son of God who endured the fury of hell, felt the white-hot wrath of God for our sins and transgressions, and gasped out His life nailed to a crossbeam. But He gave Himself anyway.

We don't deserve an Advocate, an eternal counsel for the defense who stands at the Father's side and pleads our case at the very throne of the universe. Yet He is there, for us, and He is not silent.

We don't deserve the gift of the Holy Spirit, a constant Comfort and Companion to walk with us and teach us and hold our hands down through the years. Just the same, He is ours.

We don't deserve heaven. An inheritance that can never perish, spoil, or fade where we will enjoy our loved ones and the fellowship of God Himself forever. Yet because of Jesus, we have a secured reservation.

No, we don't deserve to escape the great wrath that will fall on all the world. But it's just like our God to grant it in spite of us.

Putting aside for the moment our "just desserts," let us examine some of the Bible's promises that Christians will indeed be raptured before the Tribulation begins.

The Promise of Revelation 3:10

One of the best promises guaranteeing the church's rapture before the Tribulation appears in Revelation 3:10. As you read it, keep in mind that it is one of our Lord's own promises:

> Because you have kept My command to persevere, I *also will keep you from the hour of trial* which shall come upon the whole world, *to test those who dwell on the earth* (emphasis added).

This text represents Christ's message to one of His seven churches, the church at Philadelphia. It must transcend the one little church of Asia to which He wrote, for the church at Philadelphia has long been extinct, and the hour "which shall come upon the whole world" has not yet come.

In my commentary on the book of Revelation (Grand Rapids: Zondervan, 1974), I pointed out that the seven churches of Asia were selected out of hundreds of young churches at that time because they were types of the seven church ages that would exist from the first century to the present. The whole message of Revelation chapters 2 and 3 is to all the churches, not just the seven churches of Asia. Otherwise, the majority of churches would have been excluded. The message of Christ to the church at Philadelphia was not only for that little church, but also represented the church age that was an "open door" church—that is, the evangelistic, missionary-minded church that started about 1750 and will exist right up to the time Christ comes to rapture His church.

During the past 50 years or so, some opposition has arisen to interpretation of Revelation 3:10. Adherents to the mid- and post-Trib positions suggest that the Lord will keep us *through* the Tribulation. This is difficult to reconcile, however, with other passages that teach that few, if any, believers will still populate the earth when He comes with power and great glory at the end of the Tribulation. Instead, the saints who have been kept from wrath are with Him as He descends to this earth.

The word "from" in Revelation 3:10 literally means "out of." God is saying, "I will keep you out of the wrath to come." Derived from the Greek word *ek*, it is used more than 800 times in the New Testament, and as one scholar has noted, the only instance when *ek* is used to mean anything other than "out of" appears in Galatians 3:8, where it is rendered *"through* faith." And even there it literally means "by faith." This scholar, editor of *Our Hope Magazine*, wrote in August 1950,

> *Ek* is rendered "out of" hundreds of times, as for example: "Out of Egypt have I called My Son" (Matthew 2:15); "First cast out the beam out of thine own eye" (Matthew 7:5); "for out of the heart proceed evil thoughts" (Matthew 15:19); "And [many bodies of the saints] came out of the graves after His resurrection" (Matthew 27:53); "I will spew thee out of My mouth" (Revelation 3:16); etc.[1]

Revelation 3:10 teaches that the faithful church of the open door—which will not deny His name, but will practice good works, evangelism, and missions—will be kept out of the hour of trial (the Great Tribulation) that will try the whole earth. The guarantee of rapture before Tribulation could hardly be more powerful. No wonder one writer labeled it "a cardinal scripture."

The Promise of 1 Thessalonians 1:10

Another cardinal Scripture text was given by the Holy Spirit through the apostle Paul to a young church planted on his second missionary journey. Paul had only three weeks to ground this church in the Word of God before he was driven out of town. Many of his teachings during that brief period pertained to Bible prophecy and end-time events. This letter—one of the first books of the New Testament to be written—emphasizes the second coming, the imminent return of Christ, the Rapture, the Tribulation, and other end-time subjects. This may indicate that

Paul felt it was essential for new converts to understand what they could expect in the future.

The epistle of 1 Thessalonians was occasioned by the death of some of this church's loved ones. Naturally, since Paul had predicted that believers would be raptured, they wondered about loved ones buried in the ground. Evidently they wrote Paul a letter of inquiry and his answer appears in the book of 1 Thessalonians, written not only for that church but for the saints of all ages.

So that no one can doubt the main subject of the book, the second coming is mentioned in every chapter. The significance of this book for Bible prophecy can hardly be exaggerated, which makes the promise in verse 10 of chapter 1 so important. After complimenting the Thessalonians on their faith and testimony, he commended them for "how [they] turned to God from idols to serve the living and true God, and to wait for His Son from heaven, whom He raised from the dead, even *Jesus who delivers us from the wrath to come*" (1 Thessalonians 1:9-10, emphasis added).

The context of this passage is the Rapture, for Christians are not waiting for the glorious appearing. Paul tells them in 2 Thessalonians 2:1-12 that the latter will not occur until the Antichrist or "lawless one" is revealed (verse 8). No, the Christians in Thessalonica were awaiting the coming of Christ for His church, the Rapture. They already knew the Tribulation (or "wrath to come") would follow the Rapture, and that is what Christ has promised to keep the Christian "out of."

In his classic book *Kept from the Hour,* theologian Dr. Gerald B. Stanton clarifies that the wrath of 1 Thessalonians 1:10 is reserved for unbelievers, as is the Tribulation period. Stanton is a pre-Trib scholar and a former professor of systematic theology at Talbot Theological Seminary and Biola University. He writes:

> Romans 8:1 assures that there is no condemnation, or judgment, to them that are in Christ Jesus. Romans 5:9 (KJV, emphasis mine) declares plainly: "Much more then, being now justified by his blood, we shall be *saved from wrath* through him." Here, being saved from wrath refers primarily to salvation from eternal punishment, from hell. But does it not also include deliverance from that time of judgment on earth which

is primarily characterized by the pouring out of the vials of the *wrath of God?* First Thessalonians 5:9 confirms the fact that tribulation wrath is in view also, when it speaks of the appearing of Christ for His own in the clouds, and when it declares of those who have put on the helmet of salvation [deliverance] by our Lord Jesus Christ. *Suffering* is often the portion of the Christian (Romans 8:17; 2 Timothy 2:12; Philippians 1:29), but not *wrath!* Wrath is reserved for unbeliev-ers....

Tribulation and vengeance fall upon them that know not God:

Seeing it is a righteous thing with God to recompense tribulation to them that trouble you; and to you who are troubled rest with us, when the Lord Jesus shall be revealed from heaven with his mighty angels, in flaming fire taking vengeance on them that know not God, and obey not the gospel of our Lord Jesus Christ (2 Thessa-lonians 1:6-8 KJV).

Christians, however, are to serve the living and true God, and "to wait [not for tribulation, but] for his Son from heaven" (1 Thessalonians 1:10). Paul exhorted the Thessalonian believers:

> Brethren, pray for us...that we may be deliv-ered from unreasonable and wicked men: for all men have not faith. But the Lord is faithful, who shall stablish...your hearts into the love of God, and into the patient waiting for Christ (2 Thessalonians 3:1-5 KJV).[2]

Christians Not Appointed to Wrath

First Thessalonians 5:9 contains still another strong promise that the believer will not pass through the Tribulation: "God did not appoint us to wrath, but to obtain salvation through our Lord Jesus Christ." This passage, which follows the strongest passage on the Rapture in the Bible, must be considered in the light of its context.

After teaching about the Rapture, Paul takes his readers to the "times and the seasons" of "the day of the Lord" (1 Thessalonians

5:1-2). Some suggest this refers to the single day on which Christ returns to this earth to set up His kingdom. But that is not consistent with scriptural references to "the day of the Lord." Sometimes this phrase does refer to the glorious appearing, but on other occasions it alludes to a period that encompasses the Rapture, the Tribulation period, and the glorious appearing.[3] In other words, the term "the day of the Lord" could refer to many end-time events.

For our purpose here, 1 Thessalonians 5:9 makes it clear that God did not "appoint us to wrath" (the Tribulation) but to "obtain salvation" or deliverance from it. Since so many saints will be martyred during the Tribulation, there will be few of them still alive at the glorious appearing of Christ. This promise cannot mean, then, that He will deliver believers *during* the time of wrath, for the saints mentioned there (the Tribulation saints) will *not* be delivered. Just the reverse will happen: That period will be a time of great martyrdom. To be delivered out of it, the church will have to be raptured before the Tribulation begins.

Why Is the Church Missing in Revelation 4–18?

Those who believe that Christ will appear in the middle or at the end of the Tribulation must account for the fact that the church is not mentioned in Revelation chapters 4–18. The church walks with a heavy footstep through the first three chapters, which deal exclusively with Christ and His message to His seven churches. The words "church" and "churches" are mentioned 17 times in just three chapters. Chapters 2 and 3 render a prophetic preview of the entire church age from A.D. 33 to the Rapture.

Then at the beginning of chapter 4, John is called up into heaven with the words, "Come up here, and I will show you things which must take place after this." While we cannot use this as a primary scripture to teach the Rapture, it is interesting that John, a member of the church, is called up into heaven immediately prior to the teachings about the Tribulation, just as the church will be raptured prior to the Tribulation. Calling John in vision up into heaven, where he can look down on Tribulation events, offers an allusion or picture of the Rapture. If that was not intended, it has to be an amazing coincidence.

How else can we explain that the church, the major player in the events of chapters 1 through 3 (next, of course, to our Lord Himself), is mentioned specifically 17 times but does not appear once during chapters 4 through 18, which describe in detail the events of the seven-year Tribulation? That stunning silence can easily be explained by those who believe Christians will be raptured before the Tribulation.

The church is not there!

The silence in Revelation 4–18 is inexplicable to mid-and post-Tribs.

If You Have Ears, Why Not Hear?

There is a phrase that is repeated seven times in Revelation chapters 2 and 3, at the conclusion of each of Christ's messages to His seven churches: "He who has an ear, let him hear what the Spirit says to the churches." Nothing similar to the phrase appears again until chapter 13, which describes the middle of the Tribulation, when the Antichrist will fulfill all the prophecies of his blasphemous future as he assumes the worship of God and profanes the very name of God. At that time his hatred of and martyrdom of the Tribulation saints will reach its zenith. Suddenly, in Revelation 13:9, we read, "If anyone has an ear, let him hear." Why did God not finish by adding, as He did in chapters 2 and 3, "what the Spirit says to the churches"? The answer is obvious: The church is no longer on the earth!

It's Not for the Church

Since our Lord faithfully promised to keep His Bride, the church, *out of* the "hour of trial which shall come upon the whole world, to test those who dwell on the earth" (the church doesn't need to be tested—we have already made our decision for Christ), it is a reasonable act of faith that we take Him at His word. Since the Tribulation described in Revelation 4–18 is not for the church but for the Christ-rejecting world, and since the church does not appear in any Scripture passage that describes the Tribulation, it is reasonable to conclude that the church will not pass through the seven-year Tribulation.

Besides, there is no need for the church to be on the earth during the Tribulation. The church is on earth now to preach the gospel and bring forth fruit after our own kind. During the Tribulation there will be no time to propagate, and the gospel will be entrusted into the hands of the 144,000 Jewish evangelists (see Revelation 7:1-8), the two supernatural witnesses of Revelation 11, and the angel that preaches "the everlasting gospel" (see Revelation 14:6-7). Consequently, the church is not needed during the time of wrath that is prophesied for this earth (see Revelation 6:1–18:24).

The Great Tribulation

This world only *thinks* it has seen tribulation.

The day is coming when the worst traumas in history will be eclipsed by a seven-year period that will be far more terrifying than anything man can imagine.

The Hebrew prophets were not silent on warnings to Israel of that traumatic time to come. They referred to it as least 21 times, using such awesome terms as:

> "The time of Jacob's trouble" (Jeremiah 30:7)
> "The day of their calamity" (Deuteronomy 32:35 and Obadiah 13)
> "The day of vengeance of our God" (Isaiah 61:2)
> "A time of trouble" (Daniel 12:1) and "a day of trouble" (Zephaniah 1:15)
> "A day of wrath" (Zephaniah 1:15)

So in the New Testament when we see such terms for that period as the "wrath of God," the "day of the Lord," or the "wrath to come," we are not at a loss to know what is meant. That period is so awesome that more space and details are given to it by the prophets, apostles, and John the Revelator in chapters 6–18 of the book of Revelation, than are even given to the glorious appearing of Christ Himself. That alone should warn us that it is a highly significant period. No wonder our Lord called it the "great tribulation, such as has not been since the beginning of the world until this time, no, nor ever shall be" (Matthew 24:21). Obviously this is a future event, for no such period has yet occurred in human history.

The events of the Tribulation are so gross they would be inconceivable except that our Lord Himself mentioned them. He designated that period as the Great Tribulation and identified the time sequence as just prior to His glorious appearing. He clearly said in His Olivet Discourse, "Immediately after the tribulation of those days....Then the sign of the Son of Man will appear in heaven, and then all the tribes of the earth will mourn, and they will see the Son of Man coming on the clouds of heaven with power and great glory" (Matthew 24:29-30).

The Hebrew prophet Daniel predicted that the Tribulation would last seven years. Seventy *heptads*, or seven-year periods, were determined upon the people of God, the nation Israel (see 9:24-27), meaning 70 times seven (or 490) years. They fell into three divisions: seven *heptads* or 49 years to restore the wall of Jerusalem; 62 *heptads* or 434 years until "Messiah shall be cut off" (Christ's crucifixion); and seven years that have not yet been fulfilled. Israel has been on prophetic "hold" for almost 2,000 years, but someday it will be at center stage during the final seven-year period.[1]

Jesus predicted that, due to its appalling nature, the Tribulation will be shortened. It will be a terrible holocaust because it combines the wrath of God, the fury of Satan, and the evil nature of man run wild.

Take the horror of every war since time began, throw in every natural disaster in recorded history, and cast off all restraints so that the unspeakable cruelty and hatred and injustice of man toward his fellow men can fully mature—then compress it all into a period of seven years. Even if you could imagine such a thing, it wouldn't approach the mind-boggling terror and turmoil of the Tribulation.

I have noticed that mid-Trib and post-Trib writings seldom take the Tribulation period literally. If they did, they might be more reluctant to conclude that Christians must endure it.

Many mid-Trib proponents believe that the first three-and-a-half years are relatively mild, for they place the three main judgments of Revelation in the last half of the Tribulation.

According to their teaching, Christians living at that time will escape the Great Tribulation, or the last three-and-a-half years. They see God pouring out His wrath on the earth during those last 42 months.

The post-Trib position (with four variations) also reserves much of the suffering of that period for those unfortunate enough to be alive toward the end. They save an enormous number of events for the very last day and suggest that the greatest portion of wrath is unleashed only hours or moments before Christ returns. Some even propose a rapture just in time to save believers from the worst of the devastation. This position also suggests that the Lord will receive individual Christians during that time of wrath as a testimony of His power and faithfulness.

As a general rule, those who believe the pre-Tribulation rapture accept the tribulation teachings in Revelation, 2 Thessalonians, Matthew 24, and Daniel 9 more literally than do mid- and post-Tribbers, who tend to spiritualize prophecy teachings even though they do not spiritualize other scriptures. This could be the Achilles' heel of their whole system.

The chart on page 62 is based on Revelation chapters 6 through 19. Study it carefully and see if you agree that the Tribulation will be a horrifying, grisly period. It is impossible to understand how the loving Bridegroom, as our Lord presents Himself, would permit His church (which Ephesians 5 designates ás the Bride) to suffer such a terrifying time of tribulation just prior to their wedding, marriage supper, and 1,000-year honeymoon.

This chart designates the three major judgments of the book (chapters 6, 8–9, and 16) and gives chronological and consecutive descriptions of the entire seven years. The Seal Judgments take up the first 21 months of the Tribulation; then the seventh seal introduces the seven Trumpet Judgments, which encompass the next 21 months, extending to the midway point. The seventh trumpet then introduces the woes and the seven vials, which occur over the last 42 months, which Jesus called the Great Tribulation. The numbers on the chart correspond with the numbers on the following list, showing the time these events occur and the scriptures from which they are taken.

The Events of the Tribulation According to Revelation

1. Revelation 4:1-2. John, a symbol of the church, is taken up to heaven.

2. Daniel 9:27. The Antichrist signs a covenant for seven years with the nation of Israel. This is the event that inaugurates the Tribulation.

3. Revelation 6:1-2. Christ opens the first of the seven-sealed scrolls, and the rider on the white horse (probably Antichrist) appears, using diplomacy and the promise of peace to establish his one-world government.

4. Revelation 6:3-4. The second seal introduces a great world war.

5. Revelation 6:5-6. The third seal begins the suffering of famine and inflation (the aftermath of war).

6. Revelation 6:7-8. The fourth seal results, as do all wars, in death, but in this case it totals one-fourth of the people and living creatures on the earth. By today's population standards, that would amount to one-and-a-half billion people.

7. Revelation 6:9-11. This passage introduces the martyrdom of those who are converted under the preaching of the 144,000 Jewish witnesses described in chapter 7. An innumerable number of people receive Christ and are martyred by the government leader and harlot (the religious system described in chapter 17), who gets her power from the Antichrist. Note that evangelism during this period is back in the hands of the Jews. Since the church is absent, the 144,000 apostle-Paul-type believers will make powerful evangelists.

8. Revelation 6:12-17. The sixth seal exhibits the wrath of God poured out in the form of a mighty earthquake, the like of which has never been experienced. It is so severe that people call on the rocks to fall on them.

9. Revelation 8:1-6. The seventh seal introduces the seven Trumpet Judgments, ending the first quarter of the Tribulation and preparing for an even worse part called the "day of His [God's] wrath."

10. Revelation 8:7. The first trumpet judgment results in one-third of all trees and green grass being burned up by hail, fire, and blood cast upon the earth.

11. Revelation 8:8-9. The second trumpet sees a great mountain of sulfur falling into the sea and destroying a third of the sea and all living creatures in it and a third of the shipping vessels. Think of the movie *The Poseidon Adventure* multiplied times one-third of all the world's ships!

12. Revelation 8:10-11. The third trumpet causes a great star (or meteor) called *Wormwood* (or "bitter") to fall on the fountains of water and a third of the rivers to turn bitter, resulting in the deaths of millions.

13. Revelation 8:12. The fourth trumpet results in one-third less sun, moonlight, and stars, extending the darkness of night.

14. Revelation 8:13. A special angel flies around the earth, warning that worse judgments are to come.

15. Revelation 9:1-12. The fifth trumpet introduces hideous demonlike creatures such as scorpions and locusts out of the bottomless pit. Not able to kill men, they torture them so badly that they "will seek death and will not find it" (verse 6).

16. Revelation 9:13. The sixth trumpet introduces 200 million horsemen (demon spiritlike death angels), who kill one-third of the people on earth. This will occur between the fortieth and forty-second month of the first part of the Tribulation, which brings to 50 percent the population that is destroyed by God before the midpoint of the Tribulation. These individuals have taken the mark of the Beast and are considered incorrigibles. Since estimates of upwards of a quarter of those living at that time will be saved under the preaching of the 144,000 mentioned in Revelation 7:9, it is possible that 75 percent of the population (25 percent by martyrdom) will have been destroyed during the first half of the Tribulation period.

Now do you understand why I say that even a mid-Tribulation view of Christ's coming for His church would mean enormous suffering to millions of believers?

It seems much more reasonable, particularly in the light of Christ's promises to save His church from the "wrath to come,"

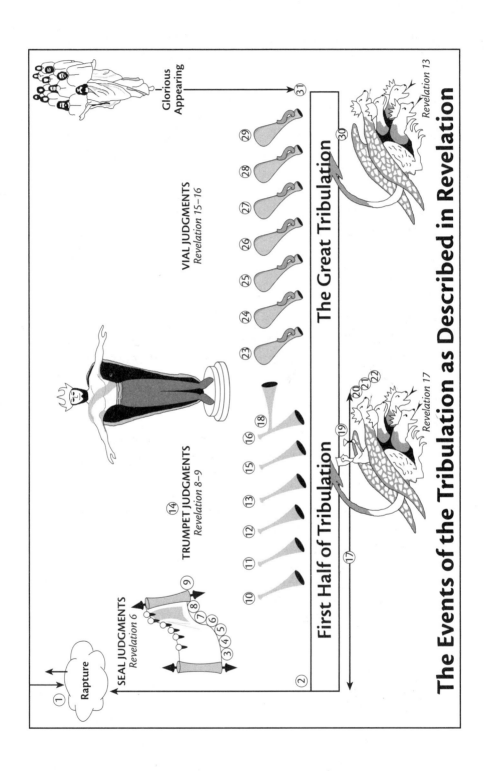

Glorious
Appearing

VIAL JUDGMENTS
Revelation 15–16

TRUMPET JUDGMENTS
Revelation 8–9

SEAL JUDGMENTS
Revelation 6

Rapture

Revelation 17

Revelation 13

First Half of Tribulation

The Great Tribulation

The Events of the Tribulation as Described in Revelation

that He would save His church from the "hour of trial which shall come upon the whole world" (Revelation 3:10). That would certainly be characteristic of our loving, merciful, forgiving heavenly Father and Bridegroom. Also, keep in mind that the saints who are martyred during the Tribulation are not part of the church. They are defined in Revelation 7:14 as "the ones who come out of the great tribulation, and [have] washed their robes and made them white in the blood of the Lamb."

17. Revelation 11:3-14. The two witnesses prophesy 1,260 days— a ministry which, if taken literally, would correspond with the 42 months of judgments already described.

Obviously, these two witnesses are real people with miraculous powers like Moses and Elijah, here to preach and witness during the entire first half of the Tribulation. It may be through their witness that the 144,000 are saved and sent out preaching. As dreadful a time as this will be, God is faithful to provide plenty of gospel preaching to the nations.

18. Revelation 11:15. The seventh trumpet judgment introduces the awesome events described in chapters 12–18 and the most severe set of judgments yet reported, the Vial Judgments.

19. Revelation 17:1-18. Describes the destruction of the Babylonish false religious system—the great harlot—which will merge all the religions of the world during the first part of the Tribulation (which will take place easily after the church is raptured). This system will be so powerful that it will dominate both the Antichrist (or the Beast) and the ten kings at that time. But because of their hatred for the harlot, at the midpoint of the Tribulation, they will make war on her and kill her.

20. Revelation 13:1-3. In the process of killing the harlot Mystery Babylon, the false religious system, somehow the Antichrist is killed and gets "a deadly wound" that is healed. In chapter 12 Satan himself is cast out of heaven, where he has been "the accuser of our brethren," and he enters Antichrist's body and resurrects him to a new and even more vicious life.

21. Revelation 13:4-10. Antichrist, now incarnated, will force the remaining people of the earth to worship him, except those

whose names are in the Lamb's Book of Life (see 2 Thessalonians 2:8-10).

22. Revelation 13:11-18. The False Prophet will replace the slain religious system, forcing people to worship Antichrist and his image or be killed. Everyone will be compelled to bear the mark or name of the Beast in order to hold a job and "buy or sell" (verse 17).

Plainly, if the church were to go through the Tribulation, she would not survive it. And I find no scriptural evidence that any believers will remain at the end of the Tribulation to be raptured, if that event is post-Trib. Remember, the worst half of the Tribulation period, which our Lord terms the Great Tribulation, has not yet begun! That last 42-month period is covered by the Vial Judgments, which take place next in this chronology.

23. Revelation 16:1-2. The first vial causes giant sores on those who rejected Christ and instead accepted the mark of the Beast, signifying their worship of him.

24. Revelation 16:3. The second vial is poured out on the sea, turning it to "blood as of a dead man; and every living creature in the sea died."

25. Revelation 16:4. The third vial turns the rivers and other sources of water to blood (an especially just judgment because the people remaining had killed so many Tribulation saints).

26. Revelation 16:8-9. The fourth vial will intensify the sun's heat until ungodly men blaspheme the name of God.

27. Revelation 16:10-11. The fifth vial will cause darkness to cover the throne of Antichrist and his entire kingdom. The sores will continue unrelentingly, producing such agony that men will gnaw their tongues in pain and blaspheme God and refuse to repent.

28. Revelation 16:13-16. The sixth vial sends lying demon spirits out to the kings of the whole world to bring them down to "the battle of that great day of God Almighty," more popularly known as the Battle of Armageddon.

29. Revelation 16:17-21. The seventh vial results in a judgment of Almighty God that destroys the entire world system and

judges all unsaved men severely. But even though enormous hailstones fall, the unregenerate still refuse to repent. This judgment is devastating and prepares the world for the coming of Christ to set up His earthly kingdom.

30. Revelation 18:1-24. The destruction of commercial and governmental Babylon—the new world order for which man has yearned ever since his rebellion at Babylon—now occurs, possibly during the seventh vial, since it fits there (verse 19) just before earth's final judgment. There will be a total collapse of the Antichrist's system and the way will be paved for the best event of the Tribulation.

31. Revelation 19:11-21. At the end of the Tribulation is the glorious appearing of Christ in power and great glory as King of kings and Lord of lords to set up His 1,000-year reign on this earth.

After reviewing these 31 traumatic events, we can understand why the Hebrew prophets and the apostles used such strong terms to identify the Tribulation. And, while God did not promise to save the Christian from daily trials and tribulations, or even the wrath of man, He did pledge to exempt us from the day of His wrath.

I simply cannot imagine the heavenly Bridegroom whispering these words to His chosen one: "Yes, My bride, My precious one, I loved you so much that I gave My life for you. I want to nourish and cherish you. I want to take you home with Me and celebrate our marriage with joy and singing and feasting. I want to be with you forever. But before I bring you home, I want you to experience seven years of the very fury of hell and seven years of the terrible wrath of My Father. But try not to worry. I'll come back for you when it's all over."

No, we can expect God to keep His promise to rapture the church out of the world before it is plunged into this awful time of tribulation. God keeps His word! And He is a God of love and mercy to those who receive Him. *Amen*

Why a Tribulation Anyway?

Everything God does has purpose, so we can expect that the horrendous Tribulation will accomplish something specific. An examination of the Word of God does not disappoint us. Like everything our Lord does, He has more than one purpose in mind.

1. *To bring time to an end.* When introducing the events that culminate with the Tribulation and return of Christ (Daniel 9:24), the prophet Daniel spoke of the consummation of time as "bring[ing] in everlasting righteousness" (9:24). The Tribulation is a fitting consummation of the grand experiment of the ages from Adam to the second coming, giving individuals an opportunity to worship God voluntarily.

2. *To fulfill the prophecies about Israel.* Many prophecies about Israel have yet to be fulfilled. The Jewish people's return to their land during this last century and the recognition of Israel as a nation in 1948 are two (described in detail in Ezekiel 36–37). The prophecies regarding the rebuilding of the temple and renewing temple sacrifices will also be consummated during that seven-year period. And there are still other prophecies that concern Israel as well. God is not through with Israel!

3. *To shake man from his false sense of security.* A stable world leads people to think that they can function independently from God. Earthquakes, plagues, and other physical phenomena from God will so shake people's natural confidence that, when they hear the gospel through the preaching of the 144,000, some of them will be more open to its offer of forgiveness and grace.

4. *To force man to choose Christ or Antichrist.* One major purpose of the Tribulation is to give the billions of individuals living at that time seven years of opportunity in which to make up their minds to receive or reject Christ. That may be part of what Daniel meant in calling it "the consummation" (Daniel 9:27). Billions of people will not have an opportunity to live out their normal lifespan, so amid these traumatic events, they will make an eternal decision. If they choose Christ, they will, as "servants of our God," receive the mark of the Father on their foreheads (Revelation 7:3). But they will then be "open season" for martyrdom at the hands of the religious system of Babylon, the government leaders headed by Antichrist, the False Prophet, and the people whose lust for sin is surpassed only by their hatred for Christians. It is doubtful that many—if any—Tribulation saints will survive to the beginning of Christ's millennial kingdom.

If, on the other hand, people accept the Antichrist, they will have the mark of the Beast, or 666, placed on their foreheads or hands. This seems to be a final, irrevocable decision. Once it is made, they will be eliminated by the judgments of God mentioned above. It is as if the followers of Antichrist become incorrigible and the earth is purged of them so that the undecided can more clearly make their choice between Christ and Antichrist.

One Last Expression of God's Love

In the midst of this awful time of physical controversy, another mighty spiritual battle will rage between the forces of Satan (in the form of the demons let loose from the bottomless pit) and the forces of God (in the form of the Jewish witnesses of chapter 7 and the two witnesses with supernatural powers described in chapter 11). The conflict will be over the souls of men and women. We will briefly glimpse the extent of this battle of heavenly hosts later in chapter 12.

Though the Tribulation is a cataclysmic time of judgment, God's love and compassion will still be evident. In Revelation 14:6-7, the "angel...having the everlasting gospel" is seen preaching to "those who dwell on the earth—to every nation, tribe, tongue, and people." We have already noted that God will offer mankind one last opportunity to accept His Son as the way of salvation through the testimony of His 144,000 witnesses. But just to make sure everyone hears and has opportunity to respond, He will send a special angel to earth to preach the gospel message within the hearing of every person. The people will be challenged to "fear God and give glory to Him...and worship Him." Those who do will be saved eternally; those who refuse will worship the Satan-filled Antichrist and be lost.

The Rapture Is Before the Tribulation

Now that we have reviewed a detailed chronology of the events of the Tribulation, I hope you have noticed something: it is not intended for the church! It is meant for Israel and the Gentiles. Israel still has seven unfulfilled years ahead of her.

(Daniel limits this period to seven years divided into two sections of three-and-a-half years each; he restricts the last half to 1,290 days [Daniel 12:9-11].) This time will allow the lost to make their decision for Christ before the ultimate battle between Satan and Christ.

There is no need for the church to be on earth during the Tribulation. Not only is Scripture totally silent about the church during the Tribulation, but in Revelation chapter 19 we find her already in heaven, coming down with Christ at the end of the Tribulation.

The church will be raptured before the Tribulation begins, thus fulfilling our Lord's promise to His church, "I also will keep you from [out of] the hour of trial which shall come upon the whole world, to test those who dwell on the earth" (Revelation 3:10). Christians don't need that test. They have already made their decision for Christ and against Antichrist. Only lost souls will proceed into the Tribulation.

It is apparent, then, that the Tribulation will be the most frightful seven years in world history.

It is anything but a blessed hope.

Chapter Five

Blessed or Blasted Hope?

M y love for second-coming teachings, particularly the Rapture of the church, was sparked as I stood at my father's grave at the age of nine. His sudden death of a heart attack left me devastated. My pastor, who also was my uncle, pointed his finger toward heaven and proclaimed, "This is not the last of Frank LaHaye. Because of his personal faith in Christ, one day he will be resurrected by the shout of our Lord; we will be translated to meet him and our other loved ones in the clouds and be with them and our Lord forever." That promise from Scripture was the only hope for my broken heart that day. And that same promise has comforted millions of others through the years.

Can you imagine saying on such an occasion to grieving saints, "And as soon as we endure part or all of the Tribulation, our Lord will rapture us and reunite us with our loved ones again"? Comfort is the essence of that primary rapture passage of 1 Thessalonians 4:13-18, for it ends, "Therefore comfort one another with these words." As we noted earlier, that passage was written early in the life of the church in answer to the concern of new believers about the future of their deceased loved ones when the Lord returns for living believers. In order to comfort these new Christians, God revealed the mystery of the Rapture.

If we locate the Rapture after the Tribulation or in the middle of it, the hope and comfort of the teaching is effectively defaced, particularly once we understand the Tribulation events as I

69

outlined them in the previous chapter. Those 31 events are cataclysms no person can await without dread and dismay. It is a mystery to me how anyone can challenge Christians to live in expectation of the Rapture if it should follow the worst period of God's wrath in all history.

Can a Christian man honestly get excited about Christ's coming if he knows that he will no longer be able to support his family or buy food for them because he refused the mark of the Beast? It would be hard for a believing father to anticipate with joy Christ's return knowing that he might watch his children starve to death.

Most mid-Trib or post-Trib teachers soft-pedal those events of the Tribulation which they prescribe for the church. And while the Lord will impart special grace to those who accept Christ after the Rapture and who must survive the sufferings of that period, it would take a masochist to look forward to it as a time of blessing.

No, the hope and comfort aspect of the Rapture demands that we escape the Tribulation, being raptured out of this world before God's wrath is poured out.

The "Blessed Hope" Is Just That

Sometimes words seem too frail to carry vast thoughts and sweeping concepts. Four English letters, H-O-P-E, are often called upon to bear the implications of a shining promise so wonderful and incomprehensible that they must surely shudder under its weight.

> Let not your heart be troubled; you believe in God, believe also in Me. In My Father's house are many mansions; if it were not so, I would have told you. I go to prepare a place for you. And if I go and prepare a place for you, I will come again and receive you to Myself; that where I am, there you may be also (John 14:1-3).

This is a prospect so staggering and so brilliant that the simple word *hope* doesn't seem adequate to bear it. Perhaps that's why Paul, in Titus 2:13, titled it "the blessed hope."

Paul's "blessed hope" is the Rapture, for it is unique to the church. No one else will take part in it. One must have a born-again relationship with Christ, through faith in His death and resurrection (see 1 Thessalonians 4:14), in order to participate in it.

The glorious appearing, on the other hand, is not for the Christian but for the remnant at the end of the Tribulation. It will primarily affect the Jews and those who have been good to them and who have somehow survived the Tribulation.

The fact that the Rapture is called the blessed *hope* by no means suggests that it is uncertain. *Hope* in this biblical context signifies confident expectation that Christ is coming. Of that there is no doubt because it is based on the certain Word of God that abides forever, will never pass away, and is settled in heaven. The word *hope* is used to denote two things: 1) a future event, and 2) something special to anticipate.

If Christ does not rapture His church before the Tribulation begins, much of the hope is destroyed, and thus it becomes a *blasted* hope rather than a blessed one.

The resurrection of all believers who have died in the Lord, and the translation of living believers to meet each other in the clouds as Paul described, have been treasured expectations for almost 20 centuries. We commit loved ones to the ground with the confident hope that we will see each other again at the Rapture and then join our Lord in the Father's house. Death for a Christian is but a temporary time of separation from friends. That is the hope of our faith.

Shouldn't We Prepare for the Tribulation?

One of the weakest arguments for rejecting the pre-Trib position is that we should be preparing the church for the coming Tribulation; otherwise, Christians will be unable to endure the sufferings of those months of calamity. After all, the thinking goes, the church today is so self-indulgent that it will crack under the attacks of the Antichrist, or will become disillusioned if it expects to be raptured prior to the Tribulation but wakes up one day to find that the church is entering the Tribulation. Some ministers even say that those of us who offer the hope of a pre-Tribulation rapture will be attacked by angry Christians if it turns out that believers have to go through the Tribulation after all.

Such a pessimistic view not only blasts the hope out of the Rapture but sells short the enabling ministry of the Holy Spirit. If the church were forced to proceed through the Tribulation, we would not be abandoned by the Spirit of God. Philippians 4:19 would not be torn from our Bibles, for God would still supply all our needs. Besides, how would one prepare for such a time of tribulation? True, we could memorize more Scripture, but you don't need the threat of tribulation for that.

All agree that people will be saved during the Tribulation. These Tribulation saints will be martyred because of their love for Christ. The Holy Spirit will provide these Tribulation martyrs supernatural grace to be faithful until death. It seems ridiculous to me to promise God's sufficiency to these new baby believers and then warn today's Christians that unless they are prepared properly, they won't be able to make it during the Tribulation.

No, a message of foreboding is hardly a message of hope. My friend, Dr. Ed Hindson, tells the story of a great preacher of another era who was defending his belief that Christ could come at any moment. The man suggested that those who no longer embrace this blessed hope should stop singing, "Glad day! Glad day!...Jesus may come today," and start moaning, "Sad day! Sad day! Jesus can't come today! I'll live out each day and anxious be, the Beast and False Prophet I soon shall see. Sad day! Sad day! Jesus can't come today."

The only way anyone could consider the mid-Tribulation rapture a blessed hope is to know nothing about the true nature of the Tribulation or to spiritualize away the gravity of such events.

Pre- or Mid-Trib Views Destroys Imminency

The believers in the first-century church believed in the imminent return of Christ, possibly during their lifetime. Paul exhorted the infant church of Thessalonica to consecrated living in view of that coming. Not only had they "turned to God from idols to serve the living and true God, and to wait for His Son from heaven" (1 Thessalonians 1:9-10), but they were challenged to soul-winning in view of the promise of His return.

That imminency-based challenge coincides with many similar directives given by our Lord to expect Him at any time. He admonishes, "Watch therefore, for you do not know what hour your Lord is coming" (Matthew 24:42), and "be ready, for the Son of Man is coming at an hour when you do not expect Him" (Matthew 24:44; see also Matthew 25:13). As we shall learn, a church filled with imminence-consciousness is a church more prone to holy living in an unholy society. John likewise predicted in his first epistle, "And everyone who has this hope in Him purifies himself, just as He is pure" (3:3).

What happens when you take away the certainty that Jesus Christ could appear at any moment?

It takes the edge off your guard. In a spiritual sense, you may not be able to sleep profoundly, but you will think that you can certainly afford a few lapses, a few catnaps. "Yes, my Lord is coming and I need to be ready...but I'll have plenty of notice—at least three-and-a-half years. Yes, I need to keep watch, but nothing is going to surprise me, because I have a list of events that have to happen before my Lord appears."

Our Lord and His apostles taught imminency to those early Christians and to us in order to counter the temptations of our world system and Satan himself. And historically, it has worked. Whenever believers have anticipated the return of the Lord in their lifetime, the result has been a higher level of consecration, a greater zeal for soul-winning, and a heightened desire to send out missionaries. It is no accident that the first three centuries of the church age were exceptional in these areas. But that zeal faded as second-coming teachings were all but abandoned under the Roman church. After the Reformation's renewed emphasis on accepting the Bible literally revived interest in prophecy and the return of Christ, belief in His imminent return again produced holy living in an unholy world.

It is a sad commentary on the church that in its twenty-century history, only five centuries have featured imminency. But those have been the most consecrated, soul-winning, missionary-minded, and spiritually productive days of the church.

Frankly, one of my principal objections to the mid- and post-Trib theories is their destruction of imminency. For if Christ cannot come at any moment, then we cannot be instructed to look for His return. Instead, we are advised to look for the inauguration of the Tribulation, when Antichrist signs a covenant with Israel for seven years, and to watch for the rebuilding of the temple, the mark of the Beast, the advent of Antichrist himself, and the 31 events listed in chapter 4 of this book. Only the pre-Tribulation view retains the promise of imminency!

Pre-Tribbers are looking for Christ, not Antichrist.

I have long been mystified that good brethren who love the Lord and His return accept the mid- or post-Trib position when it destroys a central teaching of our Lord—that "in such an hour as ye think not the Son of man cometh" (Matthew 24:44 KJV) and, "Of that day and hour no one knows, no, not even the angels of heaven, but My Father only" (Matthew 24:36). If a person adheres to the mid- or post-Trib views, then there is no secrecy about Christ's coming. Anyone can calculate precisely when He will come: He will return 1,260 days after Israel signs the covenant with the Antichrist (if the mid-Trib view is right) or seven years after that event (according to the post-Trib position). Both views effectively destroy imminency! Only the pre-Trib view retains the constant expectation that Christ could come at any moment. Lovers of biblical truth will have to be confronted with more convincing evidence than has yet been produced before they will feel compelled to embrace a teaching that destroys imminency.

No Signs Before the Rapture

Even the opponents of the pre-Tribulation position admit that the Bible teaches there are no signs associated with Christ's rapture of His church. All the sign prophecies (of which there are many)[1] relate to the glorious appearing. Pre-Tribulationists are ridiculed by some for writing books about the signs of Christ's coming while insisting that no specific signs exist for the Rapture, but these critics overlook an important fact. The signs predicted for the end of this age, which terminate in the glorious appearing, will cast long shadows before them and serve as general warnings to Christians who prepare for His coming. The time is near at hand! Like Simeon and Anna, who knew the Lord would be born during their lifetime, it is possible for diligent students of prophecy to anticipate the season of the Rapture. In fact, Scripture says that "the morning star rises in your hearts" (2 Peter 1:19). That morning star could mean a spirit of anticipation of His soon coming.

One of my associate pastors illustrated this anticipation with a story about shopping with his wife in early November. He was amazed to see the stores putting up Christmas trees and other holiday decorations so soon.

He asked me, "What does that tell you?"

"Christmas is coming!" I responded.

"Nope," he replied, "it means that *Thanksgiving* is coming! We must celebrate Thanksgiving before we can have Christmas."

So it is when signs of the glorious appearing occur. We can be assured that the Rapture is coming! And the coming of Christ in power and great glory will soon follow.

It's legitimate for us to study the signs of Christ's coming or the end of the age (see Matthew 24:3) so that we can discern the approximate time (or season) of His return. Just remember: Whatever your conclusion about how much time we have left, you must subtract at least seven years for the Rapture of the church. The blessed hope is the assurance you will be ready when He shouts from heaven—and that it will be before the Tribulation that will "test those who dwell on the earth" (Revelation 3:10).

All other views are a blasted hope.

Chapter Six

Who Says It's Obscure?

One objection to the pre-Tribulation rapture is that no one passage of Scripture teaches the two phases of Christ's second coming separated by the Tribulation. This is true. But then, no one passage teaches a post-Tribulation or mid-Tribulation rapture, either. (And no one passage teaches against the pre-Trib view.) Our task is to carefully study all the second-coming passages to see if they are talking about the same event. What we discover is that most of them talk about the coming of Christ in glory to set up His kingdom. There are, however, at least three that clearly refer to the Rapture—and several that are less plain.

Since we are deriving our position from the Word of God, one reference alone would be sufficient. But there are several. We have already considered three main rapture passages: John 14:1-3; 1 Thessalonians 4:13-18; 1 Corinthians 15:51-58. Other brief passages, such as 1 Thessalonians 1:8-10, do not clearly distinguish between the two stages of Christ's coming, but they do provide more details about the Rapture rather than the glorious appearing. In 5:9-10 of the same book, we find yet another passage. I have already stated how Revelation 4:1-2 likewise furnishes an allusion to the Rapture. In addition, we have identified four passages predicting that we will be saved "from [out of] wrath to come," or the wrath that will be poured out during the Tribulation.

In three other Bible passages I have found the two phases of Christ's coming mentioned in one verse, one chapter, and one book. The last two show the two events separated by the Tribulation period, or the activities of the Antichrist, during the seven-year Tribulation.

The Rapture and Glorious Appearing in One Verse

In Titus 2:13, Paul issues a hard-hitting challenge to God's people to live a holy and godly life. Part of that appeal is based on the second coming of our Lord: "looking for the *blessed hope* and *glorious appearing* of our great God and Savior Jesus Christ" (emphasis added).

The blessed hope is definitely a reference to the Rapture of the church. Examined from every angle, the Rapture, immediately following the resurrection of dead believers, is the blessed hope of the church. As we have already noted, our confident expectation is that one day we will be translated to be with Christ before the time of wrath begins.

I observed in a previous chapter that if looking forward to His coming means enduring the Tribulation with all its judgments, trumpets, bowls, vials, and catastrophes, it will not be a blessed hope at all. That may be why the blessed hope is always mentioned in a context of joy.

Consider our Lord's challenge to His disciples the night before He died. He did not say, "Buck up, men! Don't let your hearts be troubled just because you have to go through the Tribulation before I can take you to be with Myself." Instead He urged, "Let not your heart be troubled....I will come again and receive you to Myself; that where I am, there you may be also" (John 14:1,3). This directly parallels Paul's announcement, "The Lord Himself will descend....Then we who are alive and remain shall be caught up...to meet the Lord in the air" (1 Thessalonians 4:16-17). The Rapture is truly a blessed hope to the church.

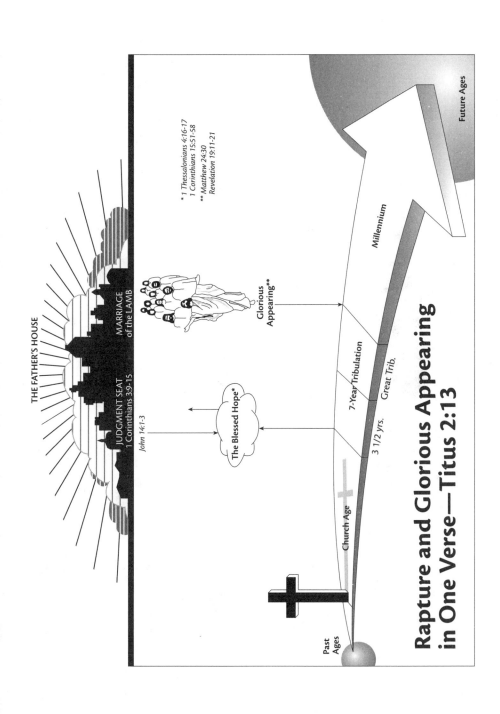

THE FATHER'S HOUSE

JUDGMENT SEAT
1 Corinthians 3:9-15

MARRIAGE
of the LAMB

John 14:1-3

The Blessed Hope*

* 1 Thessalonians 4:16-17
1 Corinthians 15:51-58

** Matthew 24:30
Revelation 19:11-21

Glorious
Appearing**

Past
Ages

Church Age

3 1/2 yrs.

7-Year Tribulation

Great Trib.

Millennium

Future Ages

Rapture and Glorious Appearing
in One Verse—Titus 2:13

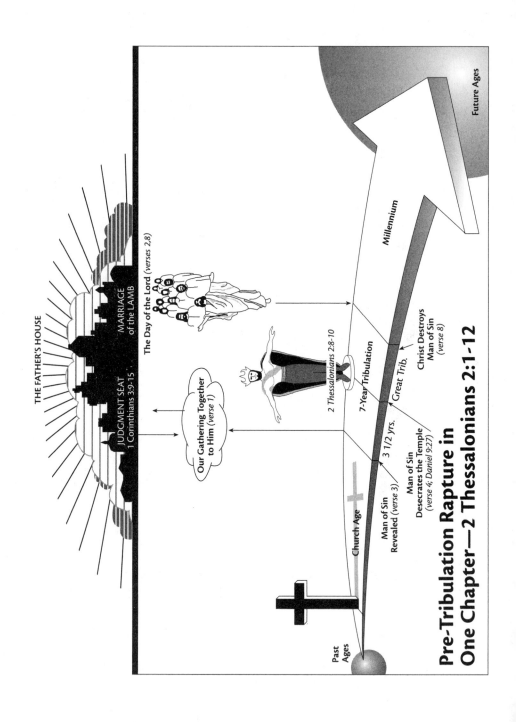

THE FATHER'S HOUSE

JUDGMENT SEAT
1 Corinthians 3:9-15

MARRIAGE
of the LAMB

The Day of the Lord *(verses 2,8)*

Our Gathering Together
to Him *(verse 1)*

2 Thessalonians 2:8-10

Christ Destroys
Man of Sin
(verse 8)

7-Year Tribulation

Great Trib.

Man of Sin
Revealed *(verse 3)*

Man of Sin
Desecrates the Temple
(verse 4; Daniel 9:27)

3 1/2 yrs.

Church Age

Millennium

Past
Ages

Future Ages

Pre-Tribulation Rapture in
One Chapter—2 Thessalonians 2:1-12

The glorious appearing is quite a different matter. It heralds that special day when Christ will return to this earth in triumph to be acknowledged by all men as King of kings and Lord of lords. The glorious appearing is Christ's literal, physical return to the earth along with His church—the second phase of His coming. The Rapture is His return in the air to receive the church. Both phases of Christ's return are mentioned in Titus 2:13, which refers in a single verse to the Rapture as the "blessed hope," and the coming to earth as the "glorious appearing."

Pre-Tribulationism in One Chapter

Second Thessalonians 2:1-12 contains the Rapture, Tribulation, and glorious appearing all in one chapter, the only time we find this in the Bible. The whole subject is referred to in the first verse as "the coming of our Lord Jesus Christ." Then Paul uses a conjunction, usually translated "and" but also rendered "even." In either case, he refers to "our gathering together to Him." The second coming refers to the two phases separated by seven years. Our "gathering together to Him" cannot refer to the glorious appearing, since that is when all living creatures are congregated for the judgment of the nations and the establishment of Christ's kingdom. The "gathering together to Him" refers to the Rapture, the event when Christ welcomes His church to be with Him. Thus in verse 1 we find both the glorious appearing and the "gathering together to Him."

Paul then follows with one of the most detailed descriptions in the New Testament (except in the book of Revelation) of the Antichrist's activities, which he places between these two distinct events. Just as John locates Antichrist's coming before the glorious appearing in the book of Revelation, so Paul in this passage does the same. "The day of Christ" is the public appearance of Christ to the earth, which will not take place until the man of sin, the son of perdition, that lawless one is destroyed by the Lord "at the brightness of His coming "(verse 8)—the glorious appearing.

In the chart on page 80 you will find the distinction between "our gathering together to Him" (already detailed in 1 Thessalonians 4:13-18) and the glorious appearing separated by the actions of the man of sin or Antichrist, all in one chapter

(2 Thessalonians 2). While we must look to Daniel and John for the time of these events (seven years), Paul mentions all three events here in one chapter.

Pre-Tribulationism in One Book

The book of Revelation was written by John about 50 years after the Lord founded His church and ascended to heaven. In it he not only revealed Jesus Christ in His present and future states, but also outlined "things which must take place" (Revelation 4:1). The book flows from the days of John all the way to the coming of Christ in power to set up His kingdom.

Chapter 1 is the introduction, and chapters 2 and 3 cover the church age, using seven historical churches to describe the entire age. (For example, the church of Ephesus is the only one that refers to apostles because the first-century church alone included apostles.)[1]

Chapters 4 and 5 draw the curtain on the drama in heaven. Then chapters 6 to 18 provide the most detailed description of the events of the Tribulation period to be found in the Bible. In chapter 19 Christ comes physically to the earth, judging the Antichrist, the False Prophet, and the nations. In chapter 20 He binds Satan in the bottomless pit, then sets up His 1,000-year kingdom on earth, followed by the judgments on the lost of all ages. The last two chapters (21 and 22) describe the eternal heaven that Christ has prepared for believers throughout history.

Now look at the end of the church age on the chart on page 83. Chapters 2 and 3 of Revelation describe events that will occur on the earth. Chapters 4 and 5 present a brief description of events in heaven, most of which have already transpired. As we have already seen, just prior to the beginning of the Tribulation, John, a member of the church age, is invited up to heaven in Revelation 4:1-2:

> After these things I looked, and behold, a door standing open in heaven. And the first voice which I heard was like a trumpet speaking with me, saying, "Come up here, and I will show you things which must take place after this." Immediately I was in the Spirit;

THE FATHER'S HOUSE

JUDGMENT SEAT
1 Corinthians 3:9-15

MARRIAGE
of the LAMB

Rapture

Judgment Seat of Christ
2 Corinthians 5:10

Believers'
Judgment

Glorious
Appearing

Great
White Throne
Judgment

Past
Ages

Chapter 1   2

Church Age

3   6–7   3 1/2 yrs.

4–5

8–9   13   16   20

10–12
14–15
17

18
19b

7-Year Tribulation

Great Trib

19a

Millennium

21–22

Future Ages

Pre-Tribulationism in One Book: Revelation

and behold, a throne set in heaven, and One sat on the throne.

This passage alone would not establish the Rapture as a pre-Tribulation event, but in light of the passages we have already studied, describing the translation of all believers (both dead and living) at this stage of Christ's coming, John being called up into heaven could certainly be construed as a preface to the pre-Tribulation rapture. John is at least representative of the church when he is raptured to be with Christ in the air while the people still living on earth proceed into the Tribulation period.

The church should not be expecting the Tribulation period, but Jewish people should. According to the prophecy in Daniel 9:24-27, seven years still remain prophetically unfulfilled for them as a nation. Those years will be completed during that period of wrath known as "the time of Jacob's trouble" (Jeremiah 30:7). Unsaved Gentiles should also anticipate that time when the new world order or one-world government will come on the scene with the cry, "Let's give world peace a chance." A charismatic world figure who has no place for God or His moral values will bring this about through the United Nations or some other major international organization.

Christians are not anticipating that time of wrath, but the coming of our Lord. Accordingly, we should so live that if He raptures His church "at an hour when you do not expect Him" (Matthew 24:44), we will be ready. Certainly every unsaved person who has heard the gospel and understands it should call on the name of the Lord for salvation, lest these days come upon him as a thief and he be left behind.

More important than any other question about Bible prophecy is this: If Christ were to come today to rapture His church and commence the Tribulation, would you be ready to be caught up with Him in the air? If not, make yourself ready by personally inviting Christ into your heart by faith.

Strong Scriptural Support

The Scripture texts we examined in this chapter demonstrate that the teaching of the Rapture of the church before the

Tribulation and the glorious coming of Christ afterward isn't so obscure. We have noted the two aspects of Christ's coming in one verse, the entire sequence in one chapter, and again in a complete book. While critics complain that the pre-Trib theory is not covered in a single passage, we have noted that Titus 2:13 gives the titles for the two events (the blessed hope and the glorious appearing); 2 Thessalonians 2:1-12 describes the two events (our gathering together to Him and the brightness of His coming) separated by the man of sin and Tribulation events; and the book of Revelation does the same (church age, John caught up to heaven, the seven-year Tribulation, and the coming of Christ in power to the earth).

No other view of end-time events can produce such passages to support its position. What others call obscure is nothing less than the plain teaching of Scripture.

Chapter Seven

The Glorious Appearing

A ll Christians agree that this world has not seen the last of Jesus Christ.

He will return to the earth, but not in the humble fashion of His first coming, when His purpose was to die for the sins of mankind. That was accomplished almost 2,000 years ago. We now await His second coming "with power and great glory!" (Matthew 24:30).

Only the doctrine of salvation is mentioned more often in the Bible than is the assurance of His second coming. Three hundred and eighteen or more such promises are recorded in the prophets, Jesus' own teachings, and the writings of the apostles. Even the angels proclaim this advent. If frequency of mention is any indication of prominence, then the second coming of our Lord is easily the second-most-important teaching in Scripture.

If Jesus Christ does not return physically and literally to this earth to set up His kingdom, Christianity will turn out to be the greatest hoax in history. His return is so intimately tied to the most central doctrines of the Bible and the church that the validity of Christianity totally depends upon it.

Without the second coming there will be no resurrection of the dead, no judgment seat of Christ, no rewards, no heaven or eternity, no final triumph of good over evil, and no casting of Satan—the old tempter of men—into eternal hell. All of these biblically predicted events await our Lord's return.

One of the most authenticated facts of ancient history is the first coming of Jesus Christ. Even today every check and letter is dated in the year of our Lord. Why was His birth selected to be the benchmark by which to date history? Primarily because of who He was—God in human flesh—and what He did for humanity in dying for the sins of all mankind. We can identify Him because He fulfilled so many Old Testament prophecies that even some of His contemporaries, such as Simeon, Anna, and John the Baptist, were looking for Him. Consequently, they recognized Him as the Lamb of God or the Messiah.

Today, no scholar of academic substance denies that Jesus lived almost 2,000 years ago. And we find three times as many prophecies in the Bible relating to His second coming as to His first. Thus the second advent of our Lord is three times as certain as His first coming, which can be verified as historical fact.

How important is His return? One indication is its universal acceptance by all Christians regardless of their denominational or theological persuasion. It forms a part of every written creed and all church doctrinal statements. Christians may disagree on the time or events surrounding His coming, and some do not recognize the different states, but all concur that He will come again to raise and judge the dead before leading them into eternity.

The World's Greatest Event

Jesus Christ's second coming will be the most significant event in the 2,000 years since His arrival on earth as a baby, for it will complete the current era of God's grace to man and usher in an entirely new program called the *Millennium*. And although many titles are given for that visible phase of His coming when He will be acknowledged as King of kings and Lord of lords, the most descriptive title for it came from the pen of the apostle Paul, who labeled it the "glorious appearing" (Titus 2:13).

That event will give purpose and meaning to the creation of this universe, to life, and to eternity. It will consummate at least 6,000 years of God's dealings with mankind, bringing him into the relationship that God originally intended for Adam and Eve when He placed them in the Garden of Eden. The people who dwell on the earth during the Millennium will voluntarily submit to God's authority and willingly serve Him.

The event that triggers that new era is the second coming of Christ "with power and great glory." It is not only called the "glorious appearing," but "the revelation" and the "coming of the Son of Man." Some label it "the second advent" or simply "the second coming." My favorite term for it is "the glorious appearing of Christ in power," for then the world will see our Savior as He truly is—not as the suffering servant of Yahweh who was rejected at birth, opposed in life, and crucified, but as He is *today*, the object of worship by both humans and angels.

Hollywood and Las Vegas and Madison Avenue speak of stellar events. But what do they mean? A B-grade country-and-western group appearing at the county fair? The release of the next music album by an aging lounge singer? The introduction of a new brand of imitation whipped cream? A glitz-and-glamour television awards program? The term has become so generic that it barely makes a ripple in the pool of our thoughts.

But there will be a Stellar Event. Celestial. Cosmic. Greater than earth. Greater than the heavens. And it will suck the air out of humanity's lungs and send men and women and kings and presidents and tyrants to their knees. It will have no need of spotlights, fog machines, amplified music, synthesizers, or special effects. It will be *real*.

This glorious appearing is the stellar event to which all Bible-taught Christians look. It will end the sin, injustice, and inhumanity that has always plagued human history. Christ's coming will inaugurate the resurrection of the saints and the establishment of the kingdom of peace and righteousness that was promised by the prophets, our Lord Himself, the apostles, the angels, and many Bible-believing Christians for almost 2,000 years. Consider...

Affirmation of Christ's Return

The Promises of the Hebrew Prophets

Isaiah 9:6-7 contains a much-loved and well-known promise that Christ will come twice to this earth, first to suffer and then to rule:

> For unto us a Child is born, unto us a Son is given;
> and the government will be upon His shoulder. And
> His name will be called Wonderful, Counselor, Mighty
> God, Everlasting Father, Prince of Peace. Of the
> increase of His government and peace there will be no
> end, upon the throne of David and over His kingdom,
> to order it and establish it with judgment and justice
> from that time forward, even forever. The zeal of the
> LORD of hosts will perform this.

Obviously, the second phase of our Lord's return has not yet occurred. But this passage points to a time when Christ Himself, the Son given of God, will be the supreme ruler of this universe.

When? At His glorious appearing.

Daniel chapter 7 describes four rapacious beasts that symbolize four successive world empires that have dominated the earth since the prophet's time (606 B.C.). This Gentile dominance will culminate in the appearance of Antichrist. The text then promises,

> I watched till thrones were put in place, and the
> Ancient of Days was seated; His garment was white as
> snow, and the hair of His head was like pure wool. His
> throne was a fiery flame, its wheels a burning fire
> (Daniel 7:9).

Revelation 1:14-15 identifies that person to be Christ Himself. In Daniel 7:13-14 the prophet provides more details:

> I was watching in the night visions, and behold, One
> like the Son of Man, coming with the clouds of heaven!
> He came to the Ancient of Days, and they brought Him
> near before Him. Then to Him was given dominion and
> glory and a kingdom, that all peoples, nations, and
> languages should serve Him. His dominion is an ever-
> lasting dominion, which shall not pass away, and His
> kingdom the one which shall not be destroyed.

This can be none other than God's own Son, the King Messiah come "with power and great glory."

Zechariah 14:1-9 provides details of the literal, physical coming of Messiah to rescue Israel and reign over the earth:

> Behold, the day of the LORD is coming, and your spoil will be divided in your midst....Then the LORD will go forth and fight against those nations, as He fights in the day of battle. And in that day His feet will stand on the Mount of Olives, which faces Jerusalem on the east. And the Mount of Olives shall be split in two, from east to west, making a very large valley; half of the mountain shall move toward the north and half of it toward the south....Thus the LORD my God will come, and all the saints with [Him]....And the LORD shall be King over all the earth. In that day it shall be—"The LORD is one," and His name one.

These are but a few of the many Old Testament verses that give details of the Lord's coming to establish His earthly kingdom.[1] As we have observed, there are eight times as many prophecies in the Old Testament for the coming of Messiah to rescue His people and to set up a worldwide kingdom than there were for His first coming. Because that initial coming is a historical fact, it follows that Christ's second coming is eight times as certain—and we haven't even begun to review the New Testament promises of His coming!

The Promises of Christ Himself

While the primary purpose of Christ's first coming was to suffer the judgment of God on man for the sins of the whole world, He accomplished many other things as well. He gave ample evidence of who He was, offered Himself to Israel, founded His church, trained His disciples, and taught Christians how to live during His absence. And He also took the opportunity to teach repeatedly about His second coming. In fact, two whole chapters are dedicated to that subject in the Olivet Discourse.[2]

Jesus also taught parables that spoke of His departure for "a long time" and an eventual return, at which time He will also exact an accounting from them regarding the manner in which they lived (Matthew 25:14-30; see also Luke 19:11-27).

Shortly after promising to build His church (Matthew 16:18-19), Jesus also promised that He would come again:

> For the Son of Man will come in the glory of His Father with His angels, and then He will reward each according to his works (Matthew 16:27).

In Matthew 24:27-31, in the midst of the Olivet Discourse, Jesus stated,

> As the lightning comes from the east and flashes to the west, so also will the coming of the Son of Man be. For wherever the carcass is, there the eagles will be gathered together. Immediately after the tribulation of those days the sun will be darkened, and the moon will not give its light; the stars will fall from heaven, and the powers of the heavens will be shaken. Then the sign of the Son of Man will appear in heaven, and then all the tribes of the earth will mourn, and they will see the Son of Man coming on the clouds of heaven with power and great glory. And He will send His angels with a great sound of a trumpet, and they will gather together His elect from the four winds, from one end of heaven to the other.

In Matthew 25:31-33 He promised,

> When the Son of Man comes in His glory, and all the holy angels with Him, then He will sit on the throne of His glory. All the nations will be gathered before Him, and He will separate them one from another, as a shepherd divides his sheep from the goats. And He will set the sheep on His right hand, but the goats on the left.

It is clear that our Lord believed and taught that He would come again to establish His long-promised government.

The Prediction of the Angels

Acts 1:11 contains the very first promise from heavenly beings that Christ will return. Immediately after our Lord ascended into heaven, angels announced to His followers where He had gone and then promised,

> Men of Galilee, why do you stand gazing up into heaven? This same Jesus, who was taken up from you into heaven, will so come in like manner as you saw Him go into heaven.

Watching a jet airliner take off is one thing. It's no big deal, really. It happens virtually every second in multiplied thousands of busy airports all over the world. The massive craft positions itself on the runway, pauses for clearance, then begins to move—slowly at first, with a throaty rumble. You could walk alongside and wave at someone in the window. Then fast as a bicycle…an antelope…a car…and even faster. Then with a scream the plane lifts into the sky. No longer seeming immense, it punches through a cloud layer or shrinks and shrinks into the deep blue. Then, perhaps with one last glint of the sunshine reflection on the airplane, like a bright star slowly fading in a sunrise, it disappears.

A technological feat, sure. But so commonplace. So ordinary. So ho-hum. Unless…someone you love with all your heart is on that plane, leaving you, vanishing into the distance. A child leaving for college. A husband and father leaving on a long business trip. A fiancée leaving for an extended stay with an ailing relative. A son leaving for dangerous military duty.

That's different. For then that disappearing plane feels attached to the flesh of your heart with a barbed hook—and the farther it flies away, the more it pulls on your chest and tears at the fabric of who you are.

That's what love does at an airport. That's what leaves folks standing on the tarmac shading their eyes and looking and looking into the depths of the heavens.

And that's where the angels found the disciples on that day when Jesus ascended to His Father. Their Lord had grown smaller and smaller before their tear-filled eyes until He was only a speck. Until He wasn't there at all.

But God didn't leave them on the tarmac. Knowing the wrenching pain in their hearts, He sent messengers—not in the sky but on the ground, standing right beside them. The disciples needn't stand gazing into the hazy horizon. They needn't be torn by grief and uncertainty. "This same Jesus, who was taken up from you into heaven" is going to come again. In the sky. The same way He left. On a return flight already booked in the counsels of the Godhead.

He is coming back! It was the first thing the Father wanted the disciples to know the moment His Son left the airways over Galilee. This wasn't a one-way flight; it was the first leg of a round trip.

The Promises of the Apostles

The apostle Paul, who wrote 13 epistles, far more than anyone else, mentioned the second coming 50 times. Here are some sample passages:

> ...and to wait for His Son from heaven, whom He raised from the dead, even Jesus who delivers us from the wrath to come (1 Thessalonians 1:10).
>
> ...so that He may establish your hearts blameless in holiness before our God and Father at the coming of our Lord Jesus Christ with all His saints (1 Thessalonians 3:13).
>
> Our citizenship is in heaven, from which we also eagerly wait for the Savior, the Lord Jesus Christ, who will transform our lowly body that it may be conformed to His glorious body, according to the working by which He is able even to subdue all things to Himself (Philippians 3:20-21).
>
> Then the lawless one will be revealed, whom the Lord will consume with the breath of His mouth and destroy with the brightness of His coming (2 Thessalonians 2:8).
>
> Christ was offered once to bear the sins of many. To those who eagerly wait for Him He will appear a second time, apart from sin, for salvation (Hebrews 9:28).

> For as often as you eat this bread and drink this
> cup, you proclaim the Lord's death till He comes
> (1 Corinthians 11:26).

It was the apostle Paul who insisted that every time we take communion, we "proclaim the Lord's death till He comes." Someone has remarked that communion is to the church what a wedding ring is to a married couple: a testimony that while they are apart, they belong to each other and will one day be joined together.

The apostle Peter added in 2 Peter 3:10-12:

> The day of the Lord will come as a thief in the night,
> in which the heavens will pass away with a great noise,
> and the elements will melt with fervent heat; both the
> earth and the works that are in it will be burned up.
> Therefore, since all these things will be dissolved, what
> manner of persons ought you to be in holy conduct and
> godliness, looking for and hastening the coming of the
> day of God, because of which the heavens will be
> dissolved being on fire, and the elements will melt with
> fervent heat?

Jude, who may not have been an apostle (though some believe him to be a half-brother of our Lord), was highly respected by the early church. Identifying himself as "a servant of Jesus Christ," he quoted this prophecy from Enoch:

> Now Enoch, the seventh from Adam, prophesied
> about these men also, saying, "Behold, the Lord comes
> with ten thousands of His saints, to execute judgment
> on all, to convict all who are ungodly among them of all
> their ungodly deeds which they have committed in an
> ungodly way, and of all the harsh things which ungodly
> sinners have spoken against Him" (Jude 14-15).

The apostle John referred to the coming again of our Lord in great glory in three of his five New Testament letters (omitting it only in the small personal letters of 2 and 3 John, which consist of one chapter each). His book of the Revelation of Jesus Christ furnishes details of the glorious appearing and the events that lead up to it. This last book of the Bible, rightly understood, is a tremendous blessing to Christians. It presents our Lord in all His power and great glory, the way He will be seen when He returns to this earth. Consider these sample passages:

> Behold, He is coming with clouds, and every eye will see Him, even they also who pierced Him. And all the tribes of the earth will mourn because of Him. Even so, Amen (Revelation 1:7).

> Then I saw heaven opened, and behold, a white horse. And He who sat on him was called Faithful and True, and in righteousness He judges and makes war. His eyes were like a flame of fire, and on His head were many crowns. He had a name written that no one knew except Himself. He was clothed with a robe dipped in blood, and His name is called The Word of God. And the armies in heaven, clothed in fine linen, white and clean, followed Him on white horses. Now out of His mouth goes a sharp sword, that with it He should strike the nations. And He Himself will rule them with a rod of iron. He Himself treads the wine-press of the fierceness and wrath of Almighty God. And He has on His robe and on His thigh a name written: KING OF KINGS AND LORD OF LORDS (Revelation 19:11-16).

> And I saw the beast, the kings of the earth, and their armies, gathered together to make war against Him who sat on the horse and against His army. Then the beast was captured, and with him the false prophet who worked signs in his presence, by which he deceived those who received the mark of the beast and those who worshiped his image. These two were cast alive into the lake of fire burning with brimstone (Revelation 19:19-20).

> Then I saw an angel coming down from heaven, having the key to the bottomless pit and a great chain in his hand. He laid hold of the dragon, that serpent of old, who is the Devil and Satan, and bound him for a thousand years; and he cast him into the bottomless pit, and shut him up, and set a seal on him, so that he should deceive the nations no more till the thousand

years were finished. But after these things he must be released for a little while. And I saw thrones, and they sat on them, and judgment was committed to them. And I saw the soul of those who had been beheaded for their witness to Jesus and for the word of God, who had not worshiped the beast or his image, and had not received his mark on their foreheads or on their hands. And they lived and reigned with Christ for a thousand years (Revelation 20:1-4).

The Promises of the New Testament

The 218 chapters in the New Testament contain hundreds of promises of Christ's return to this earth. Most of these promises pertain to the time when He will establish His kingdom on the earth after His coming, but some refer to His coming for His church in order to take them to His Father's house. To appreciate the significant coverage given this subject in Scripture, examine the chart on the next page that shows the books of the New Testament at about the time they were written. They appear as scrolls of various sizes indicating their length. Those scrolls that are shaded contain one or more promises of Christ's return. Only five do not have such a reference, and three of these are single-chapter books or personal letters to individuals.

Quite apparently our Lord wanted to assure us that He will come again and that His coming will be a world-shaking event. He will return gloriously in power, and every eye will see Him.

A Wonderful Guarantee

There is no question that the Lord Jesus Christ is coming again to this earth. It is a prophetic fact, guaranteed by the eternal Word of God. The deity and credibility of God demands it. It is a prophetic future event whose fulfillment may not be far off. Before He comes, however, He will rapture His church up to be with Him in His Father's house. That event will also mark the beginning of the stormiest time in all human history, called "the wrath of God" or "the great tribulation." The purpose of these tortuous days will be to provide humanity a seven-year period in which to make their decision to accept Christ—or to accept Antichrist, the very embodiment of evil. It is a comfort to all Christians to know they do not have to face the coming storm of judgment. That is precisely why the Rapture is called "the blessed hope."

Attacks on the Pre-Tribulation Rapture View

The pre-Tribulation rapture teaching has enriched the lives of millions of Christians during the last 170 years since it gained prominence. Still, it is not universally accepted. Over the years, most of those who have held a different view have been gracious toward those of us who believe in a pre-Trib rapture, allowing for our differences to coexist peacefully. After all, agreeing on the fact that He *is* coming is more crucial than agreeing on *when* He is coming.

But within the last few years, that live-and-let-live attitude has changed. There are some Christians who have taken it upon themselves to attack the pre-Tribulation rapture—sometimes in a vicious and carnal manner. That is particularly true of those who once held to the pre-Tribulation rapture view and for some reason decided to change. A number of these opponents have lessened their emphasis on winning souls and spend much of their time seeking to persuade other believers to change their prophetic views. As I will show in the coming pages, these attacks rob the Christian of "the blessed hope" and the constant consciousness that our Lord could come to rapture His church at any moment.

Some of these "new wave" prophetic teachings sound plausible at first hearing, confusing young Christians and troubling even mature believers who have been comforted by the blessed hope through years of walking with Christ. I have studied these assaults on the pre-Tribulation rapture, and I am convinced there are solid biblical answers to each and every challenge and false charge.

In the coming pages, we will study these attacks, beginning with the most recent. Be prepared to go into some depth with me as we look into these opposing views. Stay with me. Stay alert. Most importantly...hang on to your hope!

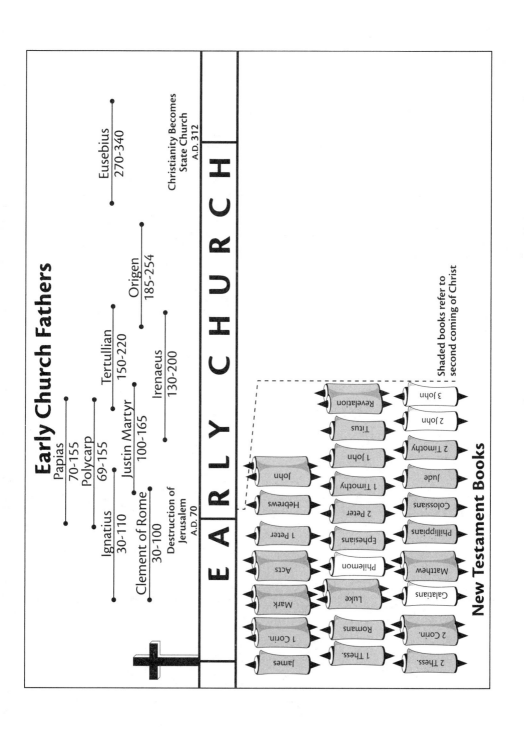

Early Church Fathers

Papias
70-155

Polycarp
69-155

Ignatius
30-110

Justin Martyr
100-165

Tertullian
150-220

Irenaeus
130-200

Origen
185-254

Eusebius
270-340

Clement of Rome
30-100

Destruction of
Jerusalem
A.D. 70

Christianity Becomes
State Church
A.D. 312

EARLY CHURCH

New Testament Books

Shaded books refer to
second coming of Christ

James

1 Corin.

Mark

Acts

1 Peter

Hebrews

John

1 Thess.

Romans

Luke

Philemon

Ephesians

2 Peter

1 Timothy

1 John

Titus

Revelation

2 Thess.

2 Corin.

Galatians

Matthew

Philippians

Colossians

Jude

2 Timothy

2 John

3 John

Part Two

THE SCRIPTURAL CASE FOR THE PRE-TRIB RAPTURE VIEW

Chapter Eight

What Are the Options?

Virtually all Christians who take the Bible literally expect to be raptured before the Lord comes in power to this earth. Yet there are hundreds of books written on this subject from at least four perspectives, several of which we have touched on already: pre-Tribulationist, post-Tribulationist, mid-Tribulationist, and partial rapture. They all teach that Christ will return physically to earth to begin His 1,000-year rule, but differ on the timing of the Rapture in relation to the Tribulation.

All four groups believe Jesus Christ to be the Son of God, the only means of salvation, and they expect Him to come again—most expect Him to appear relatively soon. Their differences lie in one major area: *when* He is coming for His church. It is a matter of timing.

While they say quite different things about the lot of believers living during the time of these prophetic events, they concur as to the time of the Millennium and eternity. But for some reason, in recent years differences among these pre-Millennialists have generated excessive heat. Some Christians barely speak to each other, and some are downright nasty to each other—which must sorely displease the Lord they are awaiting.

Distinguish Between
Dogma and Interpretation

Some Bible doctrines are nonnegotiable: the deity of Christ, for example, or salvation by grace through faith. But whether

Christ comes for His church before the Tribulation, in the middle, or at the end is not a cardinal doctrine. All Christians believe that Christ is coming with a shout from heaven and that "the dead in Christ will rise first." Believers living at the time will be changed and raised with them to meet the Lord in the air. Various interpretations of the timing of the Rapture do not constitute heresy and should not cause division among believers. Whereas some of my personal friends disagree vigorously with me on this matter, we do not show disrespect or question each other's love for the Lord.

The Bottom Line

No single verse specifically states, "Christ will not rapture His church before the Tribulation." On the other hand, no single passage teaches He will *not* come before the Tribulation, or that He will come in the middle or at the end of the Tribulation. Any such explicit declaration would end the debate immediately. It should also be noted that there is no reference of rapture in connection with the glorious appearing. Again, if the post-Tribulationists had such a verse, it would end the argument. Our task is to gather all the passages that provide details for His second coming, put them in the best order we can, and interpret them according to basic Bible study principles.

The chart in chapter 2, aligning the three major rapture passages with other passages that bear on second coming events, typifies this approach. We call that "rightly dividing the word of truth" (2 Timothy 2:15). In the absence of a definitive text, we are forced to make the best arrangement of the events that we can on the basis of biblical analysis and the leading of the Spirit of God.

Defining Views of the Rapture

The following diagrams, based on the principal scriptures, show graphically the different views of the Rapture. Since all are pre-Millennial in perspective, the primary difference lies in the timing of the Rapture in relation to the Tribulation.

The *pre-Tribulation* view holds to a seven-year Tribulation period for Israel, according to Daniel 9:27, occurring before Christ returns to this earth. The church (and, some believe, Old

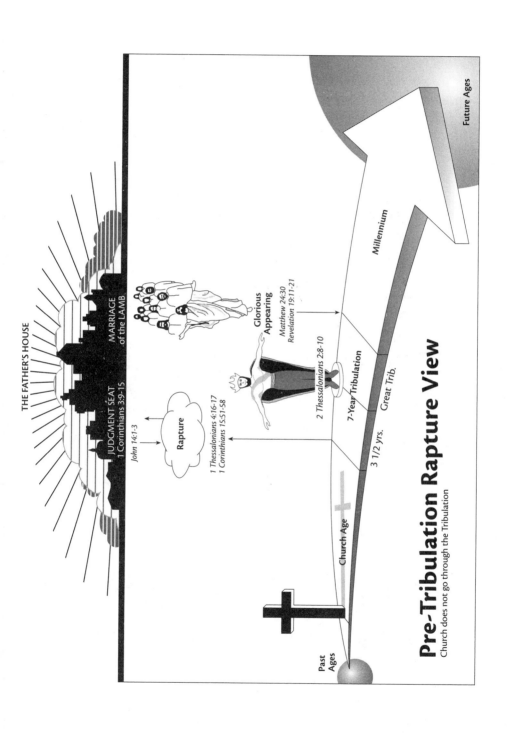

THE FATHER'S HOUSE

JUDGMENT SEAT
1 Corinthians 3:9-15

MARRIAGE
of the LAMB

John 14:1-3

Rapture

1 Thessalonians 4:16-17
1 Corinthians 15:51-58

Glorious
Appearing
Matthew 24:30
Revelation 19:11-21

2 Thessalonians 2:8-10

7-Year Tribulation

Great Trib.

3 1/2 yrs.

Church Age

Past
Ages

Millennium

Future Ages

Pre-Tribulation Rapture View

Church does not go through the Tribulation

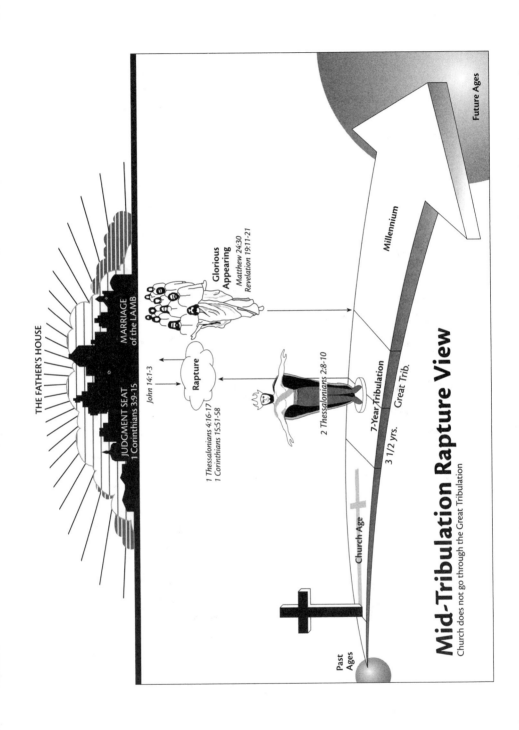

THE FATHER'S HOUSE

JUDGMENT SEAT
1 Corinthians 3:9-15

MARRIAGE
of the LAMB

John 14:1-3

Rapture

1 Thessalonians 4:16-17
1 Corinthians 15:51-58

Glorious
Appearing
Matthew 24:30
Revelation 19:11-21

2 Thessalonians 2:8-10

Church Age

Past
Ages

3 1/2 yrs.   Great Trib.

7-Year Tribulation

Millennium

Future Ages

Mid-Tribulation Rapture View
Church does not go through the Great Tribulation

Testament saints) will be resurrected or raptured prior to that Tribulation, taken by Christ to the Father's house and judged for their deeds since they became Christians, granted rewards for faithful service, conducted to the marriage of Christ and His Bride, and permitted to celebrate the Marriage Supper of the Lamb (see Revelation 19:7-9). After the seven-year Tribulation Christ will come in His glorious appearing, destroy Antichrist and the False Prophet, and chain Satan in the bottomless pit. He will then set up His kingdom and rule the world with His saints.

This view is held by most fundamentalists and many evangelicals who take prophetic scriptures literally. As a general rule, the more a person accepts the Bible literally, the more likely he is to hold the pre-Tribulation view.

The *mid-Tribulation* view is similar to the pre-Trib view except that the Rapture (1 Corinthians 15:52; 1 Thessalonians 4:16-17; Revelation 11:12) is located in the middle of the Tribulation. Rather than ascribing human personality to the two witnesses in Revelation chapter 11, this position identified them as Israel and the church; after their deaths, there will be no more witnessing.

Proponents of this view emphasize that the first half of the Tribulation features man's wrath, which the church will experience. But after that believers will be taken up, like the two witnesses of Revelation 11, and thus avoid the Great Tribulation or "the wrath of God" during the last half of the Tribulation. Mid-Trib adherents see Christians remaining three-and-a-half years longer on earth (and spending three-and-a-half years less in the Father's house) than pre-Tribbers. This position is of fairly recent vintage and has the smallest number of followers, although it seems to be growing.

According to the *post-Tribulation* view, the church will endure the entire Tribulation. The Rapture is identified with all the other end-time events: Judgment Seat of Christ, Marriage Supper of the Lamb, glorious appearing of Christ when He overthrows the Antichrist (2 Thessalonians 2:8-10), the disposition of Satan and the False Prophet into hell, the casting of Satan into the bottomless pit, and finally, the setting up of the kingdom.

This view, which has attracted many defenders, has been growing through the years. Although not the majority view of the evangelical church, it may be the predominant view of evangelicals who reject dispensationalism. Many Reconstructionists who

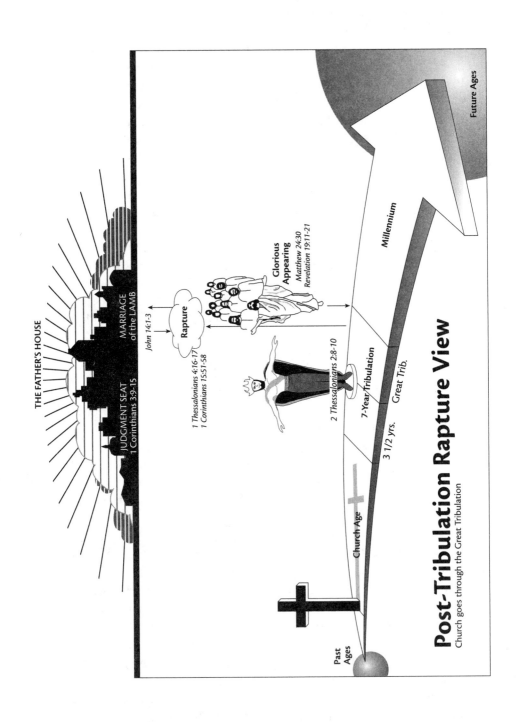

THE FATHER'S HOUSE

JUDGMENT SEAT
1 Corinthians 3:9-15

MARRIAGE
of the LAMB

Rapture

John 14:1-3

1 Thessalonians 4:16-17
1 Corinthians 15:51-58

Glorious
Appearing
Matthew 24:30
Revelation 19:11-21

2 Thessalonians 2:8-10

7-Year Tribulation

3 1/2 yrs.   Great Trib.

Church Age

Past
Ages

Millennium

Future Ages

Post-Tribulation Rapture View
Church goes through the Great Tribulation

consider themselves pre-Millennialists have accepted the post-Trib position. As a general rule, many of those who hold this view do not take prophetic scriptures as literally as they do other passages of the Bible.

The *partial rapture* view (see next page) is a relatively new theory that Hal Lindsey labels "the new Protestant Purgatory." It suggests that the best Christians will be raptured at the beginning of the Tribulation.[1] According to Hebrews 9:28, "To those who eagerly wait for Him He will appear a second time, apart from sin, for salvation." Adherents of this view believe that Christians not living consecrated lives will be left behind; repentance will afford another chance later in the Tribulation. This, of course, indicates that good works or consecration determine participation in the Rapture.

Few Christians hold this view, for it not only plays havoc with prophetic passages, but also impugns the doctrine of salvation by grace through faith. It is interesting that those who hold this view invariably believe they will be among the first to be raptured. For all practical purposes, they expect to go at the same time as the pre-Tribbers—before the Tribulation. Those who are not ready, of course, will be in big trouble—Tribulation trouble.

Where To from Here?

In the last three chapters of this book I would like to critique the two major views that oppose pre-Tribulationism—the mid-Trib position and the post-Trib view—and then summarize why I believe the pre-Trib position is still the most biblical, hopeful, and sanctifying view of our Lord's return. I will not critique the partial rapture view for two primary reasons: 1) it has so few adherents; 2) it is so obviously unbiblical.

My hope and prayer is that by the end of this book, you will be able to reaffirm with me that the Lord Jesus Christ will return for His church at any moment...perhaps today.

Let's be ready!

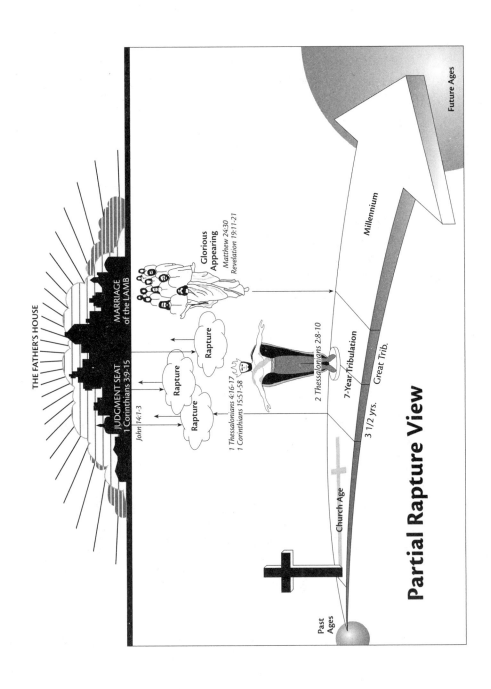

Partial Rapture View

Chapter Nine

The Case Against a
Mid-Tribulation Rapture

The newest of the three prominent views of the Rapture is the mid-Trib position. In 1941 Norman B. Harrison published *The End: Rethinking the Revelation,* subtitled, *The Rapture: Pre- Mid- or Post-Tribulation?* Although he did not invent the mid-Trib theory, his book did much to popularize it. Since then it has become increasingly favored by those who do not insist on a literal interpretation of the prophetic passages of Scripture.

Basically, mid-Tribulationism predicts that Christ will rapture His church in the middle of the Tribulation. This solves for them some of the problems of the post-Tribbers in that it allows time both for Christ to take His raptured church up to the Father's house and for other prophesied events to occur before He returns to the earth. They also respect the promise of the Lord to save Christians from "the wrath to come" by limiting the suffering of the first three-and-a-half years, confining the really difficult period to the last three-and-a-half years (or the Great Tribulation).

Many books on prophecy emerging after World War II represented all sides of the debate, reflecting each of the three positions. The more literally the author accepted the Scriptures, the more prone he was to maintain a pre-Trib rather than a post-Trib position. The mid-Trib advocates benefited by drawing adherents from both pre-Trib and post-Trib schools. They listened to the debate carefully and settled somewhere in the middle.

The Main Points of Mid-Tribulationism

Three basic tenets of the mid-Trib position need to be evaluated in light of God's Word.

1. *Adherents of this view believe that the Rapture occurs in Revelation 11:11-12.*

Essentially, they view the two witnesses described in that chapter as the witnessing church during the first half of the Tribulation. The martyrdom of the witnesses, who are then resurrected and taken to heaven, symbolize to mid-Tribbers the Rapture passages we have already studied. Thus they see the Rapture of the church taking place in the middle of the Tribulation.

2. *They equate the blowing of the seventh trumpet of Revelation 11:15 with the last trumpet of 1 Corinthians 15:52.*

Noting that the seventh trumpet is the final trumpet, they equate the two events, thus locating the Rapture in the middle of the Tribulation.

3. *They limit the time of wrath to three-and-a-half years.*

They assume that the church will be purged by going through the preliminary three-and-a-half years of the Tribulation.

A Critique of the Mid-Trib Position

1. *The Rapture does not appear in Revelation 11.*

It is puzzling that mid-Tribbers should identify the two witnesses—who have the same powers as Elijah and Moses, Old Testament Israelites—as members of the church. It is curious because although they teach that the witnesses are "raptured" when they hear a voice from heaven say to them, "Come up here," they deny that John, a member of the church who heard the same call in Revelation 4:1, could be raptured. Could it be that John's rapture, occurring before the seven-year Tribulation, does not fit their system? Can they explain why the two witnesses should be a better symbol of the church than John?

Norman Harrison makes the two witnesses symbols of two kinds of Christians: the dead in Christ and living believers. "Now, if the two witnesses are symbolic of a larger company of witnesses, then their ascension must be symbolic of the resurrection and rapture of that larger company."[1]

But there's no reason to take these witnesses symbolically or spiritualize them as the church. Besides, even if we accepted them as symbols, they would more appropriately symbolize Israel, for the Tribulation is the "time of Jacob's trouble." It's more likely that the two witnesses are Moses and Elijah. The latter was translated, never dying, and Moses' death was shrouded in mystery. No biblical literalist would transform the two witnesses into the church.

Dr. Gerald Stanton comments:

> But the two witnesses are not symbols. The normal, literal interpretation of the passage, including as it does the details of their dress, their prophecy, and their plagues, indicates that they are individual men. They are spoken of as "two prophets," and when they are killed, their dead bodies lie a definite period of time in a literal city which is identified as Jerusalem. It would not make good sense to say that symbolic bodies were killed, only to lie on literal streets, any more than to deny them literal burial in symbolic graves. The narrative of the two witnesses is evidently meant to be taken literally.[2]

> If the witnesses are only symbols, how can symbols be literally killed and lie in literal streets? Do the saints as a whole have men look on their "bodies" for "three and a half days," refusing them burial in a tomb (Revelation 11:9)? The other identifications are just as strained and unsustained by the text....Actually, there is no translation of saints at all in this chapter. The nearest approach is the resurrection of the two witnesses who are best identified as actual personalities who will live and die as martyrs at that time.[3]

We might add, how could people from all "tribes, tongues, and nations...see their dead bodies" (verse 9) over a three-day period if it applies to the entire church? They could, however, view two men via CNN cameras on the evening news. Revelation 11 must be enormously spiritualized to make it mean anything other than two human beings with Old-Testament-type powers who will come on the scene during the first half of the Tribulation, giving witness to the grace of God. In the middle of the Tribulation they are killed and translated to heaven.

If the two witnesses of chapter 11 represent the church, that would mean that the church, which played such a large role in chapters 1–3, is totally omitted from 4:3 to chapter 11. That omission makes sense only if the church is absent.

John had no difficulty identifying the church in the first three chapters. If he had meant to introduce two symbols, he would have said so. Besides, how would one witness symbolize the church that is alive at the Rapture and the other the church that "sleeps"? *Both* witnesses are killed. How can you kill saints who are already dead?

The answer is, you can't.

The church *isn't* raptured in chapter 11 for the simple reason that it isn't there! These two earthlings, endowed with supernatural powers in order to witness for 1,260 days, do not represent the church. They are literal men with literal powers, like Moses and Elijah in the Old Testament. If the Rapture appears in the book of Revelation, it is in chapter 4:1-2 at the beginning of the Tribulation, not in the middle.

2. *The seventh trumpet of Revelation 11:15 is not the "last trumpet" of 1 Corinthians 15:52.*

Identifying the seventh trumpet of Revelation with the last trumpet of 1 Corinthians 15:52 and the trumpet of God of 1 Thessalonians 4:16 is one of the most convincing arguments that mid-Tribs offer. It is the one that has convinced some of my personal friends, for trumpets obviously play a prominent part in the rapture events. But three problems arise when we attempt to merge them.

a. The rapture of the two witnesses occurs before the seventh angel blows his trumpet—three verses before! As such, their rapture is completed before the seventh angel sounds. It is therefore a part of the sixth trumpet, not the seventh. Thus, the seventh trumpet has nothing to do with the details of the eleventh chapter.

b. The seven angels blow trumpets of judgment, not blessing. Even if the seventh trumpet were the right one, it would be an announcement heralding another judgment of God on the earth. In fact, that is just what it does. It precedes the entire last half of the seven-year Tribulation, or the Great Tribulation. In practical terms, just as the opening of the seventh seal introduced the Trumpet Judgments, the sounding of the seventh trumpet prefaces the seven Vial Judgments of the last three-and-a-half years. By no stretch of the imagination could the seventh trumpet be called the trumpet of blessing sounded in 1 Thessalonians 4:16-18.

c. The last trumpet of the rapture passages is for the church, not for Israel. Trumpets were an integral part of the life of Israel in the Old Testament, not generally a part of the church's experience. But the trump of God (or the final trumpet) is the last call of God to the church on earth, beckoning her up to her initial days in heaven. The seventh trumpet, however, is for Israel and has nothing to do with summoning people to heaven. Instead, it is a clarion of judgment upon the earth. These trumpets should not be confused, for they are incompatible. One calls the church; the other announces to Israel the most catastrophic period of judgment in her history.

3. *By limiting the Tribulation to the last three-and-a-half years, mid-Trib adherents ignore the seal and trumpet judgments of Revelation 6-11.*

Go back to pages 60-63 in chapter 4 and read the first 17 events listed to take place during the Tribulation. It is not the mild period mid-Tribbers project it to be, during which the church finishes her witnessing on this earth. No, it is a season of wrath for three-and-a-half years, followed by a horribly intense period of divine fury. Although mid-Tribbers do not locate the church in the latter half of the Tribulation, they envision it going through that first part. Yet the first half is called the "wrath of the Lamb" and "the great day of His wrath" (see 6:16-17). Although our Lord designated only the last half as the Great Tribulation, that period is mentioned only once in the book of Revelation (see 7:14).

There are no biblical grounds to view the Seal and Trumpet Judgments of the first half of the Tribulation as anything but the wrath of God on an unbelieving, Christ-rejecting world.

Reasons for Rejecting Mid-Tribulationism

Many mid-Trib adherents consider themselves pre-Tribbers because they believe the Lord will come before the last 42 months of the Tribulation and rapture the church before then. Most of the reasons for rejecting the mid-Tribulation position are similar to those used to dismiss the post-Tribulation view. Here are some of the reasons why mid-Tribulationism should be rejected:

1. *It must spiritualize Scriptures that should be accepted literally.* Drs. Walvoord and Stanton say it clearly:

> The fallacy of the whole midtribulational interpretation of Revelation 1–11 is that this view forces a spiritualization of the entire passage to find contemporary rather than future fulfillment. Because of this, midtribulationists achieve an exegesis of the passages that is strained because it is subjective and arbitrary. Even a simple reading of this section will give an impression of vivid divine judgment upon a sinful world that transcends anything history has recorded. If the passage is intended to be taken with any serious literalness, its fulfillment is yet future.
>
> The Great Tribulation actually begins in Revelation 6, not in Revelation 11.[4]

> Nothing less than the most flagrant spiritualization can deny that Tribulation commences with Revelation 6 and "great tribulation" at least by 7:14....It is upon this chapter that midtribulationalists lean most heavily to demonstrate their thesis, but instead of substantiating it as true, the chapter exposes its error and breaks the theory into pieces.[5]

Daniel was specific in Daniel 9:27 that the Tribulation would be seven years long. Mid-Tribbers have no authority for reducing it to three-and-a-half years.

2. *It destroys imminence.*

If the Rapture occurs in Revelation 11, in the middle of the Tribulation, it negates the promise of the Lord's return at any moment, thereby nullifying the motivational effect that belief in the imminent return of Christ has always had on the church. As we have seen, Paul and the early church were looking for the Lord at any time. By contrast, mid- and post-Trib advocates await the Antichrist, who will sign a seven-year covenant with Israel. This means mid-Tribbers can count the days until Christ comes to rapture His church. For mid-Tribbers it is 42 months, for post-Tribbers it is seven years. How can Christ's coming be like a thief in the night if one knows the day it will happen?

3. *Such belief leads to date setting, which our Lord warned was impossible* (see Matthew 24:36).

4. *It cannot find the church anywhere within Revelation chapters 6–11 unless it spiritualizes the two witnesses and equates them with the church.*

Frankly, once a person starts to spiritualize Scripture, any conclusion at all can be reached.

5. *See objections number 1, 5, 6, 8, and 9 to post-Tribulationism in the next chapter.*

The objections, while applying here to mid-Tribbers, are even more appropriate for post-Trib adherents.

Reevaluating the Plain Teaching of Scripture

The mid-Trib position, much like the post-Trib view, has some features to commend it; otherwise some of the good men who espouse it would not do so. But it is doubtful that a biblical literalist can believe in a mid-Tribulation rapture.

It is to be hoped that since mid-Tribbers already believe the Lord will rapture His church and save them from the wrath to come, they will reevaluate their views in the light of the Scriptures, adhere to its plain teaching, compare scripture with scripture, and return to the pre-Trib position. If they believe that God in His grace, mercy, and love for His Bride will spare her part of the Tribulation period, then why not all of it? The Tribulation was intended for Israel and the world, not the church.

I am confident that Christians today, with God's ever-sustaining help, could endure the horrors predicted for those who become believers during the Tribulation period. But why prescribe it as inevitable when the Bible does not teach that at all?

Chapter Ten

The Case Against a Post-Tribulation Rapture

It may come as a surprise to most pre-Trib prophecy students that the post-Trib position (in its primitive form) is the oldest point of view. Naturally, post-Trib believers insist that their system should be believed because of its antiquity—because it is a part of "historic Christianity."

But that idea is suspect because, while history is important, it does not provide an absolute basis on which to formulate doctrine. Doctrine must be provable by Scripture or discarded. That is why I began this book with a careful study of the subject from a biblical perspective. History is not sacrosanct, the Bible is. Pre-Millennialism, for example, is not believed today because it was the predominant view of the church for three centuries. It is accepted by the evangelical church because it best fits the teachings of Scripture when interpreted literally.

Why Early Post-Tribulationists?

Early Christians held the post-Tribulational view because of their life circumstances. The average Christian did not have the entire New Testament until well into the second century, so comparing scripture with scripture was not possible for many of them until some doctrinal understanding had already been formulated. The book of Revelation, written by the apostle John around A.D. 95, did not receive wide circulation immediately. In fact, it was the last book to be accepted as authoritative and admitted into the canon of Scripture. Early-church views of the coming of Christ were established somewhat before believers had free access to the book, which provided the most extensive details of the Tribulation period.

Additionally, second- and third-century Christians experienced the severest persecutions of the entire church age. They judged they were already living in the Tribulation and concluded that the Lord would rapture His church at the end of that time. Since they believed they were already in the Tribulation, it never occurred to them that Christ would come before the Tribulation. But their great suffering did cause them to anticipate and pray for His coming during their lifetime.

During the fourth century, the teachings of the Alexandrian school of theology from Egypt that seemed to merge biblical theology with Platonic philosophy (contrary to Paul's warnings in 1 Corinthians 1–3 and Colossians 2:6-8) began to have a devastating effect on church doctrine. Dr. John Walvoord, the most prolific writer of our day on these subjects, describes that period of transition:

> Nevertheless, in the fourth and fifth centuries, with Augustine, a consolidation was achieved by separating eschatology from other areas of systematic theology. Two principles of interpretation were adopted by Augustine—a literal, historical and grammatical interpretation of noneschatological passages, and a nonliteral or figurative interpretation of prophetic Scriptures. The result was that while the Roman Church maintained many of the teachings of the Bible, it continued to use a nonliteral method of interpreting eschatology. Thus amillennialism became the accepted doctrine of the Roman Church. With the beginning of the Protestant Reformation, the Reformers returned to Augustine and built on his method of interpretation of prophecy. The Protestant Reformers accordingly were amillennial and opposed premillennialism.[1]
>
> In the aftermath of the Protestant Reformation—with the diversity of theological opinion created as Protestantism divided into various denominations and

groups—a divergent view of a millennialism known as postmillennialism emerged. Although similar views had been held by various individuals earlier, modern postmillennialism is usually attributed to Daniel Whitby (1638–1726). This new view considered the rise of the church and the preaching of the gospel as eventually being triumphant and ushering in a golden age of a thousand years in which the church throughout the world would flourish. This thousand-year period would climax with the second advent of Christ, much as is taught in amillennialism.[2]

The Protestant Reformers, returning to Augustine, delivered the church from the doctrines of purgatory and other Roman inventions but do not seem to have raised any questions about the rapture of the church as a separate event. It was only when premillennialism began to demand a literal interpretation of prophecy and reexamine the prophetic program of Israel and other issues that the question began to be raised whether the rapture, as a matter of fact, could be harmonized with the doctrines that declare that Christ will return to set up His kingdom.[3]

We have already observed that the Reformers of the sixteenth century interpreted the Bible literally. There gradually developed in the eighteenth century a realization that the literal method could also apply to prophecy. This revived pre-Millennialism and a renewed interest in the Lord's return sparked a great interest in the study of prophetical subjects. In order for Lacunza, the eighteenth-century Catholic priest and ardent student of prophecy, to read "a thousand prophetical books" before he wrote his enormously popular work *The Coming of Christ in Power and Great Glory,* obviously even the Catholic Church had to have developed prophetic literature.

The nineteenth century was a time of prophetic awareness, first in the British Isles and then in the United States. The old Historical interpretation of prophecy fell on hard times as the events of history outran prophecy, making it obvious that the book of Revelation was not past but future. Consequently, it became increasingly popular for Bible teachers to view events of the Tribulation period as yet future. During these past 200 years, a stimulating debate among evangelical Christians about the timing of the Lord's return to rapture His church has developed. All believe the Rapture will take place before He comes back to the earth, but they disagree over the interval of time between the Rapture and the glorious appearing.

Post-Tribulationists tend to take prophecy, particularly Revelation 6–19, more figuratively or symbolically than do pre-Tribulationists. As a general rule, those who take prophecy as literally as they take other scriptures are prone to hold to the pre-Trib view.

Post-Tribulation: A Definition

It is difficult to provide a simple description of post-Tribulationism because of its many variations. Basically it maintains that Christ will not rapture the church before the Tribulation. He will rapture His Bride according to the key rapture scriptures already noted in this book, but not until the end of the Tribulation. Some conceive the two events as separated by a short span of time, others by moments.

According to Dr. Walvoord,

> As ordinarily defined, posttribulationism is the teaching that the church will be translated after the predicted Tribulation, and therefore its adherents believe that the church must pass through this prophesied time of trouble. Posttribulationism is the ordinary view of practically all amillenarians and postmillenarians. It is embraced by Roman Catholic and Greek Catholic; it is followed by many Protestant conservatives as well as modern liberals....While posttribulationism in itself is a simple concept, so many variations are found within the general teaching that it is difficult to affirm a norm. At least four differing schools of thought prevail among posttribulationists in regard to their interpretation of the Tribulation. These have been called (1) classic posttribulationism, (2) semiclassic posttribulationism, (3) futuristic posttribulationism, and (4) dispensational posttribulationism.[4]

Post-Tribulationists may disagree with each other on such details as the severity of the judgments described by John in the book of Revelation, but they generally agree that Christ will come at the end of the Tribulation period.[5]

Serious Problems with Post-Tribulationism

1. *The post-Tribulation position ignores the scriptural promises of escape from the wrath of the Tribulation.*

As noted in chapter 6 of this book, God has promised at least four times that He will save Christians from the wrath to come (Romans 5:9; 1 Thessalonians 1:10; 5:9; Revelation 3:10). It is difficult to conceive of the Tribulation period as anything but a catastrophic time of wrath, for it is described as such at least ten times (Revelation 6:10; 7:14; 8:13; 11:10,18; 12:12; 13:7-8,12,14; 14:6; 17:2,8). And keep in mind that the most significant promise of salvation from this period of wrath appears in that same book (3:10). The wrath of Revelation 3:10 obviously refers to the same period of time.

Post-Tribulationists have created for themselves a major dilemma. They either have to explain away the promises of deliverance from the time of wrath (which, with all their many writings, they have so far failed to do), or they impugn the credibility and reliability of God's promises. I'm sure that even they would not grant the latter conclusion. God will keep His promises, which assures that we will be raptured prior to the Tribulation. Some holding the post-Trib position suggest that Revelation 3:10 teaches that He will deliver believers from the *effects* of the Tribulation, but that requires a bigger miracle than the Rapture before the Tribulation, and it ignores the martyrdom of the Revelation 7:9-17 saints and many others.

2. *It trivializes the second coming.*

Instead of being the blessed and glorious mystery described in the Bible, it becomes the great elevator escape: We zip up to the Father's house, take a quick peek into heaven, and zip right back down moments later with Christ in His glorious appearing.

Even though post-Trib writers do not deal with rapture scriptures at length (and some have ignored them altogether), they do draw a distinction between the Rapture and the glorious appearing. Why, then, would we have to rise up to heaven one moment and return to earth in the very next? Just to fulfill the promise of a rapture? No, Christ's pledge to return was made on the basis of what God knew would happen. His noble purpose arranged it as two separate events, detached by a period of time. The post-Trib view nullifies that purpose.

3. *The post-Trib theory allows no time for the Judgment Seat of Christ and the Marriage Supper of the Lamb.*

Two very significant, time-consuming events await the church after the Rapture and before the glorious appearing. At the Judgment Seat of Christ (Romans 14:10 and 2 Corinthians 5:10), every Christian will give account of himself to God for the deeds done in the flesh (a judgment described in detail in 1 Corinthians 3:9-15). According to 1 Corinthians 4:5, this judgment occurs after the Rapture. The Wedding and Marriage Supper of the Lamb (Revelation 19:7-9) follow the Judgment Seat of Christ, just prior to the glorious appearing. Only the pre-Trib position allows sufficient time (at least seven years) for these events to be fulfilled with dignity and grace. The post-Trib believer is forced to relegate both the Judgment Seat of Christ (which will involve millions of people) and the marriage ceremony and Supper of the Lamb to "the twinkling of an eye"—or ignore them altogether.

Of course, there is one other alternative. Post-Tribbers could allow sufficient time for these events and concede a seven-year hiatus between the Rapture and the glorious appearing. But if they did that, they would become pre-Tribulationists!

4. *The post-Trib position does not allow time for Christ to keep His promise to take believers to be with Him in the Father's house* (see John 14:1-3).

The post-Trib view obliterates one of the greatest promises regarding the second coming to be found in the Bible. In the post-Trib scheme of things, after the Rapture we immediately come back to earth with Christ for 1,000 years and then proceed to the new heaven and new earth. By contrast, the pre-Trib view places Christians in the Father's house for a minimum of seven years—John 14:1-3 and 1 Thessalonians 4:13-18 are parallel passages.

In his work *Snatched Before the Storm!* Richard L. Mayhue makes this case for pre-Tribulationism:

The parallel to 1 Thessalonians 4:13-18, John 14:1-3 refers to Christ's coming again. It is not a promise to all believers that they shall go to Him at death. It does refer to the Rapture of the church. Note the close parallel between the promises of John 14:1-3 and 1 Thessalonians 4:13-18.

Jesus instructed the disciples that He was going to His Father's house (heaven) to prepare a place for them. He promised them that He would return and receive them so that they could be with Him wherever He was. The phrase "wherever I am," while implying continued presence in general, here means presence in heaven in particular. Our Lord told the Pharisees in John 7:34, "where I am you cannot come." He was not talking about His present abode on earth but rather His resurrected presence at the right hand of the Father. In John 14:3 "where I am" must mean "in heaven" or the intent of 14:1-3 would be wasted and worthless.

A posttribulation rapture demands that the saints meet Christ in the air and immediately descend to earth without experiencing what our Lord promised in John 14. Since John 14 refers to the rapture, then only a pretribulation rapture satisfies the language of John 14:1-3 and allows raptured saints to dwell with Christ in His Father's house.[6]

5. *Post-Tribulationism places the church on earth during the Tribulation for no clear reason.*

The "time of Jacob's trouble" is the period during which Israel will fulfill its seventieth week (seven years) of Daniel, and her 144,000 Jewish witnesses and two supernatural witnesses will minister from Jerusalem. Why drag the church through that dreadful time? Besides, if millions have already escaped that period through death, why should those who are alive and remain have to endure it? The Tribulation is a time of God's wrath on the world, not on the church.

6. *Post-Tribbers cannot explain why the church is so prominent in Revelation chapters 1–3 yet totally absent during the wrath portion in chapters 6–18.*

The obvious explanation is that she is not there!

7. *The post-Trib view steals the blessed hope.*

Christians are taught to expect our Lord's return with blessed anticipation, as did the first century church. Looking for the coming of Christ *after* the Tribulation converts that hope to dread. How could any Christian father get excited about taking his family through the Tribulation?

8. *The post-Trib view destroys either imminence or literalness.*

It is impossible to expect Christ to come at any time and still accept literally the 31 events expected to take place during the Tribulation as described in chapter 4. For if Christ comes at the end, we must expect a number of events to unfold before the Rapture. Yet the Bible teaches that "in such an hour as ye think not the Son of man cometh" (Matthew 24:44 KJV). The glorious appearing will not take Bible-taught Christians by surprise, for they will expect it exactly seven years after the signing of the covenant between Israel and the Antichrist (see Daniel 9:27). By contrast, we cannot know when to expect the Rapture.

One way out of that dilemma is to spiritualize or allegorize the book of Revelation, thus reducing the significance of its judgments. But this is a very dangerous position, for historically, when one passage of Scripture is spiritualized, then others end up being spiritualized, making it easy to introduce falsehoods and even heresy into the church. Thus biblical inerrantists rarely accept the post-Tribulation position. Dr. Gerald Stanton suggests,

> Among the leading weaknesses of posttribulation-ism, aside from the intolerant attitude of many of its advocates, is the tendency to depart from the fundamental principle of literal interpretation, the failure to comprehend that the Tribulation is essentially a time of divine retribution, the tendency to take ordinary words of Scripture and force them into the mold of technical usage, the refusal to recognize the truth and appreciate the value of an imminent return, a steadfast refusal to accept Paul as the primary revelator to the church of God, and a lingering legalism combined with a failure to grasp the real character and scope of divine grace.[7]

9. *Post-Tribulationists are inconsistent about literalness.*

Because most post-Trib advocates are pre-Millennial, they read the twentieth chapter of Revelation literally (that Christ will reign on earth for 1,000 years). Yet they spiritualize much of chapters 6–19 in an attempt to reduce the horrors of the time of great wrath. That is inconsistent. We cannot give credence solely to those passages that fit our system. We must apply a literal interpretation before seeking a spiritualized solution.

John the seer speaks of earthquakes, plagues, and waters turning to blood—events that occurred in the Old Testament. Why can they not happen again during the Tribulation? Post-Tribbers are left with an impasse—justifying a literal 1,000-year kingdom and not the plagues mentioned previously. Post-Tribbers have a difficult time explaining why Revelation 18 and 19 are interpreted symbolically, but suddenly the 1,000-year kingdom of chapter 20 is to be interpreted literally. Pre-Tribulationists have no such dilemma.

While many fine Christians have embraced the post-Trib position, it creates more problems with the literal interpretation of Scripture than it solves. And while the view may at first glance seem to have the weight of history on its side, it does not mirror the clear teaching of Scripture.

Dr. Stanton sums it up well:

> Posttribulationalists accept the literal interpretation of the Bible for the fundamentals of the faith, and the literal interpretation of prophecy as the necessary basis of their premillennial hope, which is most commendable. But when it comes to the Tribulation, all has gone to pieces, all has changed, spiritualization has become the order of the day, and this only in the interest of saving a theory which cannot be made to harmonize with the literal interpretation of Tribulation passages.[8]
>
> This business of…twisting and wrenching of Scripture in the vain attempt of making it say something other than what it does say—this is a return to the methods of Plato and Origen and constitutes a dangerous departure from conservative biblical interpretation, which is literal interpretation. It is a departure which endangers all for which fundamental, premillennial men stand. Liberalism spiritualizes cardinal doctrines; amillennialism spiritualizes the Millennium; midtribulationalism and postribulationalsim spiritualize the Tribulation—but the root error throughout is the same. Nor is it impossible for a premillennial conservative,

having once given up basic defense of literal interpretation, to retreat to posttribulationalism, then to amillennialism, then on to liberalism in other areas. There are men who have trodden this pathway, although fortunately, most are arrested in their course and do not reach the apostasy which is the natural outgrowth of the principle of interpretation they have adopted....When men fail to see that the church of Jesus Christ differs in its essential nature, as well as its eschatology, from ancient Israel—when they miss the obvious fact that the Tribulation is primarily a time of God's wrath upon the enemies of His son—and when they explain away every divine promise to save the church from wrath to come—these are errors of important magnitude.

But when they fail to let the Scriptures speak and reverse the meaning of what God has been pleased to reveal concerning the coming time of trouble—when, in a word, they resort to the process of spiritualizing the Bible whenever and wherever their systems demand it—then they are involved in a clear and dangerous departure from that very method of interpretation upon which their conservative, premillennial faith is founded.

Whether historically or in the laboratory of twentieth-century exegesis, pretribulationalism alone is consistent fundamentalism and consistent premillennialism, for it alone is based on a clear commitment to the vital keynote doctrine—the golden rule of biblical interpretation—which is literal interpretation.[9]

Spiritualizing the Scriptures, even the prophetic passages, can be very dangerous, for it opens the door to private interpretations. In other words, you can conclude almost *anything* with the text. By applying the golden rule of interpretation you limit yourself to the Scriptures and plain sense, unless another sense is obvious. Most prophetic passages lend themselves to a literal interpretation—or explain what they mean.

Few who take the Bible literally hold a post-Trib position.

10. *Post-Tribulationists cannot explain the 15 differences between the Rapture and the glorious appearing unless there is a separation of time between them.*

I have located 15 distinctives between the Rapture and the glorious appearing that makes it impossible to make them both the same event. You will find them listed and explained on page 112 of my book *Charting the End Times*, coauthored with Dr. Thomas Ice. I repeat the distinctives here for your consideration:

Rapture/Blessed Hope	Glorious Appearing
1. Christ comes in the air for His own	1. Christ comes with His own to earth
2. Rapture of all Christians	2. No one is raptured
3. Christians taken to the Father's house	3. Resurrected saints do not see the Father's house
4. No judgment on earth	4. Christ judges inhabitants of earth
5. Church taken to heaven	5. Christ sets up His kingdom on earth
6. Imminent—could happen at any moment	6. Glorious appearing cannot occur for at least seven years
7. No signs	7. Many signs for Christ's physical coming
8. For believers only	8. Affects all humanity
9. Time of joy	9. Time of mourning
10. Before the "day of wrath" (Tribulation)	10. Immediately after the Tribulation (Matthew 24)
11. No mention of Satan	11. Satan bound in abyss for 1,000 years
12. The Judgment Seat of Christ	12. No time or place for Judgment Seat
13. Marriage of the Lamb	13. His Bride descends with Him
14. Only His own see Him	14. Every eye will see Him
15. Tribulation begins	15. 1,000-year kingdom of Christ begins

As you examine these lists, you are forced to face the fact that two different events are described. The pre-Tribulationist has no difficulty explaining those differences and the impossibility of their taking place simultaneously. They are not the same, and are separated in time by the seven-year Tribulation. And, according to the lists, it is impossible for Christ to come in power and glory to set up His kingdom, for the signs that precede that coming have not come to pass yet, and it cannot happen until seven years after the Rapture. But the Rapture, by contrast, can happen today! Which is why we need to do all we can to keep anyone from being left behind.

11. *A post-Tribulational Rapture doesn't tell us who will populate the Millennial kingdom.*

For years I have searched for a single reason that would convince my post-Tribulational friends of the impossibility of their position. My friend and colleague Dr. Thomas Ice has shared with me such a reason—very simply, it is this: It is impossible for the Rapture to occur at the end of the Tribulation, for if it did, there would be no one left on earth in a natural body who can populate the Millennial kingdom.

Based on several Old Testament passages and the size of the rebellion at the end of the Tribulation (Revelation 20:7-10), it is apparent that during Christ's 1,000-year reign, the world will experience an enormous population explosion. Some people believe the total population will exceed the aggregate population of the world, and today's population figures tell us there are about six billion people on earth. Whatever the case, we do know that the rebellion at the end of the Millennial kingdom will be large, and the question we must ask is this: Where do these people come from?

The Christians who are raptured and the Old Testament saints who are raised up will all be in resurrected, glorified bodies, so they can't help populate the Millennial kingdom. Jesus said in Matthew 22:30 that the resurrected "neither marry nor are given in marriage, but are like angels of God in heaven." This suggests that resurrected believers will no longer be involved in procreation. So who will populate the Millennial kingdom? It can't be believers, for they will have been raptured and given glorified bodies before entering the kingdom, and it won't be sinners, because they will not enter the kingdom. If the Rapture takes place at the end of the Tribulation, there won't be anyone on earth to populate the kingdom!

In this discussion, it's important for us to keep in mind the judgment of the nations as described by Christ in Matthew

25:31-46. The beginning of that passage says, "When the Son of Man comes in His glory, and all the holy angels with Him, then He will sit on the throne of His glory. All the nations will be gathered before Him, and He will separate them one from another, as a shepherd divides his sheep from the goats" (verses 31-32). The sheep represent believers, and the goats represent unbelievers. We then read that the sheep will "inherit the kingdom" (verse 34), and the goats will be sent into "the everlasting fire" (verse 41). Given that everyone will be sent to one of these two destinations, if we adhere to a post-Trib rapture view, we are left with no one to populate the Millennial kingdom. This is a significant problem that renders the post-Trib view impossible, or at least seriously suspect.

By contrast, the pre-Trib view says that those who become Christians *during* the Tribulation will not be raptured at the end of the Tribulation, and thus will still have their natural bodies when they enter the Millennium. The pre-Trib view, which has the Rapture *before* the Tribulation, states that the believers who are raptured will already be taken up to the Father's house and given their glorified bodies, but those who receive Christ *during* the Tribulation and survive to the time of Christ's glorious appearing at the end of the Tribulation will not receive glorified bodies. Because they still have their natural bodies, they will be able to populate the Millennial kingdom.

In the book of Revelation, the 144,000 Jews, the two witnesses, and the "angel...having the everlasting gospel to preach to those who dwell on the earth—to every nation" (Revelation 14:6) will be used to bring about a great soul harvest. The result will be "a great multitude which no one could number, of all nations, tribes, peoples, and tongues" (Revelation 7:9). Those who survive the Tribulation and endure to the end (Matthew 24:13) will enter the Millennium in their natural bodies and populate Christ's 1,000-year kingdom.

If you aren't convinced by the first ten reasons I've listed for why a post-Tribulational rapture cannot be true, surely the problem raised in reason #11, which we've discussed here, is convincing. The important question that remains unanswered by post-Tribulationists on this particular matter is well answered by the pre-Tribulational view.

Chapter Eleven

The Pre-Tribulation Rapture: Believe It!

It is unworthy of strong, mature Christians to believe that the Rapture will occur before the Tribulation if our reason for doing so is because we are afraid to trust God to take care of us during that time of trial. Happily, this is not the reason we hold such a position.

The pre-Trib view is popular because it fits so well all the Bible passages that touch on end-time events. One of the reasons it commends itself to biblical literalists is that it provides a logical, believable, and unforced sequence for all those events that must come to pass. The following chart, for example, locates the main second coming passages in a pre-Tribulational sequence.

While the pre-Trib view may not be perfect (none of the existing theories are), I believe it provides the best explanation of how our Lord will rapture His church, take them to the Father's house for their appearance before His judgment seat, and then celebrate the Marriage Supper of the Lamb. Meanwhile, the inhabitants of earth (including Israel) will go through the Tribulation, designed to be so traumatic that during those seven years millions of people will respond to the call of the gospel. During that time the Antichrist, long predicted by the Hebrew prophets, will unite the world and lead it in opposition to the sovereign God, but Christ will destroy him with the "brightness of His coming" in "power and great glory" when He returns to the earth to set up His 1,000-year kingdom.

Not only does the pre-Trib view logically locate and explain these important future events, but there are sound reasons for believing it. Following are 14 reasons that I find the pre-Trib view

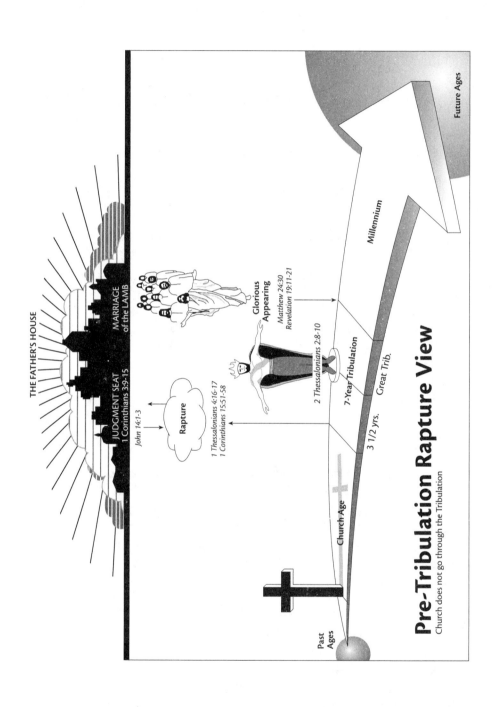

THE FATHER'S HOUSE

MARRIAGE
of the LAMB

JUDGMENT SEAT
1 Corinthians 3:9-15

John 14:1-3

Rapture

1 Thessalonians 4:16-17
1 Corinthians 15:51-58

Glorious
Appearing

Matthew 24:30
Revelation 19:11-21

2 Thessalonians 2:8-10

7-Year Tribulation

Great Trib.

3 1/2 yrs.

Church Age

Millennium

Past
Ages

Future Ages

Pre-Tribulation Rapture View

Church does not go through the Tribulation

satisfying and that convince me it rightly divides and arranges biblical prophecy.

Fourteen Reasons for Being a Pre-Tribulationist

1. *The pre-Tribulation view is the most logical view of second coming scriptures when taken for their plain, literal meaning whenever possible.*

Many of the details of the second coming must be pieced together from various passages of Scripture, no matter what view you take. The pre-Trib position finds a logical place for every second-coming passage. Like a completed puzzle, all the pieces fit. As Dr. Walvoord notes,

> It is rather significant that, without any attempt to establish uniformity in eschatology, the Bible Institute movement of America is predominantly premillennial and pretribulational. This has come from taking Scripture in its plain, ordinary meaning and explaining it in this sense. By contrast, educational institutions that have approached the Bible creedally tend to make Scriptures conform to their previously accepted creed with the result that most of them are liberals or, if conservative, tend to be amillennial.[1]

> The pretribulational interpretation allows the interpreter of both the Old and New Testaments to establish an order for endtime events that makes sense. While many details may not be revealed, the major events of the endtime as commonly held by pretribulationists can be established. By contrast, it would be difficult to find two posttribulationists who agree on any system of events relating to the endtime. The reason for confusion among the posttribulationists is a lack of uniformity in principles of interpretation that results in disagreements as to the extent of spiritualization required. While large prophecy conferences are held by pretribulationists with evident agreement of the speakers on major events of the endtime, no such conference has ever been held by posttribulationists for the simple reason that they do not have any major agreement among themselves. Accordingly prophecy conferences

are almost the exclusive domain of the pretribulational interpretation.[2]

The evident trend among scholars who have forsaken pretribulationism for posttribulationism is that in many cases they also abandon premillennialism. For those who wish to think consistently and logically from principles to interpretation, the options continue to be (1) a pretribulational rapture followed by a pre-millennial return of Christ to the earth, or (2) abandoning both for a posttribulational rapture and a spiritualized millennium.[3]

Dr. Walvoord, now in his nineties, has been a Bible scholar more than 60 years and personally knows most of the living scholars on this subject. He warns that "it is not uncommon for scholars who defect from pretribulationism in favor of posttribulationism to also defect in their doctrine of the inerrancy of Scripture."[4] I would add that some reject the pre-Trib position because it is not spelled out in detail in one single passage, but they often end up with a position more complex and less logical and not in keeping with the plain sense of Scripture. When taken literally, the prophetic passages of Scripture produce a pre-Millennial view of the kingdom, a futuristic view of the Tribulation as described in the book of Revelation, and a pre-Tribulation rapture.

2. *It clearly and logically untangles the contrasting details of Christ's second coming.*

As already demonstrated, Christ cannot come in the air suddenly for the church and come to the earth publicly at the same time. In the pre-Trib view, the coming of Christ in blessing for His church and His return to the earth in judgment are two distinct events separated by time. The book of Revelation and 2 Thessalonians 2 clarify what takes place between those events.

The criticism that Christ's coming for the church and His coming to the earth comprise two comings is not valid in view of the precedent set by the Hebrew prophets in the Old Testament. The coming of Christ to this earth is obviously two events separated by at least 2,000 years. What seemed like one coming turned out to be two events—the first coming to suffer, and then His second coming some 2,000 years later in power and great glory. Why should it now be thought strange that Christ's coming for His Bride in blessing and His coming in judgment to the earth be separated by seven years?

3. *It allows sufficient time to interject important end-time events.*

The pre-Trib view allows adequate time for Christians to be taken to the Father's house, experience the Judgment Seat of Christ ("each of us shall give account of himself to God" [Romans 14:12]), and participate in the Marriage Supper events in heaven before Christ returns with power and great glory to the earth. Post-Tribulationists offer various periods of time, but all are too brief to allow adequate time for these important events.

4. *This is the only view that distinguishes between Israel and the church.*

"The confusion of Israel and the church is one of the major reasons for confusion in prophecy as a whole, as illustrated in both amillennialism and posttribulationism."[5] Pre-Tribulationism is the only position that clearly outlines the program of the church.

5. *It is the only view that makes "the blessed hope" truly a blessed hope.*

Even the mid-Trib position destroys that hope by forcing the Christian to anticipate the trauma of the Tribulation. Post-Tribulationism, of course, is even worse in that it requires Christians to go through the Great Tribulation. No reading of Bible prophecy requires the presence of Christians during that seven-year period of judgment that is clearly intended for Israel and the Gentile world.

Remember: Rapture teaching was given to comfort those who mourn! The threat of going through the Tribulation is hardly a doctrine of comfort to the saints.

6. *It is the only view that takes God at His Word and claims His promises literally to save us out of the wrath to come.*

As the New King James Version phrases it, "I also will keep you from the hour of trial which shall come upon the whole world" (Revelation 3:10; see also Romans 5:9; 1 Thessalonians 1:10; 5:9). The Tribulation, which our Lord described in Matthew 24, is that period of trial.

7. *Only the pre-Trib view preserves the motivating power of imminency teaching found in the New Testament that was such a challenge to the early church.*

In John 14:1-3, Acts 1:11, 1 Corinthians 15:51-52, Philippians 3:20, Colossians 3:4, and many other passages, the apostles taught that Christ could come at any moment. When the church loses this anticipation, she tends to become carnal and spiritually dead.

8. *Pre-Trib Christians are looking for the coming of the Lord.*

Other views have them awaiting the Tribulation, Antichrist, and suffering.

9. *It makes a major event out of the Rapture.*

Since at least four passages of Scripture describe the Rapture, it must be a significant event. The post-Trib view trivializes it, treating it as an express elevator trip—zip up and zip right back down. The pre-Trib view makes it a dignified, blessed event commensurate with a heavenly Bridegroom who comes to take His Bride to His Father's house for their wedding.

10. *This view most clearly fits the flow of the book of Revelation.*

Taken literally, the book of Revelation is a pre-Tribulational book. Revelation 4:1-2 by itself never would unlock the mystery of the Rapture, but since that event is revealed in other passages, one may appropriately identify John's call up to heaven as a rapture event that takes place before the Tribulation.

By contrast, if post-Tribbers reject Revelation 4:1-2 as a reference to the Rapture, they must explain why the Rapture was not mentioned and where it fits. Since Revelation is the most detailed sequential account of end-time events in the Bible, it is unthinkable that such a joyous event as the Rapture, mentioned in other books of the Bible, would be completely omitted.

Interestingly enough, Revelation 19:11-20 describes the glorious appearing. At no time hinting at the resurrection of the church so the Bride can join her Lord as promised, it just assumes they are already with Him. According to the pre-Trib view, they have been with the Lord for seven years.

11. *The pre-Trib view explains why the church is not mentioned from Revelation 4:3 through Revelation 18.*

There must be a reason why the church is so central in the first three chapters of Revelation but disappears until the glorious appearing. Pre-Tribulationists insist it's because she has been raptured. Mid-Tribbers and post-Tribulationists ask us to find the church in the Tribulation even though she is not mentioned in chapters 4–18.

12. *It preserves the credibility of Christ's word that Christians will be kept from the Tribulation.*

The pre-Trib view is the only one that resolves the contrasting difficulties of Revelation 3:10 and 7:14. For if Christians are among the martyrs of 7:14 who are killed during the Tribulation, then the Lord has not kept His promise in Revelation 3:10. And that is unthinkable! Pre-Tribulationists explain that there are no Christians on the earth during the Tribulation to be martyred. They were raptured before it began—fulfilling the Lord's promise.

13. *The pre-Trib view maintains 1 Thessalonians 4:13-18 as a comfort passage and explains why the young Christians at Thessalonica were so upset about the deaths of their loved ones.*

Richard Mayhue offers these interesting comments:

> For argument's sake, let us suppose that posttribulation is true. What would we expect to find in 1 Thessalonians 4? How does this compare with what we do observe?
>
> First, we would expect the Thessalonians to be joyous over the fact that loved ones are home with the Lord and will not have to endure the horrors of the tribulation. But, we discover the Thessalonians are grieving because they fear their loved ones will miss the rapture. Only a pretribulation rapture accounts for this grief.
>
> Second, we would expect the Thessalonians to be grieving over their own impending trial rather than grieving over loved ones. Furthermore, we would expect them to be inquisitive about their future doom. But, the Thessalonians have no fear or question about the coming tribulation.
>
> Third, we would expect Paul, even in the absence of interest or questions by the Thessalonians, to have provided instruction and exhortation for such a supreme test which would make their present tribulation seem microscopic in comparison. But, there is not one indication of any impending tribulation.
>
> First Thessalonians 4 fits the model of a pretribulation rapture. It is incompatible with posttributation-ism.[6]

14. *It explains why there is no Bible instruction on preparation for the Tribulation.*

Doesn't it seem strange that although the Bible advises Christians how to face ordinary, everyday troubles, it submits absolutely no instructions related to the worst time the world will ever face, a period filled with frightening events that have never even come close to being fulfilled? Pre-Tribulationism has a simple answer: We won't be there!

In a discussion about the two main passages on the Rapture (1 Thessalonians 4 and 1 Corinthians 15:51-56), Mayhue states,

> The exhortations of the major passage on the rapture in 1 Corinthians 15:51-56 are similar in their implications. Not a word of warning is given concerning a coming tribulation, but they are exhorted to be living in the light of the imminent return of Christ. This hope is defined by Paul in Titus 2:13 as "that blessed hope, and the glorious appearing of the great God and our Savior Jesus Christ." The hope of a rapture after enduring the great tribulation is hardly a happy expectation, and this passage is difficult for posttribulationists to explain. The hope is not that of resurrection after death and martyrdom, but rather the coming and revelation of Christ in His glory to them while they are still living on the earth. The exhortations relating to the rapture constitute a major problem to posttribulationism.[7]

You Can Still Trust the Pre-Tribulation View

I would readily give up this treasured prophetic position if the Bible required it, but it does not. In fact, I trust I have proved by now that neither Scripture nor the facts of history lead us to abandon this blessed hope.

The late Dr. Wilbur Smith was one of the greatest scholars I have ever sat under. I studied Bible doctrine with him at Moody Bible Institute and the book of Revelation at Fuller Seminary. He possessed a photographic memory, was an avid reader, owned a large personal library, and was esteemed by many as an authority on Bible prophecy. Near the end of his life he wrote a review of two books on the Tribulation—the pre-Tribulation work of Dr.

Gerald B. Stanton, *Kept from the Hour,* and the post-Tribulation volume by Dr. George E. Ladd, *The Blessed Hope.* Here is his conclusion:

> I must say for myself that I have never seen any arguments or biblical exegesis of relevant passages that would persuade me to abandon the view I have held for many years, that the Lord Jesus may come at any time, and the church will not go through the Tribulation. If the church is to experience the Tribulation, the idea of the imminency of Christ's appearing must be given up. I think that no man can say from the Scriptures that Christ cannot come today. And if He could return today, it is not necessary to argue that He will come at the end of this dreadful period of suffering and satanic rule.
>
> For the millions of believers living on earth in any one generation to be convinced that the next experience for them will be a seven-year period of suffering and anguish, rather than the Lord's coming for them in glory, would certainly cast dark shadows over the church as a whole, shadows which I do not think belong to the Christian's hope for the Lord's return.[8]

Indeed, there is no reason to let go of the blessed hope of Christ's return before the Tribulation!

Part Three

ANSWERING THE ATTACKS ON THE PRE-TRIB RAPTURE VIEW

Chapter Twelve

Target Number One

All attacks on the teaching of the Rapture before the Tribulation come down to one man.

John Darby is the individual most attackers credit with first promoting this prophetic view. Some, as we have seen, accuse him of getting it from the vision of a Scottish girl. The more vicious say it was demon-inspired or that he received the teaching from a defrocked minister named Irving, or even a renegade Jesuit Catholic named Lacunza.

Whatever the charges and assertions, John Darby figures to be a central figure in any study of the pre-Tribulation rapture. There is little question that he did more than any other man to organize and popularize the view both in the United States and Great Britain. Born in 1800 and single all his life, he dedicated his boundless energies to advancing the cause of Christ through soul-winning, preaching, Bible teaching, church building, conference teaching, and publishing. He was a compulsive writer of letters, tracts, booklets, articles, and books (some 52 volumes),[1] many of which are preserved in libraries throughout the Western world.

Though slight and unimpressive of stature, Darby was a powerful personality. He was brilliant, tireless in his missionary zeal to teach the Bible, and very strong willed. As such he may have been intolerant of those who refused to agree with him. He seemed to exercise amazing patience with earnest seekers after truth, but he was not always as temperate with those who refused to consider his position seriously.

We are forced to gain our impression of Darby from those who knew him personally. Dr. James Brookes, an outstanding Presbyterian pastor of his day, considered him "one of the greatest Bible teachers of his generation."[2] C.I. Scofield and D.L. Moody became American disciples of Darby's teachings. (Although Moody promoted the pre-Trib position as much as anyone through his own ministry, his Northfield Bible Conferences and the Bible Institute that bears his name, he had a falling out with Darby over another doctrine, that of extreme Calvinism, which contrasted with Moody's emphasis upon free will.[3]) Most of the early fundamentalists and founders of the late nineteenth-century missionary movements, colleges, and Bible institutes accepted and taught John Darby's concepts, creating many second-generation disciples.

Darby did not invent the pre-Tribulation rapture, the separation of Israel and the church, dispensationalism, types and symbols, and other distinctives which have made him the most quoted prophecy teacher since the apostle Paul. Many Bible scholars had mentioned one or more of these concepts before Darby. He did, however, pull them together into a cohesive body of thought.

Darby adapted some of his Rapture concepts from those before him who separated the Rapture and the second advent as two distinct events. He then established a specific time period between them and bolstered his ideas with Scripture. By traveling far and wide, he was able to popularize his views, which were accepted by the Bible-believing church not because of the power of his persuasion but because his convictions were based on Scripture.

In a sense, I followed his precedent with the centuries-old four-temperament theory that I have been privileged to popularize in this country. I didn't invent it, but I borrowed from thinking before me, added two concepts—temperament blends and the power of the Holy Spirit to strengthen a person's inherited temperament weaknesses—and popularized it by writing and speaking on the subject. Darby was influenced by many biblical literalists before him. Some taught the dispensations, some viewed the church as distinct from Israel, and some became

Futurists. He then added nuggets of discovery from the Word of God and popularized the whole through his many writings and speaking tours.

Darby's Background

Darby was born in London of Irish parents. His family was wealthy and could afford to send him to the famous Westminster school. In 1815 the family moved from London to its ancestral castle in Ireland. In that same year Darby began his matriculation at Trinity College, Dublin,[4] where he was trained in law, and graduated in 1819 as a Classical Gold Medalist (highest honors). He passed the Chancery Bar in 1822 but abandoned the legal profession one year later. "Apparently he was in the grip of a deep spiritual struggle from 1818 to 1825 which led to his conversion. Even during those tempestuous years Darby's mind was struggling with the nature of the true church."[5] He said of those days, "In my own case, I went through deep exercise of soul before there was a trace of peace, and it was not till after six or seven years that I was delivered."[6]

During that search he came to a personal relationship with Christ, perhaps inspired by the fiery preaching of Professor Richard Graves at Trinity. Due to his deep spiritual struggles, Darby became disillusioned with the legal profession.

> In 1825 he entered the ministry within the Church of England and was given an Irish parish. Darby engaged in a tireless ministry within the parish, such that Catholics were becoming Protestants at the rate of 600 to 800 a week. Within a year he was ordained as a minister in the Church of England. Soon after ordination he was disillusioned by a decree from his bishop that all converts to the Church would have to swear allegiance to the king of England. Darby saw this as a compromise with the lordship of Christ and the bishop's decree greatly reduced his success with Catholics.[7]

In late November of 1826 Darby broke one of his legs, which provided convalescent time for him to study the Scriptures avidly and coalesce in his mind all his previous studies.

During this time he recognized the clear distinction between the church and Israel and his present position in Christ. He also came to believe in the imminent return of Christ:

> I saw that the Christian, having his place in Christ in heaven, has nothing to wait for, save the coming of the Saviour in order to be set in fact in the glory which, is already his portion "in Christ."
>
> The coming of the Lord was the other truth which was brought to my mind from the word, as that which, if sitting in heavenly places in Christ, was alone to be waited for, that I might sit in heavenly places with Him. Isaiah 32 brought me to the earthly consequences of the same truth, though other passages might seem perhaps more striking to me now; but I saw an evident change of dispensation in that chapter, when the spirit would be poured on to the Jewish nation, and a king reign in righteousness.[8]

Thus very early in his life, by the time he was 27 years old, he had formulated the basic elements of those principles upon which he would build his entire system of thought. Today it is called *dispensationalism,* and it automatically assumes pre-Tribulationism.

Within four to six years Darby was active in a series of Bible study consultations that came to be called "the Powerscourt Conferences" and practically took over the second and third meetings. During this period he and other dissenters from the established state church inaugurated the Brethren movement. One unfortunate experience during the development of this movement occurred after he had been in Switzerland for a time. He had become more entrenched in his views on the separation of the church and Israel and the pre-Tribulation rapture of the church, but his good friend and fellow Bible teacher, B.W. Newton, who pastored the Plymouth Brethren Church in his absence, did not accept these two premises. The discussions between them became so fierce that, like Paul and Barnabas, they were torn asunder. This led to an acrimonious debate that became the first of many schisms within the Brethren movement.

Each was joined by supporters, and the nineteenth-century fad of fighting paper wars intensified. Darby's insistence on a rapture separated from the glorious appearing caused his opponents to taunt him with believing in two comings of Christ—a criticism still used by post-Millennialists and post-Tribbers.

By 1845 a growing controversy within the Brethren movement prompted Darby and some of his followers to withdraw from the fellowship. Later, Newton was excommunicated for teaching a faulty view of the person of Christ.[9]

It doesn't take much imagination to foresee Newton's resentment of Darby. According to one researcher, "He spent the second half of his life on a crusade to disprove the pre-Trib rapture and thus had repeated clashes with J.N. Darby. He wrote scores of books advocating his views."[10]

Almost all modern attacks on the pre-Trib position can be traced to this source or to S.P. Tregelles, Newton's brother-in-law! Tregelles sided with Newton not only because of their personal relationship but because he was a Historicist and post-Trib, vigorously opposing both dispensationalism and the pre-Tribulation rapture view. Tregelles even suggested that Darby's teachings came from demons or false spirits.

At best, Tregelles and Newton were hostile witnesses who created the majority of the attacks on the "blessed hope" teaching.

Where Did Darby Get His Theory?

Most of the attacks on Darby relate to the source of his teaching. Fortunately, these attacks have been dated, and church historian Roy Huebner verifies that these sources were too late to have influenced Darby. He had come to accept the imminent return of Christ and the separation of the church and Israel between 1826 and 1827. Huebner proves that it took several years for Darby's teachings to become definitive, but the awareness of the coming of Christ at any moment was one of the earliest matters Darby had settled in his mind.

Huebner also updates a suggestion that he has been researching for many years—that young Darby received help from a godly minister named Tweedy, who enabled him to locate the

Rapture in 2 Thessalonians 2:1-2. It is important to note that Darby received this information before the dates of the attacks that we shall soon examine.

Many Bible translations obscure the true meaning of 2 Thessalonians 2:1, making it difficult for students to appreciate the significance of the Rapture as part of the expression "our gathering together to Him." That Mr. Darby saw it as such is evident by his own translation of that scripture:

> Now we beg you brethren, by the coming of our
> Lord Jesus Christ and our gathering together to him,
> that ye be not soon shaken in mind....[11]

I am firmly convinced that Darby was influenced by the new wave of prophetic awareness in his day—the godly influence of his teachers at Trinity College, who were biblical literalists; quite possibly the writings of Gill and others before him (particularly Reverend Morgan Edwards, a Baptist minister in Philadelphia already mentioned on page 42 of this book, who described a pre-Trib rapture 70 years before Darby); the leading of the Holy Spirit, who wanted to bring that truth to light for these last days in preparation for the event; and from his intense personal study of the Word of God. The character of the man impels us to take him at his word when he says that he derived the concept from his study of the Word of God.

Darby himself said he got his theory in the following way:

> The careful reading of the Acts afforded me a practical picture of the early church, which made me feel deeply the contrast with its actual present state, though still as ever, beloved by God. At that time I had to use crutches when moving about, so that I had no longer any opportunity for making known my convictions in public....In my retreat, the 32nd chapter of Isaiah taught me clearly, on God's behalf, that there was still an economy to come, of His ordering; a state of things in no way established as yet. The consciousness of my union with Christ had given me the present heavenly portion of the glory, whereas this chapter clearly sets forth the corresponding earthly part. I was not able to put these things in their respective places or arrange

them in order, as I can now: but the truths themselves
were then revealed of God, through the action of His
Spirit, by reading His word.

What was to be done? I saw in that word the coming
of Christ to take the church to Himself in glory.[12]

Church historian Ernest R. Sandeen wrote the following
words in 1970 about Darby's source (before the modern-day
attacks on Darby surfaced and before Huebner's first book in
defense):

> Darby never indicated any source for his ideas other
> than the Bible....In later years he seems to have felt that
> he was convinced about the doctrine as early as 1827.
> Darby's opponents claimed that the doctrine origi-
> nated in one of the outbursts of tongues in Edward
> Irving's church about 1832. This seems to be a ground-
> less and pernicious charge. Neither Irving nor any
> member of the Albury group advocated any doctrine
> resembling the secret rapture....Since the clear inten-
> tion of this charge is to discredit the doctrine by
> attributing its origin to fanaticism rather than
> Scripture, there seems little ground for giving it any
> credence.[13]

Another scholar, William E. Bell, who does not accept the pre-
Trib position, nevertheless gives this objective comment in his
book *A Critical Evaluation of the Pretribulation Rapture Doctrine in
Christian Eschatology*:

> It seems only fair, however, in the absence of eyewit-
> nesses to settle the argument conclusively, that the
> benefit of the doubt should be given to Darby, and that
> the charge made by Tregelles be regarded as a possibil-
> ity but with insufficient support to merit its accep-
> tance....On the whole, however, it seems that Darby is
> perhaps the most likely choice—with help from
> Tweedy. This conclusion is greatly strengthened by
> Darby's own claim to have arrived at the doctrine
> through his study of 2 Thessalonians 2:1-2.[14]

Anyone interested in reviewing the details concerning the events of 1826–1845 is advised to get Huebner's book *Precious Truths Revived and Defended,* which is filled with information from notes, letters, and rare documents.[15] His work demonstrates that Darby came to the pre-Tribulation rapture position by the year 1827. This date is important because *none of the current attacks suggesting Mr. Darby derived the pre-Trib position from unsavory sources provide dates before 1831!* It is likely that, had Huebner's book been available earlier, some of the attacks of the past 30 years would never have surfaced.

Did Lacunza Influence Darby?

One recurring charge that merits extended attention is the idea that Darby was influenced by the writings of a renegade Jesuit priest. The year 1826 saw the translation into English of the amazing book *The Coming of Messiah in Power and Glory,* written by Manuel de Lacunza. Edward Irving, who translated the book, was still popular and respected at this time, having not yet succumbed to the heresies that led to his defrocking in 1834. Irving translated the book and wrote a lengthy foreword while he and his wife were on a holiday leave from their church in 1826. He completed the work just in time to present it to his congregation for Christmas. Thus the book could not have been edited, typeset, and published before late 1827.

This first English translation was not available until after John Darby had already come to his conclusion about the Rapture coming prior to the Tribulation. Nevertheless, this has not stopped evangelist John Bray (who read Lacunza's book sometime around 1985, after he had become an ardent post-Trib advocate) to do his best to discredit the pre-Trib theory by suggesting that it was first conceived by Lacunza. Apparently we are to infer that Lacunza was part of some evil plot of the Jesuits to subvert the Protestant Church.

Mr. Bray acknowledges on page 2 of his booklet *The Origin of the Pre-Tribulation Rapture Teaching* that his interest in Lacunza's book was first ignited by now-deceased minister Duncan McDougall's scurilous attack on Darby, titled *The Rapture of the Saints.* Thus we discover that the modern attacks on the pre-Tribulation rapture theory are only a bitter regurgitation of a century-old assault on the early Brethrens, dispensationalism, and the Rapture. The attacks go back to 1845 and the calumnies of Newton and Tregelles.

My Bray's booklet inspired me to visit the Library of Congress in Washington, D.C., where I photocopied Lacunza's work. Viewed in the light of his times and background, I came away extremely impressed with the book, author, and its incredible concepts. His research is clearly evident on every page. It is clear to the objective reader that the book is the work of a brilliant and devoted servant of Jesus Christ whose basic purpose was to glorify Him and cause men to prepare for His soon coming. I seriously doubt it could have been inspired by some satanic conspiracy.

Lacunza Was Not a Pre-Tribulationist

One thing is certain: John Darby could not possibly have borrowed his ideas from this Jesuit source, for Lacunza never taught a pre-Tribulation rapture! He had little or no understanding of the Tribulation. His great vision was the glorious appearing, which he always located as pre-Millennial. It is true that he also saw a rapture for some believers distinct from the glorious appearing, but he did not postulate a Tribulation separating the two. In fact, he envisioned between the two events a partial rapture of a very few holy saints going to heaven for 45 days while the earth was renovated by fire (2 Peter 3:10).

In all my review of pre-Trib literature, I have never found anyone else who propounded such a theory. There is simply no way that Darby could have appropriated Lacunza's ideas as his own. As for the Rapture, I commend Lacunza for finding in 1 Thessalonians 4:16-18 a rapture for some of the believers living and dead, though he is not unique in this. Others held the same interpretation of 1 Corinthians 15:50-58 and 1 Thessalonians 4:16-18.

A careful analysis of Lacunza's view reveals that he expected the Antichrist to come to the earth for 1,260 days (according to Daniel the prophet). Then Christ would appear for "a very few" Christians both dead and alive, rapture them, hold them in the atmosphere for 45 days, and then destroy the earth by fire, finally establishing a new earth. After that He would return to this earth to set up His Millennial kingdom.

We can laud Lacunza for this progressive view in the light of his times, but it is really nothing more than a post-Tribulational coming of Christ with a 45-day partial rapture twist for a few holy people. To suggest that John Darby, who had not even seen the book when he reached his conclusions, acquired his view of the Rapture from Lacunza is really begging the issue. Lacunza's interpretation of the book of Revelation proves that, for he held that chapters 4–19 precede the coming of Christ.

As much as I am drawn personally to the dedicated author of *The Coming of Messiah in Power and Glory*, I cannot conclude that Darby lifted his view from that source. There is little similarity between Darby and Lacunza, for Darby preached that Christ would rapture His church and take it to His Father's house for seven years, during which the world goes through the Tribulation and after which Christ will come to set up His Millennial rule. Darby's position in no way duplicates that of Lacunza for two reasons: 1) Darby propounded his view before Lacunza's book was printed in English; 2) a careful reading of Lacunza proves Lacunza did not see a pre-Tribulation rapture of the church.

Lacunza was a partial rapture post-Tribulationist. He was not even close to being a pre-Tribulationist.

Rightly Dividing the Word of Truth

Despite the controversies just highlighted, Darby's teachings began to grow in popularity among those who took the Bible literally. Many Independent, Baptist, and Methodist pastors readily saw the biblical justification for Darby's teachings on dispensations, the separation of Israel and the church, Futurism, imminency, and a pre-Tribulation rapture. Since they were biblical literalists who already believed in the pre-Millennial return of Christ, it was a small step to incorporate these concepts into their views of end-time activities.

Since the pre-Tribulation rapture view did not affect their other doctrines, few felt it necessary to leave their churches to join the Brethren movement. Consequently, as the teachings became popular, their churches saw growth instead of defections, which kept the Brethren movement from becoming a visible manifestation of the acceptance of Darby's teachings. Spreading throughout Ireland, England, and Scotland, "Darbyism" eventually came to North America and Canada.

Darby's travels to the United States (seven times) and Canada were even more productive to the spread of his concepts than in Britain. Many of the Bible institutes and other schools took up his teachings and used them in preparing the next generation of ministers. His views were always supported by Scripture, making them readily acceptable to Bible believers and explaining why they became the predominant view of the pre-Millennial church.

Some of those Bible teachers recognized the Rapture for Christians both dead and living before the revelation of the "man of sin" (2 Thessalonians 2:3). However, Darby is probably the first to identify it before the entire Tribulation, which he perceived as a seven-year period. Darby was helped to see this truth by Mr. Tweedy, "a spiritual man and most devoted ex-clergyman among the Irish Brethren."[16] They were discussing 2 Thessalonians 2:1-2, which evidently revealed to him the identity of the phrase "our gathering together in Him" as a reference to the Rapture. Huebner locates this no later than 1830, before the dates of any of the accusations normally raised against Darby.

Why Not Until the Nineteenth Century?

It is true that the pre-Trib position was not formed in detail until 1826–28, but we should ask, When was the post-Trib position delineated? Dr. Walvoord asserts that post-Tribulationism as taught today is also of recent vintage. Both positions agree that the glorious appearing follows the Tribulation, as our Lord predicted, and the apostle John locates the event just before Christ sets up His kingdom. All pre-Millennialists agree on this. But the timing of the Rapture and the events of the Tribulation generate extensive debate.

As far as I can judge from church history, post-Tribbers just assumed that the Rapture and glorious appearing were synonymous. For post-Tribbers to get mileage out of the criticism that the pre-Trib position is suspect because it is of recent vintage (in contrast to the supposed long-term history of their view), most resort to a simplistic view of the second coming. Not until the pre-Trib position began to be popularized did post-Trib advocates take the Rapture seriously and develop the details of their own position. Thus the historical beginning of either view are really not relevant to the discussion.

If Darby had not located the Rapture before the Tribulation, someone else in his generation probably would have done so. The electrifying acceptance of this teaching by Bible-believing churches was due not to Darby, but to the support offered by the literal teaching of the Scriptures.

One twentieth-century Bible writer suggests,

> F.F. Bruce's conclusion as to where Darby got the pre-Tribulational rapture seems to be correct. It was in the air in the 1820s and 1830s among eager students of unfulfilled prophecy.[17]

Note again that John Darby did not invent the Rapture. Huebner is correct when he explains, "The word 'rapture' was in use, to designate the catching up of the saints, long before 1832. For example, Joseph Mede (1586–1638) wrote, 'Therefore, it is not needful that the Resurrection of those which slept in Christ, and the Rapture of those which shall be left alive together with them in the air....' "[18]

This clearly indicates that Mede, a great seventeenth-century literalist, understood 1 Thessalonians 4:13-18 to teach the catching up of the saints and used the word *rapture* to designate that catching up. His statement was made over 200 years before Darby taught the Rapture! Thus we see that the term *rapture* was not unique to Darby, but had been in use by others before him. For every printed reference to rapture teachings that have been preserved to this day, there were doubtless many other comments in print and in the messages of faithful teachers of end-time subjects that remain undiscovered or are lost.

For example, as early as A.D. 270, St. Victorinus, Bishop of Petau, wrote a commentary on the book of Revelation in which he said,

> And I saw another great and wonderful sign, seven angels having the seven last plagues; for in them is completed the indignation of God. For the wrath of

God always strikes the obstinate people with seven plagues, that is, perfectly, as it is said in Leviticus; and these shall be in the last *time, when the church shall have gone out of the midst*[19] (emphasis added).

So it is clear that the teaching of the church being taken out "in the last time," meaning the coming of Christ, was known as early as the third century.

When you add to this list of existing evidences of those who saw the Rapture long before Darby (such as Morgan Edward back in 1742 and Pseudo-Ephrem in A.D. 372), you come to realize it's clear that Darby did not invent the pre-Tribulational rapture view of the return of Christ. Rather, this view has been treasured and mentioned by others earlier in church history.

Darby's Views Were Based on Scripture

Opponents of the pre-Trib view like to make it sound like a revolutionary teaching, whereas the only real difference between pre-Tribulational and post-Trib teaching is the location of the Rapture before or after the Tribulation, a distinction of seven or more years. It is an important distinction, however, for it determines whether Christians will miss those tribulations or go through them.

It is safe for us to conclude that Darby did not receive his view of the Lord's return from any of the sources attributed to him by his detractors. Modern researchers have found nothing to prove otherwise, and their attacks, which have unfortunately deceived the unsuspecting, are nothing more than a regurgitation of old, discredited attacks.

Be assured that this biblically based view of end-time events is trustworthy and deserving of your continued confidence.

Chapter Thirteen

A Case Study
in Slander

There is one form of attack that is not worthy of Christians. Unfortunately, this form of attack was launched immediately after the death of a well-known pre-Trib teacher. The attack generally proceeds in this fashion: Once the body is lowered into the grave, the attackers suggest that in his last moments the deceased repudiated his belief in the imminent return of Christ. Of course, this disavowal was known only to one or two persons—and never by those closest to the deceased.

The shabbiest of this sort of assault was a scurrilous attempt to dishonor the name of one preeminent pre-Trib advocate during the first half of this century. It serves as a classic example of what we might call the *dead hominem* attack. Since the offensive was not mounted until after his death, he could not personally defend himself.

Dr. Harry A. Ironside (1876–1951), pastor of Moody Memorial Church in Chicago, was a Bible teacher, pastor, writer, and conference speaker extraordinaire. He was my number-one hero in the ministry, the one man after whom I unsuccessfully tried to pattern my own ministry. A brilliant man, largely self-taught (even learning Chinese on his own), he was an avid student of the Bible. His messages were always saturated with Scripture, and he was famous for Bible exposition with a practical application that culminated in either an evangelistic challenge or an appeal to consecrated living. A deeply spiritual and humble man, he was committed to making the Bible clear, exciting, and practical.

The first gift my wife gave me for Christmas six months after we were married was his entire set of commentaries on all 27 books of the New Testament. I have worn them out. In fact, I would never preach on a text until I reviewed Dr. Ironside's insights. Through his books, conferences, and preaching, he inspired as many young ministers as anyone in this century. And he always spoke clearly of the imminent return of Christ for His church.

The Attack on Dr. Ironside

I personally objected to the attack on Dr. Ironside when it surfaced more than 30 years *after* his death. To my surprise, it originated with a man who loves the Word of God and is, like Dr. Ironside, an evangelist. This antagonist has shifted from a pre-Trib to a post-Trib position on the Rapture, and like so many of his persuasion, he is not merely content to lose the blessed hope for himself but feels obligated to steal that hope from others. It is my overwhelming conviction that some people have left the pre-Trib position because they have overexposed their minds to arguments for post- or mid-Trib positions and underexposed their minds to the biblical reasons for holding the pre-Trib view.

John L. Bray has attacked the integrity and reliability of Dr. Harry A. Ironside in two of his works.

> I first read of this new interpretation of this "70th week" in a book by Dr. Harry A. Ironside, former pastor of Moody Memorial Church in Chicago, back in 1946. In the preface to this book, Dr. Ironside said, "It is not with any pretension of having discovered something new that I have prepared this volume." Then in chapter 2, which deals with this particular prophecy of Daniel, he said, "We have here the backbone of the entire prophetic system of the Bible." So you can see the importance of this particular interpretation of this prophecy to the dispensationalists and the Pre-Tribulation Rapture teachers. Dr. Ironside said, "between the sixty-ninth and the seventieth weeks we have a Great Parenthesis which has now lasted over nineteen hundred years....The moment Messiah died

on the cross, the prophetic clock stopped. There has not been a tick upon that clock for nineteen centuries. (*The Great Parenthesis* [Grand Rapids: Zondervan Publishing House, 1943], 33). Not until the Rapture will that clock start ticking again, according to this viewpoint.

No, Dr. Ironside had not discovered something new when he wrote the book, *The Great Parenthesis*. This had already been taught by an earlier person, none other than J.N. Darby, who wrote, "We are properly nowhere, save in the extraordinary SUSPENSION of prophetic testimony, or period, which comes IN BETWEEN THE SIXTY-NINTH AND SEVENTIETH WEEK of Daniel" (Letters of J.N.D., 1, 131).

I think it might be helpful again at this point to repeat what I said in my little book on *The Great Tribulation?* Back in the fall of 1943, Dr. Ironside said to a friend who was working with the radio staff where Dr. Ironside occasionally went to speak (and the friend personally told me this) that there were grave questions about the whole teaching relating to dispensationalism; but he felt he was too far along in years to make any changes, having written too many books on those subjects. Dr. Ironside said that the system was "full of holes."

Just keep in mind that Dr. Ironside, himself having had much association with the Plymouth Brethren assemblies, got this teaching from J.N. Darby.[1]

Notice that Bray offers this hearsay evidence without identifying Dr. Ironside's accuser—evidence that would never be admissible in court. But that doesn't deter Bray from slandering a great man, affectionately known during his life as "the bishop of fundamentalism," by circulating such an unfounded statement long after his death.

Dr. Robert Sumner, editor of *The Biblical Evangelist*, is a careful researcher who was able to uncover the identity of John Bray's witness.

Another who has attacked the memory of Dr. Ironside is Dave MacPherson, a man who has seemingly made a ministry of attacking pre-tribulation and pre-tribulationists—possibly because of past personal problems relating to this issue. He, like Bray, has been saying that Ironside admitted to "a close associate" he had known the teaching was "full of holes," and MacPherson also adds that Ironside explained "he was too old to make any book changes." Unlike Bray, however, MacPherson has named the so-called "close associate" as Mr. Stanley Payne, a man unfamiliar to us or to any of Ironside's surviving relatives. But MacPherson's position, too, makes Ironside out to be an insincere hypocrite who pretended in print to hold a position he did not really believe.

Be that as it may, it was our understanding that Payne had given MacPherson a statement, authorizing him to publish it, so we wrote and requested a copy. The latter cordially responded, noting that he was using it in a book of some 300 pages which is being published "by a well-known Christian publisher," expecting release of the book about August. However, this additional flood of erroneous publicity only makes it doubly imperative that we defend Ironside's good name to a new generation of literates. In Payne's letter to MacPherson, he said about the incident:

> In the 1940s I was on the radio staff of the Moody Bible Institute working as supervisor of traffic. The late Dr. Harry Ironside, then pastor of the Moody Church, would come down to the studios and bring a half-hour message whenever we needed him to fill in. One day after one of these broadcasts, I began to question him about many of the predictions which he and other Bible teachers had made in the late '30s just prior to WW2. He answered with this comment: "I know that the system I teach [the pre-trib secret rapture and related subjects] is full of holes, but I am too old and have written too many books to make any changes."

Those were his exact words.

Frankly, we would more easily believe that the sun rises in the west than believe those words ever fell from the lips of that great man of God.

Why do men do things like this? We think A.J. Pollock put his finger on the key, in his *Will the Church Go Through the Great Tribulation?*, saying: "It appears to us a very likely trick of the lawyer with a bad case, who, to make up his deficiency, resorts to abusing the other side."

The late William R. Newell...discussing this same strange and evil habit, said: "Again—why do the post-tribulationists keep claiming that men who held Christ's imminent coming while on earth, made some statements to him, 'just before death,' declaring the opposite?

"Robert Cameron, of *Watchword and Truth*, whose later life was largely a proselytizing campaign for post-tribulationism, used to claim that Dr. Brookes, of St. Louis, had given up this hope 'before he died, in an interview with him'! But both the last books and the later associates of Dr. Brookes deny this. Others claimed that Professor W.G. Moorehead gave it up, etc., etc. Someone told me that R.A. Torrey weakened. I challenged him. He could produce no proof whatever! Mrs. Torrey, when told that a Canadian magazine had claimed that her husband had given up the hope of Christ's imminent coming for the whole Church, was much distressed, and wrote the editor to publish her denial of such a false report." [Which request that journal has never granted. Why?][2]

Dr. Ironside Never Changed His Mind

When I first read John Bray's claim that Dr. Ironside had changed his mind, I knew it was untrue, for he dates this so-called conversation "back in the fall of 1943." I was a ministerial student at Bob Jones University during the last four years of Dr. Ironside's life, during which he was the most popular Bible conference speaker two of those years. I took copious notes on his sermons because, as pastor of a country Southern Baptist church, I had to prepare three new sermons every week. During my senior year, he warmed our hearts with a message on Christ's return for His church, and you can be sure that Dr. Bob Jones, Sr. would never have invited him to the university if he had changed his position! Suggesting that he preached the pre-Tribulation rapture in 1950 after disavowing it in 1943 is unbelievable!

Bray and other post-Tribbers who would gather (if they could) strength for this position by besmirching the testimony of a leading Bible teacher of the past are on the horns of a dilemma. They either purposely have slandered a great Christian leader on flimsy and unconfirmed hearsay evidence (which potentially impugns their Christian integrity), or they are grasping at straws to justify their position. Some post-Tribbers will do almost anything to gain converts to the belief that Christians will go through the Tribulation, even to the point of claiming a biblical literalist has changed his view.

Recently I contacted a man who had been an official at Moody radio for many years. He was irate that anyone would make such a spurious charge. He told me on the phone that R. Stanley Payne was "a paper pusher who filled out logs and is hardly remembered by anyone who works there, and that it is unlikely that such a conversation ever took place." Later I discussed the matter with a former president of Moody Bible Institute, who also found the charge dubious. He added, "Dr. Ironside was a great kidder. I'm sure if he ever said such a thing, he must have been kidding." Personally, I cannot imagine that he would do so to an obscure traffic manager in a then-small radio station. To this date, since the publication of this spurious charge, while many people have stepped forward to deny this statement, no one has substantiated Payne's allegations!

The Witness of Dr. Ray Stedman

One of my longtime pastor friends was the late Dr. Ray Stedman, who for years pastored the Peninsula Bible Church in Palo Alto, California. While a senior at Dallas Seminary, he worked closely with Dr. Ironside when Ironside came to deliver a series of lectures on the book of Isaiah. Stedman later helped a publisher edit and prepare the tape-recorded messages for publication after Dr. Ironside's death. During part of the last year of Dr. Ironside's life, Ray traveled with the Bible teacher and his wife. You will find his testimony very interesting:

> I did travel with Dr. Ironside for the entire summer
> of 1950. I was with him constantly as I served as his

chauffeur, secretary, and personal companion since he was suffering from eye cataracts and was almost blind. I had, of course, many occasions to hear him preach and to talk with him personally about his past experiences and beliefs. During all that time I never heard him express the slightest doubt about his views of a pre-tribulational rapture and other prophetic issues. On the contrary, since this was only shortly after the rebirth of Israel as a nation, I found him very excited about what was taking place in Palestine, and very convinced that it was leading to the fulfillment of long-standing Old Testament prophecies.

Certainly he never uttered in my hearing anything like the statement that the pretrib rapture was a theory with "a lot of holes" in it, nor did he ever suggest that he would like "to rethink his position." We often discussed these matters as we drove across the country, and he constantly commented to me that I was very fortunate to have been trained in these teachings at Dallas Seminary. I left him in August, 1950, to take up my work as pastor in Palo Alto, and he left shortly after that on a voyage to New Zealand, where he died in January, 1951, unexpectedly, of a heart attack.

I am glad you are taking up the defense of the pre-trib rapture teaching, as I am greatly troubled by the ease with which contemporary pastors are ignoring the Scriptures in this respect and drifting into amillennial-ism, with its necessity for performing exegetical gymnastics on many Old and New Testament Scriptures to sustain their position.[3]

Ray Stedman, July 18, 1991

Dr. Ironside's Family Denies the Charge

In preparation for writing an article, Dr. Sumner contacted Dr. Ironside's family to see if they could confirm the hearsay evidence of John Bray. Without exception, they denied it vociferously.

Dr. Sumner says this about the response from Sally Gentry Ironside, Dr. Harry Ironside's daughter-in-law:

The quote about Dr. Ironside saying "the system was full of holes"—which both Bray and MacPherson attribute to him—elicited the response, "I can say that statement or expression is one I never heard him use." And in her letter to us, she explained: "My husband, John, and I were very close to his Dad during the years 1939–1950. In fact, he lived with us after his first wife died. Never did his Dad voice any such doubt. If he had such a doubt, I am sure he would have discussed it with us."

Mrs. Ironside gave us this statement in defense of her father-in-law:

> During his last 12 years we often heard him preach on the 70th week of Daniel, and related subjects, with passion and conviction. No man could have preached with such power from the Holy Spirit if he were daring, knowingly, to preach a lie.
>
> His character was such, and his love for the Lord and the truth so great, he would be incapable of perpetuating a lie.
>
> If he doubted a teaching, or even if he didn't, he would accept no man's word and blindly follow it, but would search the Scriptures to see if these things were so.
>
> If he found himself teaching an error, he would have been the first to acknowledge it, rather than do despite to the Name of his Lord.
>
> He was indeed an honest and an upright man, a meek and humble man, and a man without guile.
>
> He was a man who lived what he preached at all times.
>
> We think the above would be the testimony of all who knew him, even his theological enemies.[4]

Lillian Ironside Koppin, the daughter of Dr. Ironside, said this:

> I am happy to reply concerning my father's integrity although I will say, after some thirty years his being in heaven, it does seem a bit incongruous to have to defend his ministry and stand.

Never to my knowledge did he ever make such a statement as appears on page 25 of this book....

I do believe that my father was honest enough that, if he felt strongly concerning this teaching, he would have published something to reveal his stand. I personally refuse accepting a statement of one person to another. What does Scripture say about "gossip"? I believe that the person involved in the article better go back and do some heart searching before he takes a saint and says what he thinks he said, or thought.[5]

Ironside's Post-1943 Books Deny the Charge

Some of the books by Dr. Ironside that teach the pre-Trib position very clearly were written after the so-called 1943 statement. For example, his commentaries on 1 and 2 Thessalonians, published in 1947, included the following teaching:

> After unfolding the truth concerning the rapture—which will take place when our blessed Lord rises from the Father's throne, descends in the air and gives that awakening shout, and the dead in Christ shall rise first; then we which are alive and remain will be changed, and we will be all caught up together to meet Him in the air—the apostle turns to consider the Day of the Lord.
>
> Following the catching away of the saints there will come upon this world the darkest period it has ever known—that which is designated in many places in the Old Testament as the "day of the Lord"; and also the "time of trouble," or "great tribulation," as it is called in both the Old and New Testaments.[6]

The last book by Dr. Ironside, completed by Ray Stedman from tape recordings after the Bible teacher's death, presents the sixty-first chapter of Isaiah in the same way as any pre-Trib theologian would:

> We are living now in the parenthesis between the sixty-ninth and the seventieth weeks of Daniel,

between the beginning of the acceptable year of the Lord and the day of vengeance of our God (341, 342).[7]

As Dr. Sumner points out,

> Obviously if Dr. Ironside wrote these words after he said what John Bray claims he said back in 1943, he is the worst kind of hypocrite. No man of God would purposely teach one thing while believing another. And all those who knew him will testify that Harry A. Ironside was indeed a man of God![8]

Correcting a Mistake

Critics of the pre-Trib position will have to do better than bring accusations against a great biblical literalist several decades after his death. Since they cannot prove their position from a literal interpretation of the Scriptures, they seem desperate to steal—from those who have it—the hope of Christ's blessed return for His church before the Tribulation holocaust.

It's about time for some of those who have retreated from the pre-Trib position to admit their mistake and restudy the Scriptures. And some of them owe the memory of Dr. Ironside an apology.

Chapter Fourteen

MacPherson's
Vendetta

The most publicized and possibly best-known attack on the pre-Tribulation rapture view was launched during the seventies by a newspaperman named Dave MacPherson. Through a number of books and his regular periodical, this committed post-Tribulationist has pursued a 20-year vendetta against a time-honored position whose followers, MacPherson feels, have caused him and his family devastating pain. He seems to view the pre-Trib position as so dangerous to the body of Christ that he cannot allow the Holy Spirit to protect His church. Instead, he is impelled to dredge up the discredited post-Trib attacks of the nineteenth century, suggesting there has been a gigantic cover-up that for 150 years has endeavored to protect the origins of the theory. In short, he attributes J.N. Darby's thesis about the Rapture to either a demonic spirit, a deluded Scottish girl of 15 years (in 1830-32), or the followers of Edward Irving. (Please see chapter 12 for a full discussion of J.N. Darby, a godly, insightful Bible teacher.)

I read MacPherson's books when they first came out and was impressed with his gifted writing style. Since then I have read much on both sides, and have concluded that Mr. MacPherson's theories are both unproven and unconvincing and cannot be substantiated by the facts.

In addition, many careful researchers have studied MacPherson's books and have put rebuttals into print. On the following pages are portions of these reviews, used with permission from these scholars. You be your own judge of the facts.

Examining What Others Say

Dr. Gerald B. Stanton

Dr. Gerald Stanton devotes five pages to this issue in the book we looked at briefly a number of pages back. Let's take time to examine his potent arguments in detail.

> In 1973, Dave MacPherson, then a newspaperman of Kansas City, Missouri, published a vigorous repudiation of pretribulationism under the title *The Unbelievable Pre-Trib Origin*. It was revised and expanded in combination with another booklet by the same author, *The Late Great Pre-Trib Rapture*, and published in 1975 under the title *The Incredible Cover-Up*.
>
> In MacPherson's widely distributed "A Letter to Southern Christians," yet another title by the same author was promoted, *The Great Rapture Hoax*, "packed with the sort of shocking data that's been known— and covered up—by Pre-Trib leaders for decades." This letter further claims that "the Pre-Trib view wasn't heard of anywhere on earth before the 1800s," that it was "originated by a young lassie in Scotland in the *spring* of 1830," and that it was "pirated" and spread by John Darby, a Britisher who "regarded Americans as inferior creatures, worthy of exploitation." Among other nasty declarations, MacPherson goes on to attack the honesty and morality of C.I. Scofield and promises that his book "will turn you inside out!"
>
> It will immediately be apparent that his book titles are provocative, if not abusive. There has been no "cover-up" or "hoax," for pre-Trib authors and leaders have arrived at their conclusion from biblical exegesis rather than from any presumed history of the doctrine, and most certainly with no desire to defraud. Furthermore, to attack the morality and

integrity of fellow believers just to further an eschato-
logical opinion is a disgrace to the Name and cause of
Christ.

What then is MacPherson's primary thrust throughout these several paperbacks? In his own words, "the
two-stage teaching is an early nineteenth-century
invention which first saw the light of day in Great
Britain and does not reflect the teaching of the New
Testament" (1975, 6). "The pre-trib rapture theory
ascended from the mists of western Scotland in the
spring of 1830" (1975, 138). It had a "hidden background," a "bizarre origin" (1975, 90, 101), when a
"dangerously sick" young woman by the name of
Margaret MacDonald came under the influence of the
Scottish revival and had a revelation in which she
proclaimed an utterly new view that the Church would
escape the coming Tribulation.

Extensive quotations from Robert Norton, at the
time of M.M.'s "revelation" a 22-year-old medical
doctor, indicate that she, her sister, and brothers were
members of the Catholic Apostolic Church of Edward
Irving and came under early charismatic influence with
the "gifts of prophecy" and "speaking in an unknown
tongue." Under such influence, Margaret MacDonald
supposedly revealed that the Church would escape the
Tribulation. Some have gone so far as to attribute her
declaration to demonic forces. This "utterance" of
M.M., MacPherson states repeatedly, is the origin of the
pretribulational view that the Church will escape the
coming Tribulation.

The true facts of the case prove otherwise. The
recorded declarations of Margaret MacDonald show
clearly that she was not trying to establish the details
of the prophetic future, but rather lamenting the weak
and sinful condition of the professing church. She
cried over "the awful state of the land," the "distress
of nations," the need for "purging and purifying of the
real members of the body of Jesus." She prays for "an
outpouring of the Spirit" upon the church so that
believers will be "counted worthy to stand before the
Son of man." "Those that are alive in him...will be
caught up to meet him in the air." But she declares
also that the Church will go through "fiery trial" for

the "wicked" one, who shall be revealed "with all power and signs and lying wonders." Then, even more clearly, she declares "the trial of the Church is from Antichrist"—which to say the least is hardly a pretribulational concept![1]

Many Post-Tribulationists Buy the Lie

It is easy to understand why post-Trib writers quote and requote MacPherson as though he were a credible reporter. He attempts to make his witnesses, long dead, say what he wants them to say. We cannot read MacPherson without being impressed with his literary ability. However, his facts do not stand up in court. Stanton contends that the significance of the Margaret MacDonald vision has "been blown far out of all proportion by those who seek to discredit pre-Tribulationism."

> Alexander Reese traces the Pretrib view to the "separatist movements of Edward Irving and J.N. Darby." George Ladd, quoting Tregelles, traces "the idea of a secret rapture" to an "utterance" in Edward Irving's church, which "came not from Holy Scripture, but from that which falsely pretended to be the Spirit of God." J. Barton Payne says that "soon after 1830 a woman, while speaking in tongues, announced the 'revelation' that the true church would be caught up [raptured] to heaven before the tribulation" (156). Even Robert Gundry declares "pretribulationism arose in the mid-nineteenth century. The likelihood is that Edward Irving was the first to suggest the pretribulation rapture" (185).
>
> However, Gundry in all fairness observes that "the origin of an interpretation of Scripture is not the measure of its correctness." He says also of Irving that "tongues and prophetic utterances did not begin to appear in his church until late 1831, i.e., after the appearance of pretribulationism" (187). It remained for MacPherson to try to demonstrate that beyond question the pretribulation view began with an 1830 "utterance" of Margaret MacDonald.[2]

Unfortunately for MacPherson, he was unable to prove his point, but that does not deter post-Tribbers who have not done their homework from quoting him.

Poor Margaret MacDonald

Some suggest that Margaret was only 15 years old when she became a follower of Edward Irving and began to have these visions. Anyone who reads her vision will be impressed with her deep concern for the worldliness of her day and earnest attempt to call the church back to holiness in view of the Lord's imminent return to the earth. But she knew nothing about the Rapture before the Tribulation. Stanton compassionately said of her,

> It is cruel to imply that her utterance was purely emotional, or perhaps Satanic. She was a young and humble Christian endeavoring to call a cold and careless church back to the power and control of the Holy Spirit. The writer thoroughly concurs with Hal Lindsey when he says: "Although I don't agree with the authenticity of her vision, records show her to be a beautiful sister in the Lord, filled with love and compassion for others" (1983, 173).
>
> There is nothing in the M.M. quotation to indicate that she was a pre-Tribulationist. She did not distinguish between the Rapture and the second coming of Christ, but rather divided the Rapture itself into two or more parts based on spiritual readiness. This is the Partial Rapture position, very different from pre-Tribulationism. MacPherson is forced to admit this: "Margaret saw a series of raptures (and she was actually a partial rapturist, with or without the label)" (1975, 85). Indeed, she seemed to believe that the Church had already entered the Tribulation, a possibility strengthened by a statement published by Irving in December 1831 in *The Morning Watch:* "We have, blessed be God, lived to see the commencement of the seventh vial, DURING THE OUTPOURING OF WHICH THE LORD WILL COME!" (Huebner, 23, emphasis his). This is certainly not pre-Tribulationism![3]

What Is MacPherson's Personal Vendetta?

One wonders what prompts MacPherson to resurrect such withered charges. Perhaps Stanton can shed some light:

> It is MacPherson's contention that the Pretrib Rapture view is a relatively modern heresy with a plot on the part of its adherents to hide its dubious background. He makes the awful charge that in China "the Pre-trib Rapture view has caused the deaths of thousands of persons" because missionaries did not warn the people of coming persecution (1975, 103). His final conclusion seems to be that "the Pre-trib rapture view is on its last legs—if it ever had a leg to stand on!"
>
> Why such a tirade from a young newspaperman? Is it possible that we are witnessing a personal vendetta?
>
> Dave learned his posttribulationism at an early age from his father and pastor, Norman Spurgeon MacPherson, a fine gentleman but an enthusiastic follower of Alexander Reese, whose arguments he considered unanswerable and whose viewpoints he actively promoted. He even wrote his own book on the subject: *Triumph Through Tribulation*, dated 1944.
>
> Dave writes openly about the "prophetic narrow-mindedness periodically erupting in my father's California pastorate" and its effect upon his mother's health. He recounts his own dismissal from a Bible Institute because he discussed prophetic viewpoints "differing in detail from the school's official position." Two weeks before the end of the semester, he says, "I was dismissed from the premises....My dismissal was possibly the last straw. A few days later my mother died" (1973, 15).
>
> While all of this is most regrettable, one must not respond to personal sorrow by breaking fellowship with fellow believers over prophetic detail, nor by attacking them and impugning their integrity because they support an alternate viewpoint.[4]

Dr. John Walvoord

One of the most respected pre-Trib scholars in the country is Dr. John Walvoord, author of numerous books on prophecy and for many years the president of Dallas Theological Seminary. In two of his books on the Rapture, he addresses this old attack on the pre-Trib position. He notes as spurious MacPherson's charge that John Darby borrowed his pre-Trib theory from Edward Irving and Margaret MacDonald in 1832.

> There is evidence that this is a false story told by Tregelles in 1864, thirty-two years after this supposed incident. As R.A.Huebner demonstrated by a careful analysis of the documents attributed to Irving and MacDonald, nine years before Tregelles told the false story, he had charged the origin to Judaizers and apparently had not started his later story. Both of the allegations of Tregelles are without any support, and he was obviously a prejudiced witness.[5]

Walvoord adds that the most serious weakness of Mac-Pherson's colorful argument is that his own writings quote both Irving and MacDonald sufficiently to prove that neither is even close to being pre-Trib. They were both post-Trib!

> It is quite amazing, in reading posttribulational literature, to find how many worthy scholars have quoted the origin of pretribulationism as coming from MacDonald and Irving without any research supporting it, and these include scholars such as Ladd, Reese, and Payne. Now that research has demonstrated by the work of MacPherson himself that they were not actually pretribulational, it illustrates how far a contention can go without support.
>
> In contrast to the assertion that Irving was a pretribulationist, Huebner has demonstrated that what Irving actually believed was that the Rapture would occur at the end of the Tribulation, after the seventh seal, after the seventh trumpet, and after the seventh bowl in the Book of Revelation, which practically all posttribulationists recognize brings one to the end of the Tribulation. According to Huebner, Irving published a statement in *The Morning Watch* in December 1831 as follows: "that the seventh seal had been opened, the seventh trumpet sounded, the

seventh vial commenced; but it is only to this last-mentioned portion of prophecy that we shall at present direct our attention. We have, blessed be God, lived to see the commencement of the seventh vial, DURING THE OUTPOURING OF WHICH THE LORD WILL COME!"

In the light of this statement, how could anyone assert that Irving was a pretribulationist? It is also worthy of note that this statement came a year after he was supposedly the recipient of the pretribulational rapture. MacPherson's contention that Irving was a pretribulationist has by his own research demonstrated exactly the opposite.

Margaret MacDonald, likewise, left behind no clear record that she ever held to a pretribulational rapture. It is possible from some of her statements to arrive at the conclusion that she was garbled in her view of prophecy and could possibly be identified with the partial rapture view. None of her statements, however, placed the Rapture before the Tribulation begins. At best, it can be demonstrated that the Rapture would be included in the series of events that climax the Great Tribulation.[6]

After marshaling this impressive evidence, Dr. Walvoord calls upon MacPherson to set the record straight:

> The whole controversy as aroused by Dave MacPherson's claims has so little supporting evidence, despite his careful research, that one wonders how he can write his book with a straight face. Pretribulationists should be indebted to Dave MacPherson for exposing the facts, namely, that there is no proof that MacDonald or Irving originated the pretribulation rapture teaching.[7]

> Under the circumstances, it would seem that common honesty would call for Dave MacPherson to write another book confessing that his entire point of view has no basis in the charge that pretribulationism is recent, however, posttribulationists choose to ignore facts, and this greatly limits the pertinence of this point.[8]

Roy A. Huebner

Brethren Church historian and Bible teacher Roy A. Huebner has published two books about Darby and the teachings he revived, defended, and popularized. The first was released in 1973, the second in December 1991. In the latter volume, titled *Precious Truths Revived and Defended Through J.N. Darby,* he puts this matter to rest once and for all. His book quotes almost 500 original sources and is the most carefully researched volume on this subject to date. Lengthy quotes of very old documents, books, and letters make it an invaluable resource for the careful student.

Huebner (probably because he, like Darby, is a Brethren) took great exception to MacPherson calling Darby a liar and accusing him of getting his ideas from an occult source. In one of his quotes, he uses MacPherson's own words to show the twistedness of his thinking:

> In a paper dated Jan. 23, 1990, wherein D. Mac-Pherson is touted as "the world's leading authority on the origin of the Pre-Trib rapture theory," he wrote:
>
> 1830 "The Occult Connection"
>
> Darby didn't originate any rapture view in 1827 or any other year. Pre-trib leaders know that Prior Rapturism began in 1830. But they're also aware that both the originator and the first group to adopt it (that is, the Irvingites—followers of Edward Irving) were all heavily influenced by the OCCULT! So leaders today do everything they can to draw attention away from 1830....
>
> "For This They Willingly Are Ignorant Of..."
>
> Darby knew that in 1830, Margaret (whom he had visited) had given birth to the Prior Rapture. He also knew that the Irvingites had soon echoed her ideas and given her credit. Too many people knew about this even in 1850. If Darby had dared to claim in 1850 that he'd come to these ideas BEFORE 1830, he would have been the laughingstock of Britain! In effect, the Pre-trib Darby of 1850 contradicts

> today's Pre-tribs who deviously emphasize
> 1827. Such history revisionism allows them to
> detour around 1830 (even though Darby
> himself pinpointed it!) and thus escape the
> stigma of the OCCULT! (I'll reveal such
> connections later on.) Their claim that Darby
> was the originator in 1827 is groundless.
> Neither Darby nor any other early developer
> ever made such a claim.

Here it comes out plainly that the purpose is to stigmatize. However, if there is a valid stigmatization by an *occult* source, as D. MacPherson indicates that there is, then notice that M.M.'s "revelation" expounded post-Tribulationism. At any rate, chapters 2.4 and 5.1 show that it is "the world's leading authority on the origin of the Pre-Trib rapture theory" that has distorted and revised history. He did not at all profit by reading the alleged utterances of Margaret MacDonald. Instead of apprehending the plain import of her statements, which has affinity to the post-Tribulational scheme and no real resemblance to the interlocking church truth, pre-Tribulation rapture and dispensational truth, he has read into her statements what he appears so anxious to find. He has calumniated and slandered Darby for about 30 years now, as well as attributing unsavory motives to those who have not fallen for his obvious untrue statements (Luke 12:2-3; 2 Corinthians 5:10).

MacPherson's attributing Margaret MacDonald's "revelation" to an occultic source is particularly interesting in view of the fact that at least three of his books have been published by those who are previsionary-revelations, namely Logos International and New Puritan Library. Indeed, one of the books has a Foreword and a Postlude by Pat Brooks of New Puritan Library. Then, too, the post-Tribulationist James McKeever, who seems to be constantly receiving "revelations," has touted the line of calumny put out by MacPherson.

MacPherson stands in a line of discredited calumniators of Darby in regard to the recovery of the pre-Tribulation rapture, beginning, it seems, in 1855, when the supporter of B.W. Newton (i.e., S.P. Tregelles), in his effort to attack the recovered truth, said the doctrine came from Judaizers. In 1864 he said it came from a spirit.

From S.P. Tregelles, MacPherson received that idea but subsequently shifted to M.M. of Port Glasgow, Scotland; hence his baseless allegation, "So Plymouth Brethren organizer John Darby rejected Margaret's 'miraculous gifts' but accepted her novel two-phase coming." It is interesting how some who are hostile to dispensational truth have fallen for the obviously absurd misrepresentations. Consider the following by the "reconstructionist" postmillennialist Gary North:

> The students are not told of Dave MacPherson's discovery that Margaret MacDonald, a girl about twenty years old, went into trances in 1830 and announced the pre-tribulation rapture doctrine. We are still waiting for Professor John Hannah, a competent and talented church historian, to go into print and show from original source documents that MacPherson's thesis is nothing but a sham. Strangely, he has decided to remain silent. Or not so strangely, as the case may be.[9]

North no longer needs to wait for Professor Hannah to show from original documents that MacPherson's thesis is false; it "is nothing but a sham." *Sham* is a strong word, meaning "an imitation that is meant to deceive; a counterfeit; a deception; a fake."

A writer with amillennial leanings, J.R. Boyd, wrote:

> To provoke thought and still researching we have even circulated some challenging, system-wrecking material from Dave MacPherson in his "Incredible Coverup."...blockbusters for destruction of phony pretense....
> Notice the alleged reason for circulating what is in reality obvious calumny.[10]

The "obvious calumny" of MacPherson has turned out to be anything but system-wrecking. It is only persuasive when we read his statements but do not examine the increasing evidence that Darby could not have received his ideas from man or demon, for they did not themselves believe the pre-Trib position. It is easier to believe that Darby derived them from the Scriptures, as he claimed.

Post-Tribulationist John Bray

One post-Tribulationist who admits that neither Irving nor MacDonald announced the pre-Tribulation rapture theory is evangelist John Bray, who abandoned the pre-Trib for the post-Trib position. I do not share his enthusiasm for Lacunza being the source for the pre-Trib position, simply because Lacunza did not see it. However, I do appreciate his candor in not ascribing deception to John Darby but treating his memory with respect as a brother soul-winner who looked with anticipation to the appearing of Christ.

John Bray clearly admits that in spite of Dave MacPherson's claims to the contrary, Margaret MacDonald did not see anything like a pre-Tribulation rapture in her vision, but was, like him, a post-Tribber. On page 20 of his booklet *The Origin of Pre-Tribulation Rapture Teaching,* he candidly refers to Robert Norton's 1861 book (from which MacPherson draws heavily) and provides his own analysis:

> In his book, Robert Norton said of Margaret Mac-Donald's account of her prophecy, "...HERE we FIRST see the distinction between that final stage of the Lord's coming, when every eye shall see Him, and His PRIOR appearing in glory to them that look for Him."
>
> However, my own mind at this point is not definitely satisfied that Miss MacDonald was saying that Christians will be taken out of the world before the time of tribulation. It seems to me that Margaret MacDonald was saying that Christians WILL face the temptation of the false Christ (antichrist) and be in "an awfully dangerous situation," and that only the Spirit IN US will enable us to be kept from being deceived; and that as the Spirit works, so will the antichrist; but the pouring out of the Spirit will "fit us together into the marriage supper of the Lamb," and those filled with the Spirit would be taken while the others would be left. She definitely taught that only those who are Spirit-filled will be caught up to meet Christ when He

comes; this is the partial rapture theory, the same as Lacunza taught, except that Lacunza's qualifications for worthiness to be caught up at the Rapture were somewhat different that [sic] Margaret's. In this "revelation" she did not say what will finally happen to the other Christians who are not Spirit-filled and not caught up, though Lacunza did finally get around to it in his book by placing their resurrection at the time of the general resurrection following a Millennium. In fact, in this "revelation" she did not say anything about what happens between the time when the Spirit-filled Christians are raptured and when the Lord descends on to earth, nor even if there is any time element in between; whereas Lacunza taught there was much time involved between the appearance of Christ and the resurrection of Christ and the resurrection of the worthy Christians, and the time when He comes on down to the earth. Perhaps that was not "revealed" to her, that is, as to what would happen to the others!

Margaret MacDonald plainly said, "This is the trial through which those are to pass who will be counted worthy to stand before the Son of Man." The trial she referred to was that of the antichrist being "seen on earth" who will imitate the work of the Holy Spirit, "so that if it were possible the very elect will be deceived."[11]

So it seems to me that while Norton was a Pre-Tribulation Rapturist, MacDonald was a Post-Tribulation Rapturist; while both believed in a partial rapture—a rapture of only certain Christians, as Lacunza had also taught.[12]

I am surprised to find that Bray can admit Darby could not have borrowed his views from Irving or MacDonald, yet Bray does believe that Darby adopted his views from Lacunza. That is most interesting because Lacunza did not hold these views either, and even Bray admits that Lacunza's views were similar to those of Irving—which explains why Irving translated his book and wrote the foreword to it.

Dr. Thomas Ice

A graduate of Dallas Theological Seminary and author/ pastor, Dr. Ice has addressed this subject in *Bibliotheca Sacra* (April/June 1990) and his own *Biblical Perspectives* (January/ February 1989). He agrees that the two reasons for rejecting the thesis that Darby gleaned his views from Irving or MacDonald are: 1) Darby established his in 1827, five years before MacDonald's vision; and 2) Irving and MacDonald never did believe in a rapture of the church prior to the Tribulation and the appearance of the Antichrist.

Among Dr. Ice's contributions to this study is his rejoinder to MacPherson's assertion that a number of pre-Trib leaders respect his writings and research.

> True, many scholars have complimented Mac-Pherson on his effort; however, most have not endorsed or agreed with MacPherson's thesis. F.F. Bruce's comments are typical: "This makes most interesting reading....It is an illuminating book." MacPherson takes such general statements about his book as agreement with what he is saying. Most scholars, however, while saying that MacPherson's work is valuable, stop short of agreeing with his conclusion. Bruce, long associated with the Brethren movement but one who does not agree with the pretribulational rapture view, says, "Where did he [Darby] get it? The reviewer's answer would be that it was in the air in the 1820s and 1830s among eager students of unfulfilled prophecy...direct dependence by Darby on Margaret MacDonald is unlikely."
>
> Various scholars reveal that they think, in varying degrees, that MacPherson has not proven his point. Most if not all of the following six writers whose statements are quoted do not hold to the pretribulation rapture teaching. Ernest R. Sandeen declares,
>
>> This seems to be a groundless and pernicious charge. Neither Irving nor any member of the Albury group advocated any doctrine resembling the secret rapture....Since the clear intention of this charge is to discredit the doctrine by attributing its origin to fanaticism

rather than Scripture, there seems little ground for giving it any credence.

Historian Timothy P. Weber evaluated the dilemma as follows:

> The pretribulation rapture was a neat solution to a thorny problem and historians are still trying to determine how or where Darby got it....A newer though still not totally convincing view contends that the doctrine initially appeared in a prophetic vision of Margaret MacDonald....
>
> Possibly, we may have to settle for Darby's own explanation. He claimed that the doctrine virtually jumped out of the pages of Scripture once he accepted and consistently maintained the distinction between Israel and the church.

American historian Richard R. Reiter adds,

> [Robert] Cameron probably traced this important but apparently erroneous view back to S.P. Tregelles....Recently more detailed study on this view as the origin of pretribulationism appeared in works by Dave MacPherson.... Historian Ian S. Rennie...regarded MacPherson's case as interesting but not conclusive.

Postribulationist William E. Bell asserts,

> It seems only fair, however, in the absence of eyewitnesses to settle the argument conclusively, that the benefit of the doubt should be given to Darby, and that the charge made by Tregelles be regarded as a possibility but with insufficient support to merit its acceptance....On the whole, however, it seems that Darby is perhaps the most likely choice—with help from Tweedy. This conclusion is greatly strengthened by Darby's own claim to have arrived at the doctrine through his study of 2 Thessalonians 2:1-2.

John Bray does not accept the MacPherson thesis either:

> He [Darby] rejected those practices, and he already had his new view of the Lord coming FOR THE SAINTS (as contrasted to the later coming to the earth) which he had believed since 1827....It was the coupling of this "70th week of Daniel" prophecy and its futuristic interpretation, with the teaching of the "secret rapture," that gave to us the completed "PreTribulation Secret Rapture" teaching as it has now been taught for many years. [This] makes it impossible for me to believe that Darby got his Pre-Tribulation Rapture teaching from Margaret MacDonald's vision in 1830. He was already a believer in it since 1827, as he plainly said.

Brethren scholar Roy A. Huebner considers MacPherson's charges as "using slander that J.N. Darby took the [truth of the] pre-tribulation rapture from those very opposing, demon-inspired utterances." Huebner concludes that MacPherson did not profit by reading the utterances allegedly by Miss M.M. instead of apprehending the plain import of her statements, as given by R. Norton, which has some affinity to the post-tribulation scheme and no real resemblance to the pretribulation rapture and dispensational truth, he has read into it what he appears so anxious to find. It seems, then, most likely that Margaret MacDonald did not teach any of the features of a pretribulation rapture doctrine as MacPherson suggests, and therefore she could not have been a source for the origin of that doctrine.[13]

Why Does MacPherson Do It?

As I have read the documentation, studied Margaret's vision, and validated for myself that it does not say what MacPherson claims it does, I have had to ask myself, *Why does he do it? Why would an obviously intelligent person waste 30 or more years of his life trying to tear down a concept that has been such a blessing to millions of believers?* He certainly has nothing better to offer in its place! Post-Tribulationism is a doomsday concept.

Through it all I have developed a compassionate view of this man who has spent much of his life in a futile attempt to undermine an instrument of blessing for the body of Christ. Thomas Ice offers some background information that may be helpful:

> Dave MacPherson is dedicated to disrupting belief in the pre-tribulation rapture, since, according to his interpretation, it has been the cause for great disruption in his own life. "Back in 1953 I had a jolting encounter with the Rapture" is the first sentence in one of MacPherson's books. This is a reference to his expulsion from a Christian college in California for propagating views that conflicted with the pretribulational view. He suggests that this experience was so devastating that it accounts for a setback in his Christian life. Because of his discouragement MacPherson and a friend got drunk in Mexico and passed out. MacPherson says this was a brush with death because of the many dangers that could befall someone in that condition in Mexico. Later he was involved in a wreck with a car while riding his motorcycle, and he almost lost his left arm. But these were not the beginning of his nor his family's troubles because of the pretribulational rapture.
>
> Trials and tribulations due to this doctrine seem to run in the MacPherson family. Dave's father, Norman, had planted a church in Long Beach, California, and was doing quite well until a group of new people in the church caused a commotion over the timing of the rapture. Norman MacPherson was forced out of this prospering church because he had shifted from the pretribulational to the posttribulational view of the rapture. He then started another, less successful church in Long Beach.[14]

Ice includes the following footnote:

> Robert L. Sumner has noted that "MacPherson has a bad habit of attributing all kinds of personal tragedies

to the pre-trib teaching: his mother's death, his sister's inability to have more children, his own failure to follow through on his calling as an evangelist, and other matters" ("Looking for the Blessed Horrible Holocaust!" A book review of THE LATE GREAT PRETRIB RAPTURE," *The Biblical Evangelist* [May 1975], 8). Sumner also states that MacPherson's lovable dog, Wolf, apparently became demon possessed just about the time MacPherson was about to write his first anti-pretribulation book, savagely biting his writing hand several times" ("Hope? Or Hoax?" *The Biblical Evangelist* [February 1984], 7).[15]

What Did Margaret MacDonald Really Say?

Ice and others who have studied Margaret MacDonald's vision carefully find it difficult to understand how MacPherson found the pre-Tribulation rapture in it.

> MacPherson now admits that this is not the pretrib rapture but that she saw two comings, with a gap between them, and one of the comings preceding the revealing of Antichrist. However, every one of those points have to be assumed from her statements. She does not clearly say those things. For example, Mac-Pherson has to equate M.M.'s use of "sign" with the Rapture. That is not what she is saying. She is saying that those who are spiritual will see the secret sign of the Son of man, which will precede the single second coming of Christ. She is still very much a one-coming posttribber. *It is amazing to think that posttribber Mac-Pherson is saying that posttribber M.M. came up with the pretrib Rapture.* Only if you do those kind of tricks with her statements can you even come close to what MacPherson is suggesting. [16]

Note: If you are interested, you may read Margaret MacDonald's actual vision for yourself and see if she held to a pre-Tributionist perspective. It is found in Appendix C.

A Summary of the Facts

These researchers, we may conclude, have fully explained the facts of the case. John Darby gained his views primarily from his study of the Word of God, the inspiration of the Holy Spirit, and the influence of emerging premillennial biblical literalists, who were moving from the Historical school of interpreting prophecy to the Futurist position. But even if he didn't, that doesn't change anything. The pre-Trib position is supported by Scripture. Surely that is enough!

Chapter Fifteen

The Pre-Wrath Rapture Myth

The most recent major attack on the pre-Tribulation rapture view occurred in the 1990 publication of *The Pre-Wrath Rapture of the Church* by Marvin Rosenthal.[1] A 319-page book by a formerly reliable publisher of pre-Trib material, it features a beautiful cover and was promoted by the best marketing plans I have seen from that company in years.

The book is original, to say the least. In all of my review of end-time resources, I have never seen anything like it. The author, who claims he was a pre-Tribulationist for 30 years, blends material from all three of the most popular views on the Rapture: pre, mid, and post. He retains the Rapture before the time of wrath, as his title suggests, but locates it 21 months after the time designated by mid-Tribs and five-and-a-half years after the pre-Trib position.

Thus he formulates the most confusing interpretation of end-time events ever put together, a concept that no one except this author would come to on his own—unless he just wanted to be different. It certainly does not represent the conclusions of an earnest prophecy student humbly trying to unravel the prophetic sequence of end-time events from a literal reading of Scripture.

Rosenthal enthusiastically claims his view "has the Word of God to sustain it," and "within two years many men will be teaching the pre-Wrath rapture. Within five years it will be a recognized position. And, if God pleases, within fifteen years it will become a major position of the believing church."[2] Most of us remain unconvinced, however, and the book has been rejected by most prophecy scholars.

In the dozen years since its publication, I know of no credible authority who has adopted its views, but I have read several damaging critiques. I doubt the author will live long enough to find pre-Wrath rapture perspective a major position. It may appeal to those seeking prophetic innovation, but after the first blush of fadism passes, it will likely be forgotten. Despite the book's initial success due to originality and marketing hype, its major flaws will drop it in the sea of oblivion rather than make it a major contribution to prophecy studies.

Because the author failed to have his manuscript evaluated by other biblical literalists with a better grasp of Greek, Hebrew, and prophecy before he rushed into print, it may well serve as an instrument of confusion, robbing some of the blessed hope, the promise of the at-any-moment return of our Savior. Fortunately, this mishmash of concepts does not seem to have caught on in the church, for if it had, it would help deaden the body of Christ.

One of the first things that troubled me about Rosenthal's book was his dogmatic arrogance. Instead of the usual "It would seem" or "The text suggests," the author writes autocratically in espousing his new theory. Dr. Gerald Stanton, whom I quoted earlier, agrees with this assessment:

> The 13 chapters of argumentation in support of these claims are frequently tedious and repetitious, with a dogmatism that earns the book a unique place in the literature of the rapture debate. Rosenthal set forth John Walvoord, J. Dwight Pentecost, and Charles Ryrie as his former "heroes" in matters of prophecy and eschatology (Rosenthal:25), whose logic in his judgment is now faulty and whose interpretation of the Bible can no longer be trusted. Rosenthal's own opinions, however, are "indisputable" and "beyond refutation" (105, 109). His facts "cannot be set aside," and for his primary conclusions "there simply is no question"(110). The doctrine of imminence, which he calls "a major pillar of pretribulation rapturism," is "untenable," and that is a "clear, unassailable truth that cannot be dismissed"

(150). He declares that pretribulationists are locked in an "unsolvable dilemma" (112). Such dogmatism is, to say the least, both unwholesome and irritating, for many of his statements warrant further investigation.[3]

What the Book Teaches

As the title states, the book mainly deals with the timing of the Rapture in relation to the Tribulation or Daniel's seventieth week of seven years. As one who loves charts that help illustrate biblical truth, I commend the author for the 25 color charts in the book. The main one, found on page 241, provides a description of his central concept. The upcoming chart, my own reproduction, basically conveys his new theory.

As you can see, Rosenthal transfers the first half of the Tribulation to the "beginning of sorrows," which is usually ascribed to the time before the signing of the covenant with Israel and the beginning of the seven-year Tribulation. This allows him to make three sections out of that period which our Lord divides into two sections: the Tribulation (see Matthew 24:9) and the Great Tribulation (see Matthew 24:21). He then places the Rapture five-and-a-half years into the seven-year period of "Jacob's trouble" and follows that with the "Day of the Lord," to which he designates the final 21 months.

In fairness to Rosenthal, he tries valiantly to preserve the reliability of the Lord's promise to keep us from the hour of wrath during that time, but in so doing he necessarily has the Christian going through the first three-quarters of the Tribulation. Then he would have us believe that "the beginning of sorrows" (Matthew 24:8) and the "great tribulation" (Matthew 24:21)—the first five-and-a-half years of that seven-year period—are not God's wrath (which he reserves until after the Rapture). He places that period of wrath at the beginning of the last 21 months, designating it the "Day of the Lord." In other words, according to the chart on page 197 of his book, he sees the Seal Judgments taking up three-quarters of the Tribulation period and then jams the Trumpet and Vial Judgments into the last 21 months. This seems terribly forced in the light of the logical flow of the judgments as described in the book of Revelation, which I outlined in chapter 4.

Dr. Stanton says of Rosenthal's analysis:

Almost every point of the summary chart on page 197 is open to question. A comparison with the chart on page 147 reveals that Rosenthal contradicts himself on the extent of God's wrath and the time of the second coming of Christ. While his sincerity may be beyond question, many of his definitions appear to be homemade and supporting evidence is completely inadequate....

Rosenthal is in serious error when he attempts to set the time of the Rapture three-fourths of the way through the seven years of judgment and wrath, some 1,890 days after the Antichrist makes his unparalleled covenant with Israel. Among evangelical Christians from all major rapture perspectives, Rosenthal walks an isolated path when he asserts that these six signs unite in setting the timing of the Rapture. Believers are to watch for Christ's coming and live accordingly, for it is their blessed and purifying hope, evidently next on the prophetic program of God. The Lord's people should not be confused by vehement argumentation designed to set the day of His appearing, adding yet a fifth and doubtful position to an issue that has already been subjected to more than its share of debate.[4]

What Others Have Said About Pre-Wrath

Rosenthal's book has certainly not lacked reviews in major Christian magazines. As we would expect, because he takes a little from each of the prevailing views and disagrees with them all, he alienates himself from representatives of the other positions. So far I have not read one positive review, but have placed several negative critiques of his theory in my files. Consider the following excerpts.

Dr. James O. Combs, editor of the *Baptist Bible Tribune* and prophecy preacher for 50 years, exclaims,

What amazes me is that so many great Bible expositors have been so wrong for 100 years or longer, according to Mr. Rosenthal. In fact, the whole idea of imminency so clearly taught by Christ Himself and echoed by Paul (see Mark 13:34-37 and Titus 2:13) is repudiated by this author!...Are we to believe that finally in 1990 Marvin Rosenthal has found the truth

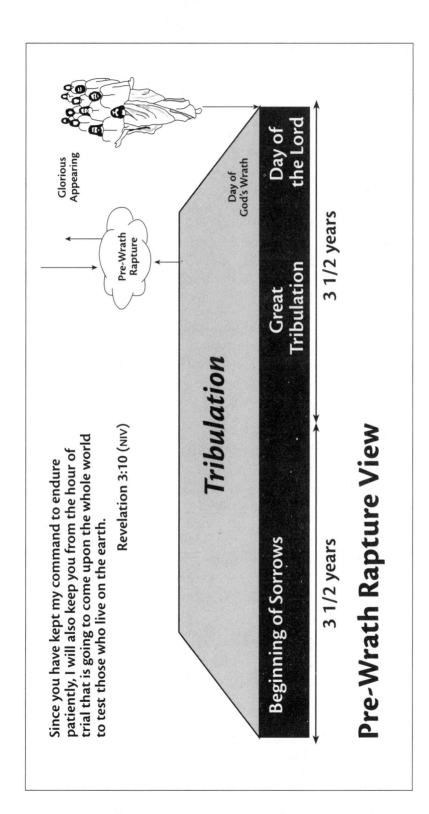

Since you have kept my command to endure patiently, I will also keep you from the hour of trial that is going to come upon the whole world to test those who live on the earth.

Revelation 3:10 (NIV)

Glorious Appearing

Pre-Wrath Rapture

Tribulation

Beginning of Sorrows

Great Tribulation

Day of God's Wrath

Day of the Lord

3 1/2 years

3 1/2 years

Pre-Wrath Rapture View

that all the rest of us missed? What great super revelation did Mr. Rosenthal receive? Why has he been so singly chosen to advocate this new variation on "mid-trib" rapture thought and tens of thousands of us allowed by the Holy Spirit to be blinded in this area? Does he fancy himself to be the "true prophet," he himself, alone?...His new theory demolishes the real meaning of THE BLESSED HOPE.[5]

Dave Hunt, a popular author on many prophetic subjects and a research and consulting expert, states in *The Omega Letter*,

[The book's] ideas cannot be supported by Scripture, and Rosenthal's attempts to do so create numerous contradictions....

Numerous problems immediately arise. Since the Antichrist, according to Rosenthal, must appear first, the church is no longer watching and waiting for Christ but for Antichrist. Moreover, even after the Antichrist takes control of the earth the church cannot look for Christ until she has suffered considerably under that "Wicked" one.

Yet the early church was definitely watching for her Lord, not for Antichrist: "From whence [heaven] also we look for the Saviour" (Philippians 3:20); "And to wait for his Son from heaven" (1 Thessalonians 1:10); "and unto them that look for him shall he appear" (Hebrews 9:28), etc.

If Rosenthal is correct, then one can no longer expect Christ at any moment. Imminency has been lost, and with it the "blessed hope" that sustained believers for centuries....

A "pre-wrath rapture" would hardly be a "blessed hope." In fact, it would be a non-event, for there would be few if any Christians left alive to rapture at the time. Could any Christian take Antichrist's mark and thus survive to be raptured? Indeed not! Revelation 14:9-10 makes it clear that those who "worship the beast and his image, and receive his mark" will be consigned to hell.

In building his unbiblical thesis, Rosenthal falls into a number of other errors.[6]

Dr. Paul Karleen, Bible and linguistics scholar (ancient Greek), Bible college professor for 20-plus years, and author of such books as *The Handbook to Bible Study* (Oxford), has written a most detailed examination in his book *The Pre-Wrath Rapture of the Church—Is It Biblical?*[7] This work is highly commended by Dr. John C. Whitcomb and Dr. Charles C. Ryrie. After penning a 102-page review on Rosenthal's book, Dr. Karleen concludes,

> Joining many bad arguments never makes a good argument, but put together enough weak claims and anyone can be fooled. Rosenthal presents his position by adding one conclusion to another in a chain-like effect, writing in such a way that, if the reader accepts each part, he is likely to conclude the pre-wrath position is valid. But many partial truths do not make a whole truth. The total of anything can be no better than the quality of each of its components....There can be no question that Rosenthal has wrestled with significant issues in biblical interpretation. *But the pre-wrath rapture is not justified in its claim to be the true explanation of the unfolding of the seventieth week of Daniel and of associated events.*[8]

Theodore W. Ertle, in his review for *The Baptist Bulletin*, September 1990, notes,

> A new twist to the prophetic scene has appeared with the publication of this book. The danger is that some may be swept into sympathy toward the author's position because of a lack of research or conviction. This reviewer is unmoved from his pretribulational mooring.
>
> Here are several objections:
>
> 1. Rosenthal is in error in his major premise that "the Day of the Lord" lasts only a few months and is the "wrath time" at the close of the seven years of Daniel's seventieth week. His whole system falls here and can be rejected at this one point....
>
> Rosenthal says the term "that day" is not a technical term parallel to the Day of the Lord (129). This is no small error. The terms are often synonymous in the Major and Minor Prophets (Isaiah 2:11,12; Jeremiah

30:7,8; Ezekiel 30:3,9; Joel 3:14,18; Amos 5:18; 8:3,9; Zephaniah 1:7-10; 2:2; 3:11; Zechariah 14:1,4; Malachi 4:1,5). Even when these dual terms are not in proximity, "that day" is still obviously "the Day of the Lord" in many prophetic Scriptures (e.g., Jeremiah 25:33; Zechariah 12:9)....

2. Rosenthal makes an unprecedented and, I believe, forbidden overlap of covenants between Israel and the Church. He thereby sees the Church in Matthew 24 and most of the Tribulation.

The rent veil (Matthew 27:51) indicated that a new covenant position began at the cross without overlap. Hebrews 10:9 says pointedly that the first covenant was taken away so the second could be established. Romans 11:19 teaches that Israel was broken out of the covenant stock so that we could be grafted in and that Israel would one day be grafted back in nationally (verses 23-26). Daniel 9:24 says that the seventieth week of prophecy belongs expressly to Daniel's people and city—certainly not to the Church.

No greater prophetic rationale exits for a supernatural removal of the Church than the requirement that there be the clearing away of a redeemed people who have a covenant that conflicts with the covenant of national Israel. Israel functions without overlap with us in her wrath and renewal stage called the seventieth week of Daniel....

The fact is clear: Marvin Rosenthal has bought into the presuppositions of the midtribulation position and has refined them in his book. His book has challenged but has not changed the presuppositions into which I have bought, namely, that Israel is always Israel—distinct and separate from the Church; second, that the Lord Jesus Christ may come for us at any moment in the grafting out event we call the Rapture, so that He may keep His unfulfilled covenant promises to Israel.[9]

Dr. Stanton thoroughly reviewed Rosenthal's book and raised the following objections:

It is evident that the *timing* of the rapture, and not its relationship to divine wrath, is uppermost in the mind of Rosenthal in the writing of this volume. Coming perilously close to advocating a date-setting scheme, he defends with enthusiasm the view that the rapture will be three-quarters of the way through the "70th week of Daniel," with divine wrath to be found only in the final quarter. His evidence for such conclusions is lengthy and complicated, based squarely on his personal division of the "70th week of Daniel" into three clearly recognizable periods, the "Beginning of Sorrows," the "Great Tribulation," and the frequently predicted "Day of the Lord."

The rapture is then placed immediately between the Great Tribulation and the Day of the Lord, which according to his definitions is after the Tribulation but still "pre-wrath." Rosenthal proceeds to support these views by some 200 pages of strong and somewhat overbearing argumentation, with a sharp attack against any response that reminds him of his previous pretribulational position.

His terminology and unique division of the "70th week" are central to his argument. He tries, with several notable exceptions on his own part, not to use the expression "the Tribulation period," saying that it contains a predisposition toward pretribulationism when it is used of the entire 70th week of Daniel. Rather, he prefers to call the coming seven years of judgment and wrath the "70th week of Daniel." These seven years he then subdivides as follows: (1) The first three and one-half years are "the Beginning of Sorrows." (2) The first half of the second three and one-half years (which would be one and three-fourths years or 21 months), he calls "the Great Tribulation." (3) The final 21 months, the fourth quarter of the seven years, he designates as "the Day of the Lord," in which is found the "wrath of God." Just before the day of the Lord, at the sounding of the "seventh trumpet," the rapture will occur. Hence the rapture of the church takes place between the third and fourth quarters of the 70th week of Daniel, just before the outpouring of the wrath of God. Therefore to Rosenthal the rapture will take place at a sharply defined moment of prophecy, and it is postribulational but pre-wrath.[10]

Stanton then adds,

> It is a serious error to claim, as Rosenthal does, that "the first three and one-half years are not part of the Tribulation period" (106-7) because God's wrath does not start until "considerably further" into the 70th week. In his words, "the seals are not God's wrath; they are God's promise of eternal protection during man's wrath" (145). Moreover, "the first five seals relate to man's activity under the controlling influence of Satan. God's wrath has not yet begun" (247). But this is not entirely true, for the seals also reflect the judgment of the sovereign God. All seven seals are broken by Christ, and the riders of the first four seals and their accompanying judgments are initiated by four "living creatures" who descend from the very presence of God (Revelation 4:6-8). They are responding to divine holiness when they command these riders, not to "come and see," but simply come!"...
>
> It is a denial of Scripture to declare the first four seals the activity of men rather than the judgment of God. And a rapture placed after the first six seals would certainly not be a "pre-wrath rapture."[11]

Then Stanton takes eight full pages to detail Rosenthal's fallacies, which include his view of the Tribulation, the future of the church, the Day of the Lord, the last trump, the location of the Rapture, and other major events of the future. He has some penetrating comments about one particularly interesting chapter:

> In chapter 18 Rosenthal asks the question, "Are Pretribulation Rapture Arguments Really Unanswerable?" While admitting that "pretribulationism has more than its share of notables of the faith" he adds that "church history is replete with men of distinction who had blind spots in their theology" (243). Then he gives 11 pretribulational arguments and his rebuttal of each, taking what comfort for his own position he can from each issue.
>
> Space does not permit a further discussion of these arguments, nor a rebuttal of Rosenthal's rebuttals. Suffice it to say that some of the arguments are not

entirely representative of normal pretribulational positions, and many valid pretribulational arguments are not introduced at all. Both Walvoord and Pentecost present a substantial summary of pretribulational arguments, and these issues have been abundantly discussed in the literature on the rapture debate. Moreover Rosenthal's rebuttals are largely a restatement of positions earlier defended.[12]

Stanton then highlights a very serious difficulty:

A problem runs throughout this book. Continually Rosenthal quotes Scripture, which is commendable, but almost invariably in the midst of the quotation he interjects his own definition or explanation, sometimes in brackets and sometimes in parentheses. The impression is given that the reader cannot understand each Scripture passage unless he is helped along or prodded by Rosenthal. While separate commentary is legitimate, Scripture is inspired by the Spirit with the potential of being taught by the Spirit, even "the deep things of God" (1 Corinthians 2:10-12). This is even true of prophetic material, for "when He, the Spirit of truth comes, He will guide you into all the truth...and He will disclose to you what is to come" (John 16:13).[13]

In summary he concludes,

Rosenthal testifies that the writing of his book caused him "the most difficult, tension-filled, heart-wrenching two and a half years" of his life (17). He speaks of sleepless nights and excruciating tension, of strained and somber board meetings, of agony of soul and the trauma of lost friendships and a lost job. While readers respond to this agony with deep regret and empathy, it is hardly the mark of being taught and led by the Spirit. One would think that a new clarification of a divisive problem of eschatology which has troubled the church for more than a hundred years, with the Spirit finally fulfilling the promise of Daniel 12:4 and shedding new light and understanding, would be accompanied by the joy of illumination and the peace of divine guidance. Such was evidently not the case.

Rosenthal should be commended for his diligence and thanked with appreciation for every insight which bears the clear stamp of truth. But my considered conclusion is that Rosenthal's published views are a distortion of prophetic truth, sometimes curious, sometimes strange, and frequently false. Taken as a whole, they are an unworthy replacement of the blessed hope of Christ's imminent return for the church at the rapture.[14]

Pre-Wrath Destroys Imminency

Almost every reviewer highlights the major problem of the book: the pre-Wrath view destroys imminency, the very force that has produced so much dedication in times of persecution, worldly environment, and theological confusion. From the days of the apostle Paul through today, the Christian who was convinced his Lord could come at any moment was motivated to holy living, soul winning, and missionary zeal. And that motivation helped him live above adversities and the circumstances of life, prompting him to invest his life in things above, not on things on the earth, as our Lord instructed us. While I doubt that Marvin Rosenthal or the others who attack the pre-Tribulation rapture view really want to demotivate the Body of Christ with their teachings, that does seem to be the result.

Locating the Rapture and the period of wrath three-quarters of the way into the Tribulation forces it to occur 21 months *after* the Antichrist desecrates the temple (see Daniel 9:27; Matthew 24:15; 2 Thessalonians 2:4). This would cause the church to watch for the coming of Antichrist, which is obviously unscriptural. It also destroys imminency, which Rosenthal claims the apostle Paul did not teach (249). He then would have us believe that we can gain comfort (see 1 Thessalonians 4:18) from the fact that the church will be raptured before the battle of Armageddon.

Rosenthal does not seem to realize that surrendering the church to five-and-a-half years of Tribulation—which includes the four horsemen, a world war, famine, the death of a quarter of the world, and the martyrdom of millions of Christians—is a betrayal of our Lord's promise to "keep [us] from the hour of trial which shall come upon the whole world, to test those who dwell on the earth" (Revelation 3:10).

Suggesting as he does that these first six seals of prophetic judgment are not Tribulation events is to reject the words of Scripture at their primary, literal meaning, even though he claims he does not do that.

Rosenthal admits that Christ breaks each seal, but then, without warrant, he calls these judgments the "wrath of antichrist." He even suggests on page 247 that "a strong case can be made for the thesis that the blessed hope is *enhanced* if a time of difficulty were to precede it" (see Romans 5:2-4,9). Thus he identifies the first five-and-a-half years as "a time of difficulty"! But he is wrong—they will be *tribulation!*

The strongest term in the book of Revelation for describing that period is used in Revelation 6:16-17, where it is called "the wrath of the Lamb! For the great day of His wrath has come, and who is able to stand?" Yet Rosenthal puts the Rapture between the sixth and seventh seals. Apparently "the wrath of the Lamb" is not, according to Rosenthal, "a time of difficulty." This point alone destroys the entire premise of his book. Most reasonable, Bible-loving, pre-Trib rapturists would abandon their position if a better theory based on Scripture came along. Pre-Wrath rapture is not that theory.

Many other faulty assumptions could be brought to the witness stand, particularly Rosenthal's failure to make a clear distinction between the church and Israel. His novel suggestion that the archangel Michael is the restrainer mentioned in 2 Thessalonians 2:7 (256) does nothing to strengthen his position. If Michael was no match for the devil when contending for the body of Moses (see Jude 9), he will scarcely be able to restrain his adversary during the Tribulation. The restrainer in 2 Thessalonians 2:7, and the only restraining influence in society today, is the Holy Spirit within the church. When the church is raptured at the beginning of the Tribulation, the Holy Spirit, who dwells in the church, will be gone. Consequently the world will be given over completely to evil (see Revelation 9:20-21).

Now, because the Holy Spirit is God, and because God is omnipresent, He will still be in the world (as He was in the Old Testament). The great soul harvest predicted for the first half of the Tribulation (Revelation 7:9) will demonstrate His presence, but He will not be in the church, restraining the world during the Tribulation.

Although Rosenthal claims that "there is, however, substantial evidence to identify the Restrainer" (256), he offers none. He seems to interpret Scripture texts as he wishes, then claim dogmatically and with certitude that they prove his point.

Rosenthal uses the pre-Trib argument that the church is mentioned 19 times in the first three chapters of Revelation but is not mentioned again until chapter 22. He suggests that such an omission "creates a significant problem" (244) for post-Tribbers. However, he apparently does not realize that five-and-a-half years of church silence during "the wrath of the Lamb" likewise poses a significant problem for him. Actually, the entire pre-Wrath rapture theory creates a series of significant problems.

The *pre-Wrath rapture* is a misnomer. It isn't *pre*, for Rosenthal locates the Rapture 63 months into the Tribulation period. And it isn't *wrath* because the author refuses to acknowledge it as Tribulation wrath until five-and-a-half years of the Tribulation have passed. Both tenets are unscriptural, opening the theory to most of the objections I will offer in chapter 15 against the other forms of post-Tribulationism. Rosenthal's theory is essentially another form of the post-Trib view, of which Dr. Walvoord says there are four variations. Rosenthal throws in a few mid-Trib points and includes the rapture scene taught by pre-Tribbers, but he has actually developed a fifth variation of the post-Trib view.

The pre-Tribulation rapture view that has captivated most of the Bible-believing church for the past 170 years or more is not in danger of being replaced by the pre-Wrath rapture view. I have a hunch that the author, instead of making converts, will probably spend most of his time defending and revising his position. Dr. H.A. Ironside used to say, "Be careful of any teaching that is new; it might not be true."

Another Pre-Wrath Book

I received a surprise in June of 1992 while attending the Christian Booksellers Convention. Under my hotel room door, someone had slipped a multicolored and very expensive advertisement of a new book identical in concept to the pre-Wrath rapture, called *The Sign.* At first glance I assumed Rosenthal had made his first convert, two full years after the publication of his book! *The Sign* appeared to reaffirm the idea that the Rapture would occur about two-thirds of the way into the Tribulation.

Not to worry! The late Robert VanKampen, the author of *The Sign,* was no convert to the pre-Wrath view. He was the originator! Rosenthal admitted in his book that a friend suggested the concept to him; VanKampen was that friend and was more than able to subsidize the expensive ad campaign that impressed many booksellers. Fortunately the book weighs in at two pounds and runs 518 pages, which should discourage even some ardent prophecy buffs from reading it. What's worse is that the book presents some original and bizarre concepts not even put forward by Rosenthal.

VanKampen claimed to have ardently studied this subject for the better part of eight years before putting his ideas in print. That means he held the view long before Rosenthal. Perhaps the plan was to let the student come out with the first book, get a response from the critics, then have the teacher come out with a more thorough presentation.

In my view, the book falls far short of that goal. It answers few criticisms, confirms many objections to Rosenthal's book, and further weakens its own credibility by the bizarre suggestion that the Antichrist will be a reincarnation of Adolph Hitler (208-213). If the Christian community buys that idea, we're really in trouble!

A much more reasonable suggestion is that the demonic spirits that indwelt Nebuchadnezzar, Nero, Attila the Hun, Adolph Hitler, and other ruthless, would-be world rulers will indwell the Antichrist during the first half of the Tribulation. This would account for his unreasoning hatred for the Jews and others who worship God. This more simple explanation demands no unscriptural reincarnation. No, the Antichrist will be a real person who will not be identified until after the Rapture of the church.

VanKampen Is Anti-Imminency

The Tribulation begins at the signing of a seven-year covenant between Antichrist and the Jewish nation—even VanKampen admits that. But timing that event *before* the Rapture destroys the at-any-moment expectation of Christ's coming that God intends to be a consecrating, soul-winning motivator for the church. VanKampen instructs people to look for Antichrist and the Seal Judgments of Revelation—not the coming of Jesus. I believe this to be the most dangerous part of his whole concept.

Sadly, VanKampen was not content simply to deny the time-honored concept of the imminent coming of Christ. He is actively hostile to it! He actually says, "Christ is indeed coming! But His return will not be imminent until the church is undergoing the fiery testing of Antichrist" (304). This and similar statements mark a departure from the traditional mid- and post-Tribulation positions that do not attack imminency. Normally, they simply ignore the fact that His coming will be absolutely predictable if we are around to see the covenant signed between Israel and Antichrist. In such a case we will know the day of the glorious appearing, for it will be exactly seven years later. VanKampen's blatant attack on imminency won't do anything to endear his theory to the Christian community. It is clearly unscriptural.

Space does not permit a more thorough examination of this book—I will leave that to others—but there is much that disqualifies it from being a serious threat to the pre-Tribulation rapture position. One problem that needs to be expounded is the author's refusal to acknowledge that the Rapture is not found in the Olivet Discourse. The sign from which he takes the book's title is not the Rapture, but the glorious appearing at the end of the Tribulation. No signs are necessary for the Rapture. Just because the disciples later became members of the church is no reason to expect the Rapture in Matthew 24. The church wasn't even founded when Jesus gave the Olivet Discourse.

Is VanKampen Another MacPherson Victim?

Could it be that VanKampen is another tragic victim of Dave MacPherson's vendetta against the pre-Trib view? We will explore that savage, unfounded attack in the following chapter. VanKampen was obviously aware of MacPherson's spurious assaults against the imminent coming of the Lord Jesus. His footnotes on pages 445 and 446 make that clear, for he parrots the MacPherson line about the origin of the pre-Trib position (which I will show to be an incredible hoax).

If VanKampen indeed accepted MacPherson's hoax, he started his whole investigation on a faulty premise—that the pre-Tribulation rapture is untrue. And one fundamental truism of logic is that if you start with a false premise, you end up with a false conclusion.

VanKampen evidently started out thinking the Rapture does not occur prior to the Tribulation; therefore, he had to find another place for it. Not satisfied with the mid-Trib or post-Trib positions, he decided to locate it *between* them. And while he did a great deal of creative thinking during his eight years of research, it is still true that no matter how long you study, a faulty premise guarantees a faulty conclusion. *The Sign* is a prime example of this.

We have reached a time in history when the Christians in the church need to be challenged to a life of holy living and commitment. Nothing accomplishes that better than belief in the imminent return of Christ for His Bride. The pre-Wrath rapture destroys that, and instead instructs the church to look for the signs of the Tribulation, the Antichrist, and the wrath of God— hardly positive motivators!

I believe that if the complex arrangement of end-time events found in *The Sign* (for the first time in church history!) were to become the prevailing view of Christendom, it would not only shatter the blessed hope, but produce a carnal, worldly, and disinterested body of believers.

Fortunately, after several years of public scrutiny, it looks as if this view is going nowhere. Except for VanKampen and Rosenthal, I know of no serious prophecy student who has embraced it. I predict it will prove to be an aberrant brainstorm that, despite its deep-pocketed promotional campaign, will fade away in time.

Chapter Sixteen

The Most Absurd
Charge of All

O f all the attacks on the Rapture, easily the most ridiculous is the one which finds it an instrument of the Illuminati (the Master Conspirators) to put the evangelical community to sleep politically so the secularizers of the Western world are free to dominate the government, education, communications industry, and other agencies of influence. The proponents of this attack would even have us believe that Dr. C.I. Scofield, author of the study Bible with notes and references that has blessed millions of Christians, was part of that plot.

Robert L. Pierce, author of *The Rapture Cult,* distributed by the John Birch Society, is the first person I have ever read who called belief in the Rapture "cultish." Even the most zealous post-Tribbers who hate the pre-Trib position have not made such a suggestion. In fact, even the post-Millennial apologists from Tyler, Texas, in their earnest attempt to rescue their system of theology from a well-deserved grave by savaging the pre-Trib position, have not, to my knowledge, made such a suggestion.[1]

A cult is a religious group that misleads people about the true identity of Jesus Christ and the means of salvation He has offered to man freely by faith. In light of that definition, a pre-Tribber is in no way cultish. Pierce is wrong in his assertion, and he is wrong about Scofield and the pre-Tribulation rapture view that Scofield helped to popularize both in this country and in Europe.

Pierce's inspiration was none other than the self-styled authority on the pre-Trib "hoax" reviewed in our last chapter, Dave MacPherson. Pierce, an activist in the John Birch Society and a student of the conspiracy theory, became a Christian in the early sixties. Using the venom-inspired distortions of history that MacPherson presented as truth, Pierce took them one step further by applying them to "the great conspiracy," all without one scintilla of fact.

I think I am well qualified to answer Pierce's attack. I myself have been a 50-year student of the satanically inspired, centuries-old conspiracy to use government, education, and media to destroy every vestige of Christianity within our society and establish a new world order. Having read at least 50 books on the Illuminati, I am convinced that it exists and can be blamed for many of man's inhumane actions against his fellow man during the past 200 years.

Dr. Adam Weishaupt, a professor at Goldestdat University, launched the Illuminati in Bavaria on May 1, 1776. For 30 years my wife and I have worked tirelessly to halt the effects of this conspiracy on the church, our government, media, and the public schools; so obviously I am not hostile to the conspiracy theory. An enormous amount of evidence proves that the secularization of our once Judeo-Christian society has not been an accident but is the result of the devilishly clever scheming carried on by this secret order.

To suggest, however, that the conspiracy used the biblical concept of a pre-Tribulation rapture is ridiculous. I include it in this book in the hope that anyone influenced by such suggestions will have an answer for the questions they raise. I would hope that the John Birch Society would disassociate itself from a book that has so little fact to support it, for the distribution of it will do nothing to endear the society to the 70 million Christians in America who otherwise identify with the society's moral concerns for our nation.

Let us first examine Pierce's rather novel view of the way pre-Tribulationism spread through America:

> John Nelson Darby, during the period 1862 to 1872, spent nearly seven years residing in and traveling through the United States and Canada.[2]

Two of Darby's most influential converts were James Hall Brookes, pastor of the Walnut Street Presbyterian Church in St. Louis, and Adoniram Judson Gordon, pastor of the Clarendon Street Baptist Church in Boston. These two men, while remaining in their established pastorates, became the leaders of the movement which was successful in spreading Darby's doctrines throughout the northeast and midwest during the last quarter of the century. Darby's doctrines also had an impact on Dwight L. Moody, the famous Chicago evangelist, although Moody appears to have accepted the doctrines slowly, and perhaps only partially.

The promotion of Darby's doctrines in America, by Americans, got underway effectively in 1875 with the establishment of a series of annual summer conferences. Beginning in a small way, the conferences expanded their membership and reach under the leadership of Dr. James H. Brookes and became semi-institutionalized as the Niagara Bible Conferences, meeting each summer from 1883 to 1897 at Niagara-on-the-Lake, Ontario. The conferences became highly successful in spreading Darby's doctrines to many influential American church leaders, especially those conservative leaders who were upset and concerned about the spread of the "higher criticism" movement in their churches....In this context Darby and his disciples made their appeal, which was always to the conservatives, since the Darbyites insisted, as did the conservatives, upon the inerrancy of the Bible as God's Word.[3]

The History Pierce Sees As Conspiratorial

Pierce draws heavily from church historian Sandeen, from whom I have also borrowed in this volume. But he takes the events of church history and gives them a conspiratorial twist. Even as he admits that the pre-Trib position swept through the evangelical Christian community, producing conservative fundamentalism, somehow he claims that such an amazing movement was accomplished by something other than the work of the Holy Spirit!

Sandeen attributes the pro-Darby victory partially to superior organizational and editorial skills, but remarks, "Some other factor seems necessary to explain the relative success of the Darbyite dispensationalists at the beginning of the twentieth century."[4]

In succeeding decades the leadership of the Darbyites further consolidated their hold on the conservative wing of Protestantism, with the Scofield Bible serving as their primary source book. They have succeeded so well that, today, the truly conservative point of view has been nearly forced down George Orwell's memory hole so far as public recognition of its existence is concerned. The term "fundamentalist" has replaced the term "conservative" in common usage, and the prime division within Protestant Christendom is now held in the public mind to be one between "liberals" and "fundamentalists," all the latter being Darbyite in doctrine. The "conservatives," those who accept neither the "higher criticism" of the Bible nor the Darbyite doctrine, are ignored completely.[5]

Let us examine further the two men who emerged as "fundamentalist" leaders at the turn of the century. Arno C. Gaebelein (1861–1945) arrived in the United States as an immigrant from Germany in 1879 and became a minister in the German conference of the Methodist Church. He attended some of the Niagara conferences and became well acquainted with James H. Brookes, who commended Gaebelein and his work in Brookes' publication *Truth*. During the 1890s Gaebelein was engaged in evangelizing the Jews on the East Side of New York City. As a result of his conversion to the Darbyite philosophy, Gaebelein decided in 1899 to leave the Methodist Church; later he gave up his Jewish mission work as well, to allow him to spend full time as leader of the Darbyite faction. Beginning in 1900 and continuing for more than thirty years, Gaebelein conducted a nationwide campaign, traveling to nearly every state in the union as well as to most parts of Canada to hold meetings and conferences, generally of one-week duration. He had no formal ties, during all this time, with any organized church, but conducted his work in each locality with the aid of any local church that would provide him facilities and an audience. His impact in spreading the Darbyite doctrine across North America was tremendous. Gaebelein and Scofield apparently became close friends and colleagues sometime during the fifteen-year duration of the conferences at Niagara-on-the-Lake.[6]

(Anyone who has read Gaebelein's books, particularly *The Conflict of the Ages,* or *Our Hope Magazine,* which he edited, could not call him a conspirator. He was a highly respected fundamentalist!)

Dr. James H. Brookes was possibly the most respected and successful pre-Tribulation pastor in all America during his lifetime. We are told that he was enormously influential in spreading pre-Tribulationism within his ranks of his Presbyterian denomination and beyond.

> Cyrus Ingerson Scofield (1843–1921) was born in Michigan but was reared in Wilson County, Tennessee. Serving in the Confederate Army during the Civil War, he received the Confederate Cross of Honor for bravery at the Battle of Antietam. At the end of the war, Scofield went to live in St. Louis with his older sister, who had married into one of the prominent pioneer French families of that city. In 1866, Scofield married Helene Labeau Cerre, a Roman Catholic and member of another prominent old French family.
>
> After studying law in St. Louis, Scofield in 1869 was dispatched by the Cerre family to Atchison, Kansas, to look after some Cerre financial interests there. Having been directed by the Cerres to hire the best legal counsel available in Kansas, Scofield engaged John J. Ingalls, a prominent lawyer and politician.
>
> In succeeding years Scofield and Ingalls became law partners as well as political allies. Both became members of the Kansas State Legislature, where Scofield was instrumental in electing Ingalls to the United States Senate in 1872. Ingalls in turn succeeded, in 1873, in having Scofield appointed at age 30 as United States Attorney for the district of Kansas and the Indian Territory.[7]

Detractors of Scofield and the Bible that bears his name always mention his unsavory past before he came to Christ—a past that included a ruined career, a plunge into alcoholism, a tragic divorce, and a profligate life. After his conversion, however, he became an illustration of the transformed life of the believer of 1 Corinthians 1:18, and later he publicly testified of his past so frequently that his evangelist friend D.L. Moody once urged him to put it behind him and stop mentioning it.

After accepting Christ, Scofield studied under Dr. James H. Brookes, the pastor of Walnut Street Presbyterian Church, who was considered one of the best biblical scholars in America. He was an ardent pre-Millennialist and an early student of John Darby. This godly man poured himself into the spiritual development of C.I. Scofield, and his investment was repaid by 40 years of pastoral work and preaching/teaching that ministered to millions of people as well as a Bible that has probably inspired more Scripture study than any other in history.

In 1882 Scofield became the pastor of the First Congregational Church in Dallas, Texas, where he remained until he transferred his work to Northfield, Massachusetts, in 1895.

> Scofield began work on his Reference Bible in 1903, after he and his friend Gaebelein had secured financial backing to enable Scofield to drop most of his pastoral duties and spend almost full time on the project. Some of his financial backers were: Lyman Stewart, president of the Union Oil Co. of California; Francis E. Fitch, a member of the Plymouth Brethren and the head of a printing company which printed the New York Stock Exchange lists; Alwyn Ball, Jr., a real estate broker and member of the large New York real estate firm of Southack and Ball; John B. Buss, a St. Louis businessman; and John T. Pirie, owner and New York representative of Carson, Pirie, Scott and Co., the large Chicago department store. Pirie owned a large estate at Sea Cliff on the north shore of Long Island, and it was there, in the summer of 1902, that the decision was made to proceed with the Reference Bible.
>
> The Scofield Reference Bible was completed in 1908 and was published early in 1909 by none other than the Oxford University Press, one of the most prestigious

publishers in the English-speaking world. Gaebelein relates how Scofield had met a Mr. Scott of the London publishing house of Morgan and Scott, and how, while the Reference Bible was being written, Scofield visited with Scott in England. To quote Gaebelein, "Mr. Scott said that his own firm would gladly undertake the publication, but he feared Morgan and Scott could not give to the Reference Bible the worldwide introduction it must have." He added, "There is only one publishing house which can handle your Reference Bible and that is the Oxford University Press." A few days later, Mr. Scott took Dr. Scofield to the office of Mr. Henry Frowde, the chief of the great Oxford University Press, which is so widely and favorably known throughout the English speaking world. He became at once interested.

The Scofield Bible is essentially a King James Version which has been interpreted and augmented by the addition of footnote commentaries written primarily by Cyrus Scofield, with advice and collaboration from seven consulting editors. One of these was Arno C. Gaebelein, whose field of expertise was prophecy. While the commentaries support orthodox Christian tenets in many respects, they promote, in every passage relevant to the question, the pre-tribulation "rapture" and related doctrines first espoused by Irving and Darby around the year 1830. Ernest R. Sandeen says of the Bible that it "combined an attractive format of typography, paragraphing, notes, and cross references with the theology of Darbyite dispensationalism." The book has thus been subtly but powerfully influential in spreading those views among hundreds of thousands who have regularly read that Bible and who often have been unaware of the distinction between the ancient text and the Scofield interpretation.

In the nearly seven decades since its first publication, the Scofield Bible has been promoted to the extent that today, in many fundamentalist churches, it is nearly the only Bible accepted. It has had a profound influence upon the religious thinking of millions of American Christians, bringing the doctrines of Irving and Darby into nearly every crossroads hamlet in America.[8]

The thought never seems to strike Pierce that in a free-enterprise country, where supply and demand determine what succeeds and what fails, that the Oxford University Press produced such a Bible because it was profitable to do so. If Christians did not like it, and if it had not spoken to a real need, they never would have bought it by the millions.

The Conspiracy Tie

Commenting on the Jesus movement, when thousands of hippies turned to Christ, Pierce notes,

> Although it is not directly related to the subject of this chapter, it is interesting that this blossoming of "youth religion" has coincided in time with the blossoming of the "rapture" cult.[9]
>
> Since the majority of the larger Protestant church congregations are "liberal," the Scofieldian doctrine is taught primarily in the smaller, independent congregations. Thus the spread of the doctrine has the superficial appearance today of being a spontaneous, grass-roots movement when in actuality it is just the opposite, having been promoted from the top down.[10]
>
> To a discerning observer, of course, the very fact that the doctrine is promoted by the Insider-controlled communications media is evidence enough that this is far from being a spontaneous, grass-roots movement, any more so than is the "religious youth."[11]

Pierce then goes on to make this incredible confession:

> The author recognizes that the history given in this and the preceding chapters may not be enough evidence to prove Conspiracy involvement in the phenomenal growth and perversion of the pretribulation "rapture" doctrine. Unfortunately, this is the usual situation when one delves into the more hidden recesses of the Conspiracy. Perhaps, though, it would be useful to assemble and observe at one time some of the more interesting bits and pieces of circumstantial evidence.[12]

How does one respond to an attack that is so historically weak and unprovable that even the author "recognizes that the history given...may not be enough evidence to prove Conspiracy involvement...and perversion of the pretribulation 'rapture' doctrine"? You cannot; this author is preposterous. Not only does he fail to prove his case, he even admits he hasn't proven it. Yet he wants his readers to believe it anyway just because he says it. But then he gets even more unbelievable. After a long list of more unprovable charges he makes this bizarre conclusion:

> Any one of the above [charges] taken alone might be of little significance, and each could be attributed to normal influences or to coincidence. But taken together they do indicate a pattern, or at least the possibility of one. Certainly there is *no proof* that any one of the individuals mentioned was in any way directly involved with the Conspiracy, and it is possible that none was. But, to paraphrase an expression used many times regarding circumstances obviously benefiting the Conspiracy, if there had been no pretribulation "rapture" doctrine, the Conspiracy would have had to invent one. It may be that the Conspiracy had the incredible good fortune that it all developed spontaneously. Or, it may have originated spontaneously, subsequently receiving a nudge here and a pat on the back there, as needed, from the Conspiracy. Or, it may have originated spontaneously and then was taken over and perverted at some point by the Conspiracy. Whatever the mechanism, it is certain that the vast majority of the people involved were innocent of any conspiratorial purpose, just as in most projects of the Conspiracy. But the tragic fact remains that the doctrine is having a devastating effect today in neutralizing current and potential opposition to the Master Conspiracy which seeks to enslave the world.[13]

The Possibility Pierce Missed

Since Pierce admits that he cannot prove his allegations, I will not bother to list detailed reasons for discarding each. I am inclined to think that any mature Christian will view this whole argument as a myth. Instead, I would like to offer an alternative that eliminates the conspiracy theory from consideration.

The successful spread of dispensational truth and a second-coming awareness of the at-any-moment-coming of Christ to rapture His church demands more than a human explanation. Of necessity it requires something special, something far more distinctive than the machinations of the Illuminati.

It was the work of the Holy Spirit!

"Darbyism" is really God preparing His church for the soon coming of His Son. I will admit that the spread of the movement involved hundreds of godly leaders, from great soul-winners such as D.L. Moody and R.A. Torrey to theologians such as Lewis Sperry Chafer and John Walvoord. It included thousands of pastors and Bible teachers, inspired by the Holy Spirit, who appreciated the plain biblical teaching on this subject.

C.I. Scofield and the Scofield Bible did not create the movement. Rather, the movement created them! His edition of the Bible caught on because in its time it best fit the beliefs of that group of Bible literalists who wanted to study the Word of God for themselves and hear directly from God. Besides, the Scofield Bible contains far more than dispensationalism and the pre-Tribulation rapture. It includes valuable notes on the deity of Christ, the Trinity, challenges to holy living, assurances of salvation, and hundreds of other practical helps that have nothing to do with prophecy.

The conspiracy hoax theory is itself a hoax. It denies that the real power behind the rapid spread of dispensationalism is the truth of God's Word.

Pierce's Real Problem

In the early sixties Pierce was an anti-Communist member of the John Birch Society and a patriotic activist. When he accepted Christ, he soon noted a strange phenomenon. As some equally active members also became Christians, they joined churches to grow in Christ and soon lost interest in their society activities. For that reason he lamented the Christian "who knows the score and has been putting his all into the battle but who, becoming weary or discouraged, embraces the 'rapture' idea as a welcome relief from his responsibilities. The 'rapture' cult could not operate more perfectly to neutralize patriots if it had been engineered to do exactly that."[14]

Pierce failed to recognize that it was not the so-called rapture cult that neutralized Christians, but rather. false notions of the pietistic movement. In those days many of the society's San Diego county leaders came to our church, and I had the joy of seeing many members accept Christ and follow Him in believer's baptism. I often spoke at society training seminars, knew Mr. Welsh, and shared Christ personally with him one morning at breakfast before he died. My friend, Dr. Larry McDonald, who, until tragically killed by Soviet communists in the bombing of Korean Airlines flight 007, was scheduled to become the next John Birch Society leader. In fact, I counseled the San Diego area coordinator when he came to me, irritated that so many members were joining our church and becoming "neutralized." But in the providence of God he bowed his head and prayed to receive Christ that day in my office, and later I baptized him. After attending church regularly and growing spiritually for a few years, he died suddenly of a heart attack.

The teaching of the Rapture has never neutralized a single Christian. What has done so is the pietistic movement's error that politics is evil and that heavenly minded Christians should not be involved in changing society through government. It is true that John Darby didn't believe Christians should vote, but that had nothing to do with his pre-Trib convictions.

Those who accepted the pre-Tribulation rapture view may have adopted this unscriptural idea of pietism, but the two are unrelated. In fact, one reason the Illuminati conspirators are running far behind their schedule to usher in the new world order is that the Religious Right in the 1980s registered and got out the vote of a record number of evangelical Christians in the election of Ronald Reagan as president. His election didn't solve all our national problems; it wasn't intended to. But it lit the way for other Christians who could turn the conspirators back another decade.

Christians are the only group in America large enough to vote out of office a sufficient number of liberal humanists to return this country to some degree of moral sanity. If we do so, we can continue to enjoy the same freedom to preach the gospel and advance the kingdom of Christ that our forefathers established. It would take only an additional 10 percent increase of involvement by the Christian community in registering voters, informing them of candidates' positions, and urging them to vote on election day. That should be the bottom line of Christian responsibility for people living in a free country.

Anyone who will not use his influence to preserve his freedom while he has the liberty to do so does not deserve that freedom and will surely lose both his freedom and his influence. The future does not belong to the conspirators; until Christ comes to rapture His church, it belongs to us who name the name of Christ. God have mercy on those Christians too unconcerned to use their freedom to vote while they still have that option. It will be the tragedy of the ages if 60 percent of the Christian community refuses to get involved and, by its silence, lets the liberals turn America into a Soviet-style socialist "paradise," which some have been working toward for nearly 90 years. If we let them, these liberal humanists, by overtaxation and exorbitant government spending, will do for America what communism has done to the former Soviet Union. That has nothing to do with prophecy, but it has everything to do with apathy.

The real cause of passivism is pietism's false notion that Christians should be so heavenly minded that they never get involved even with the basic elements of responsible Christian citizenship, like voting. But it has nothing to do with the pre-Tribulation rapture perspective of Bible prophecy.

Pierce and others who subscribe to his theory forget that if there had been no C.I. Scofield, and consequently no Scofield Reference Bible, the pre-Tribulation rapture theory would still be the most popular view of end-time events among evangelical, Bible-believing Christians. For if Scofield had not been available for God to promote His teaching of the imminent return of Christ, the Lord would have used someone else.

Chapter Seventeen

Why Do They Do It?

Ever since I launched into the research for this book, I have repeatedly asked myself, *Why do some opponents of the pre-Trib view attack it so vehemently?* The view doesn't promote spiritual laziness or worldliness. In fact, we have repeatedly noted its positive effect on those who hold this view: it encourages holy living in an unholy age, inspires Christians to soul-winning in view of the soon coming of Christ, and causes the church to become missionary-minded.

John Darby himself admonished, "If we study the history of the church, we shall find it to have declined in spirituality exactly in proportion as this doctrine of the expectation of the Saviour's return had been lost sight of. In forgetting this truth it has become weak and worldly."[1]

So again I return to the question, Why do they do it? Some of the attacks have been downright vicious. Others have involved lies and distortions, such as the one against Dr. Ironside. Similar attacks, all without substantiation, have been made against Dr. James Brookes, Professor W.G. Moorehead, R.A. Torrey, and even C.I. Scofield.[2] All the attacks have been refuted by close relatives and associates, but the very existence of such charges, leveled by professing Christians, makes one question the motives of the assailants.

In Fairness

I would hasten to concede that such attacks are not universal. Many honorable Bible teachers who represent the post-Trib view would never stoop to such affrontery, and I am not aware of any diatribes launched by mid-Trib proponents. All the skirmishes with which I am familiar have been initiated by a few noisy post-Trib zealots bent on trying to discredit the pre-Trib view and gain adherents for theirs.

By contrast, no pre-Tribber I know has made a fetish out of attacking post-Tribulationism. In prophetic literature we do not find pre-Trib adherents spending a major part of their lives fighting their pre-Millennial brethren. Both have so much in common regarding end-time events that the timing of the Rapture should never be a source of division and conflict.

Attacks by post-Millennialists are ineffective, and those by amillennialists are all but ignored. Anyone who is obliged to elevate his system of theology over the Word of God in order to "clarify" what God is saying cannot be a match for the humble servant of Christ who receives the Bible as the inerrant Word of God and interprets it literally. To most Bible students, accepting the Bible literally wherever possible is natural, which explains why the other theories are so unpopular; consequently, their attacks are usually ignored, for their real confusion relates to Scripture or interpretation, not to eschatology. Normally when the pre-Trib position is attacked, it is the entire pre-Millenarian concept that is attacked, not just the pre-Trib view.

It is difficult to understand why some post-Trib advocates feel it necessary to assail their pre-Trib brothers as though the opposing position is a threat to them personally. Their appeal is usually less to Scripture than to historical events that are not presented factually. Bray, MacPherson, and others seem so obsessed with their point of view that they twist dates, statements, and with reference to Margaret MacDonald and Manuel de Lacunza, attempt to read into others' writings or visions statements they simply did not make.

And tragically, many Christians are deceived in the process. There is no reason for them to abandon the blessed hope of Christ's return for His church before the Tribulation.

Hope Stealers

It is not my intent to be ungracious, but I do wish to counteract attacks on the pre-Trib view for the sake of young, impressionable Christians. Such assaults become effective hope stealers. Anytime we destroy a saint's belief that Christ will rapture His church before the Antichrist appears on the scene, we strip him of the hope that traditionally has helped the church live a life of expectancy.

How could I look a young believer in the eye and breathe courage into his heart if I believed he might very well face the fury of hell and the outpoured wrath of a righteous God on a world that has rejected His Son? How could I "comfort" him with those horrific tidings? We want believers to anticipate Christ's imminent return, not to look for the Antichrist and Tribulation.

So again we come to the exasperating question: Why? For what reason do preachers or other Christians feel they must attack the pre-Trib position?

Possible Reasons for the Attacks

1. The first could be anger. In counseling others, I have discovered that anger is a harmful motivator, for it often strips a person of sound reason and produces obsessive behavior. The attacks of S.P. Tregelles and B.F. Newton against John Darby were prompted by bitter hatred. This is why their lies and false accusations can be readily refuted. They may have been godly men in their everyday lives, but hatred seems to have clouded their rationality and promoted animosity in the area of prophetic teaching. Some of the modern-day rehearsals of those hundred-year-old false charges can easily be attributed to bitterness and wrath (see Colossians 3:8-9).

2. Jealousy is another possibility. Even a casual reading of some of the modern attacks betray an element of jealousy—hardly a worthy motivator.

3. Pride could serve as one forceful motivator of some attacks. One man who claimed to be a pre-Tribber in seminary and then changed his position seems to have been influenced by a mean-spirited author who is now dead.

After I sent for one of his booklets and perused it, I realized this former pre-Trib teacher had read these vicious attacks and, although not quite so harsh as his teacher, used the same arguments. Having announced to his supporting constituency that he had changed his position, he couldn't possibly revert without ruining his credibility. But I noted that he quoted extensively from Lacunza and others (as did his mentor), rather than validating his position from the Scriptures. Out of pride he launched offensives against the opposition, attempting to gain adherents. Unfortunately, many doctrinal conflicts through the years can be attributed to the sin of pride, the very sin that caused Satan's downfall.

4. Personal vendetta cannot be ruled out in many instances. In two books written 11 years apart, S.P. Tregelles claimed that Darby appropriated the pre-Trib theory from two different sources: the Jews and Margaret MacDonald. Obviously, it could not be both. Dave MacPherson was incensed by the way his father was treated by his church after he changed his position, and by the way he himself was dismissed from Biola College (now Biola University) for attempting to pass out post-Trib literature.

I can feel compassion for such crises in the life of a young man, but his conclusion that a church should keep a pastor even when he changes his position and that a pre-Trib school does not have the right to oust students when they refuse to stop proselytizing and spreading another view is not defensible. The school's position was clear before he became a student, so he had no one to blame but himself. Yet he has launched a publication and speaking campaign that attempts to destroy the credibility of the pre-Trib position. In the process, he has damaged his own, for he presents his arguments on a spurious foundation.

One of the kindest and most objective arguments against the twisted logic of MacPherson was written by a pastor friend of his who agreed with the post-Trib position. According to an article by Thomas Ice, this unnamed post-Trib pastor, after reading MacPherson's book, was alarmed that it would collapse under close scrutiny. He called him personally to air his concerns but reports,

He was not too happy with me. I then composed a rather lengthy paper and shared it with several authors of post-Trib books with whom I was acquainted, and told them of my apprehensions.

My major concern was that the public and pre-Trib readers would soon discern the poor foundation for the book [MacPherson's], and thus the post-Trib position would suffer embarrassment, even shame. I might say that I received almost unanimous confirmation from the post-Trib authors that they felt the same way as I....

In observation of the present dilemma caused by publication of the book, I think that the advancement of prophetic understanding could best be done by ignoring Mr. MacPherson's publication and moving along with examination of other aspects of the controversy. [Letter to Thomas Ice dated April 17, 1990, on file.]

The pastor's letter also included a summary of conclusions he had reached on the matter through his own research. They are virtually the same conclusions reached by Huebner and myself, even though he is post-Trib. I think the reason for this is that this is where true historical analysis of the matter leads.[3]

Unfortunately, to this point, the man has not acknowledged his mistakes, which could signify that a personal vendetta is more important to him than seeking after truth.

5. Shabby scholarship could also be a reason for some of the attacks. It is almost unbelievable that so many people have quoted fraudulent information from unknown sources as though it were fact. The desire to rush into print because information supported a position became more important than validating the data. An article by Thomas Ice mentions those who try to discredit the pre-Trib position by "just parroting these slanderous speculations about our theological roots." He quotes one detractor as follows:

Darby apparently drew much of his beliefs from two sources: a series of visions by a 15-year-old girl named Margaret MacDonald, and a book by Jesuit priest Emmanuel de Lacunza (Joseph R. Balyeat, *Babylon— The City of Revelation* [Sevierville, TN: Onward Press, 1991], 226).

The author of the above citation thought that he was enlightening his readers on the subject. Instead, his ignorance concerning the matter was put on display, since he was attempting to merge two conflicting views, either of which if true would exclude the other. Also, he is most likely ignorant that the champions of the "two sources" he noted vigorously blast the views of the other in their writings.[4]

I earlier referred to a book written by a prolific author who took his arguments from the slanderous charges of S.P. Tregelles, whom researcher Roy Huebner has so clearly discredited. This is shabby scholarship. And sincerity cannot compensate for error.

Honoring One Another

Not everyone who opposes the pre-Tribulation rapture view does so with malice or hostility. Many conduct themselves as true servants of Christ who honestly wish to discover what the Scripture says about the issue. We may disagree with each other on the timing of the Rapture, but we honor each other as members of the same spiritual family.

But others go to great lengths to attack the pre-Trib position with a vehemence normally reserved for heretics who deny the deity of our Lord. These persons make their false accusations and write their spiteful books out of many motivations, most of them bad.

The devil and his imps are the ones who really win. Satan has long been a sower of discord among brethren and a distorter of truth. Our Lord called him a "liar and the father of [lies]" (John 8:44). When the pre-Trib position is attacked, undermining the faith of a young Christian, or when a minister embraces a different theory and divides his church by teaching it, Satan notches another victory.

Only the devil triumphs when we no longer cling to the truth that Jesus could come at any moment, for historically when the church has lost that consciousness, she has become carnal, worldly, and callous to eternal things.

Do not let unfounded attacks upon the pre-Tribulation rapture position rob you of the blessed hope, but live every day as if our Lord will "descend from heaven with a shout....And the dead in Christ will rise first. Then we who are alive and remain shall be caught up together with them in the clouds to meet the Lord in the air. And thus we shall always be with the Lord. Therefore comfort one another with these words" (1 Thessalonians 4:16-18).

The Blessed Hope: A Treasured Truth

Few Bible doctrines have brought more hope to grieving souls during the past 2,000 years than the blessed hope, the teaching that Christ will return for His church, resurrect the dead, and translate living believers to be with Him while the world endures the Tribulation.

The apostle Paul presented the Rapture as a treasured truth that was to bring comfort to believers. This rapture doctrine has comforted many Christians in their hours of grief, just as it did me as a boy of nine.

In a church I pastored in San Diego, a husband and wife loved each other dearly. Charles, a deacon and close personal friend, had inherited a heart condition similar to that which had already taken the lives of his three brothers. One day the Lord called him home. After his funeral, which I tried to elevate into a praise service in honor of the Lord he loved, his wife sorrowed openly. At the graveside service she was accompanied by her sister, who did not share the couple's faith in Christ. The sister wept uncontrollably. Before long the grieving wife, in spite of her loss, turned to her sister with these words of comfort, "Esther, don't take on so. I will see Charles again as soon as Jesus comes for His church."

This is the blessed hope in action! It is the firm expectation of the believing church that for centuries has fueled a passion for holiness, energetic evangelism, and a powerful missions outreach.

There is no need to give up hope in this treasured and biblical doctrine! Believe it. Stand firm in it. Encourage one another in it. The Lord is coming…maybe today!

Maranatha!

The Preposition *Ek* Means "Out Of"

(*Our Hope Magazine*, August 1950, 86-88)

In the Bible, the word rendered "from" is from the Greek preposition *ek*. It has various connotations that denote *exit out of* or *separation from* something with which there has been connection—from a place, from the midst of a group, from a condition or state, etc. The preposition is used twice in John 17:15, once denoting *out of*, and once *from* (while still, as it were, in the presence of): "I pray not," our Lord says to the Father in His intercessory prayer, "that thou shouldest take them *out of [ek]* the world, but that thou shouldest keep them *from [ek]* evil" (KJV). Thus it may be seen that the post-Tribulationists have a point of argument for their view of Revelation 3:10.

Having said this much, however, suppose we examine more fully the preposition, the text, and the context.

Regarding the preposition *ek*, which is used over 800 times in the New Testament, only once can we find an instance where it is actually rendered "through." That is in Galatians 3:8, "through faith" (KJV) where the obvious sense is "by."

Ek is rendered "out of" hundreds of times, as for example: "*Out of* Egypt I called My Son" (Matthew 2:15); "first cast out the beam *out of* thine own eye" (Matthew 7:5 KJV); "for *out of* the heart proceed evil thoughts" (Matthew 15:19); [many bodies of the saints] came *out of* the graves after his resurrection" (Matthew 27:53 KJV); "I will spew thee *out of* my mouth" (Revelation 3:16 KJV); etc.

We have traced the preposition *ek*, when translated "from," 150 times in the New Testament, to find no more than five occasions when it could possibly denote "through" or "in," and only in one instance (its second use in John 17:15, to which we have already alluded) in the exact sense that the post-Tribulationists suggest for Revelation 3:10. The usual Greek for "through" is *dia*, and for "in" is *en, eis, eip*, and *kata*. It would seem that, if the Spirit of God intended to convey to the readers of this passage that the Lord would keep His own *through* or *in* the hour of trial, He would have used *dia*, or *eis*, or *epi*, or *kata* and not *ek*, which surely implies "out of" rather than "through" or "in."

It is helpful to observe the text itself as well. Those to whom the Lord is speaking are said to have kept "the word of my patience" (Revelation 3:10 KJV), an expression that suggests, at least, patient waiting *for Him*. "And the Lord direct your hearts into the love of God, and into the patient waiting for Christ" (2 Thessalonians 3:5 KJV). "For we know that the whole creation groaneth and travaileth in pain together until now. And not only they, but ourselves also, which have the first fruits of the Spirit, even we ourselves groan within ourselves, waiting for the adoption, to wit, the redemption of our body....But if we hope for that we see not, then do we with patience wait for it" (Romans 8:22-25). The redemption of the body will be at Christ's coming, and we who wait for Him are keeping the word of His patience.

It is important to note that it is not simply the temptation, or tribulation, that our Lord promises to keep His own from, but it is *"the hour of* temptation, which shall come upon all the world" (Revelation 3:10 KJV, emphasis added). While it may be proposed that the Lord can keep His own *from trial* simply by keeping them *safely through* it, it does not seem this can be stated with equal force in regard to *the hour of* temptation that the whole world will experience. The *hour* itself must be lived through by all who are in the world contemporaneous with it, when the only way that one can be *kept* from that hour is to be taken *out* of the world when it strikes.

Examine the last clause of Revelation 3:10: "to test those who dwell on the earth." Those who are to undergo this tribulation, "those who dwell on the earth," comprise a class of people that is referred to in such a way or by kindred expressions throughout the book (Revelation 6:10; 8:13; 11:10; 12:12; 13:8,12,14; 14:6; 17:2,8), and that is entirely earthly in its thinking and in no way whatever a heavenly people. There is not the slightest suggestion that the Lord's blood-purchased church must remain here for that experience, even as a protected spectator.

Finally, the context suggests that Christ's keeping of those who have kept the word of His patience *"from* the hour of temptation" will be *out of* it, called upward by His rapture shout; for the next verse declares, "Behold, I come quickly: hold fast which thou hast, that no man take thy crown" (KJV). Such a crown will be a form of reward, and when our Lord comes, He will reward His own. One of His last messages from heaven was this: "Behold, I come quickly; and my reward is with me, to give every man according as his work shall be" (Revelation 22:12 KJV).

Two Keys to
Understanding Prophecy

It has long bothered me, and probably many other Christians, that so much disunity has arisen regarding the timing and events associated with our Lord's return. Of all the teachings in the church, this second-most-frequently mentioned truth ought to be a unifying source of joy and blessing. Instead, it has become a divisive issue in the body of Christ. It is a sad commentary on the church that some Christians have been critical and intolerant because they disagree on this subject. Only the devil gains victory by such attitudes, which tend to retard rather than promote sanctification, evangelization, and world missions.

It is my hope that future disagreements can be resolved in a spirit of love and respect so that, as we draw closer to the actual fulfillment of these events, we might be of one mind. As I like to facetiously remind my mid- and post-Trib friends, their views do not determine their participation in the Rapture. When our Lord shouts from heaven, we all will rise at the same time! He will not selectively shout, "All you pre-Tribbers, come up here." He is coming according to His time schedule, not ours, and when He calls, all Christians go at the same time to be with Him forevermore.

These differences of opinion probably arise because not all Christians adhere to the two keys to understanding the prophetic Word of God. First, one must interpret the Bible literally unless the context provides good reason to do otherwise. Second, we must understand that Israel and the church are distinct! They had different beginnings, purposes, and commissions, and they have different futures. If a person fails to acknowledge these two facts of Scripture, all discussion and argument is fruitless. The issue is not so much one's view of prophecy as it is one's view of Scripture and the church.

Verbal Inspiration

The Bible was written for all people to understand, not for theologians to wrangle over or to use as raw material from which to develop comprehensive systems of theology. Some teachers seem to view Scripture as a servant to their theology rather than vice-versa. The Bible says that "all Scripture is given by inspiration of God, and is profitable for doctrine, for reproof, for correction, for instruction in righteousness" (2 Timothy 3:16). Thus the Bible is unlike any other book. Historically, whenever the Bible is not accepted as inspired, authentic, and accurate, it has been twisted to mean anything the interpreter desired. To avoid that problem, we must take Scripture passages literally in context whenever possible.

Satan successfully tempted Eve by questioning the accuracy of the Word of God ("Has God indeed said...?"), and has repeated the same deception in all ages. Whenever men have accepted the Bible literally, Satan has hurried to offer another method of interpretation; that explains how heresy has crept into the church. The first three centuries the church was so persecuted by the Roman government that heresy had no chance to develop; most believers accepted the Bible literally. Consequently, they expected Christ to come at any time to set up His kingdom here on earth. Churchmen of the first three centuries were called *chiliasts,* meaning "mellennialists."

Not until proponents of the Alexandrian School began to allegorize and spiritualize Scripture in the third century did anyone start to doubt the premillennial return of Christ. Origen, the Greek heretic, was among the first. Later, Augustine laid the foundation for destroying doctrinal integrity by introducing Catholic doctrines that have lasted until this day in a form of Christianized paganism—Christian in name, pagan in origin and practice. This never would have happened if people had continued to take the

Bible literally wherever the plain sense of Scripture made common sense. Amillennial or postmillennial positions would never have gained much influence in the church without this nonliteral system of interpreting the Bible.

For the next twelve centuries after Augustine, the Bible was either banned or hidden in monasteries until the Reformation unlocked the Scriptures and set it free.

Reformation students accepted the authority of Scripture over church doctrine. Gradually they began to accept the whole Bible literally, which naturally brought about a revival of premillennialism. Such is the logical result of accepting the scriptural promise that Christ will come back to this earth in power and great glory after the Antichrist has been revealed for a time of tribulation. And when Jesus comes, He will subdue and reign over the nations, slay the Antichrist and False Prophet, bind Satan for 1,000 years, and resurrect dead believers who will rule and reign with Him in that kingdom.

I doubt a person could arrive at an amillennial or postmillennial position simply by reading the Bible literally. Instead, a system of interpretation or theology must first be applied to explain away the many promises of the future kingdom age and the 1,000-year time period mentioned in Revelation 20. Such a system is necessary in order to conclude that no kingdom will arise or that we will take over the world and so improve it that Christ will return to an ideal world already prepared for Him.

Both amillennialism and postmillennialism require that systems of belief be imposed on the text of Scripture in order to reach certain conclusions about end-time events. In that respect they are like Christian Science, which must include Mrs. Eddy's systems of helps in order to manufacture its bizarre conclusions about the Bible. The same can be said for Jehovah's Witnesses and most other cults. As one writer has noted about those who hold to a Reformed perspective,

> For some Reformed Christians, the system of doctrine seems to be the final authority, not the Bible. Confronted by apparently conflicting passages of Scripture, they let their Reformed presuppositions decide how the apparent conflict should be resolved. Comparing, for example, Isaiah 45:23, "unto me every knee shall bow and every tongue shall swear," and the

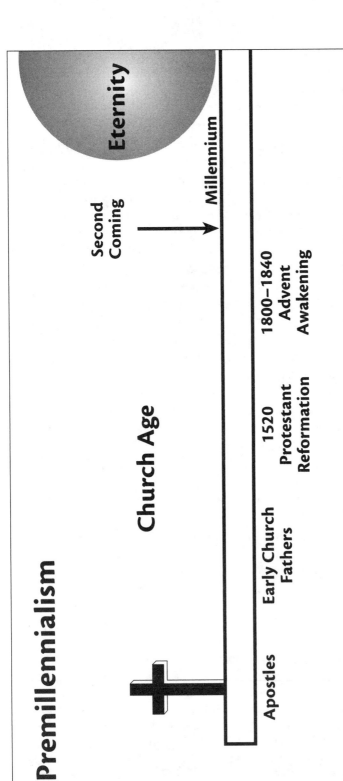

Premillennialism

Eternity

Second Coming

Church Age

Millennium

| Apostles | Early Church Fathers | 1520 Protestant Reformation | 1800–1840 Advent Awakening |

A premillennialist believes that Christ will return to the earth in power and glory to establish His kingdom for 1,000 years before the final resurrection of the dead and the final judgment. For the first three centuries of church history, it was the predominant view of the church, then was held by only a few during the Dark Ages. The popularity of this view has been increasing since the Reformation, and it is now the predominant view in Bible-believing evangelical churches.

Amillennialism

No Millennium
The Church = The Kingdom of God

Second Coming

Eternity

Amillennialism was begun by Augustine and has been the official doctrine of the Catholic Church for 1600 years. It interprets the Millennium spiritually, as it does most prophecies. Amillennialists believe Christ bound Satan during His earthly ministry, that the first resurrection is the new birth of the believer, and the millennium corresponds with the church age, which to them, is the kingdom of God. They believe Christ will come to judge and establish eternity. To them there will be no Millennial kingdom, and Israel will not see the literal fulfillment of its kingdom promises. In addition to Catholic churches, this view has prevailed in Anglican and state churches, Reformed churches, and liberal mainline churches.

Postmillennialism

The Church to
Usher in the Millennium

Second
Coming

Eternity

Conceived by Daniel Whitby, a liberal Unitarian minister, this view is based on a figurative interpretation of prophecy that permits a variety of opinions and a lack of uniformity among postmillennialists. They see the kingdom as spiritual and unseen rather than political and material. The divine power of the kingdom is the Holy Spirit; the throne of Christ is in heaven. The preaching of the gospel and spread of Christian principles signal its progress. Christ's coming is in the distant future, when Christ's kingdom (Christianity) fills the whole earth. This view assumes the world is getting better and will culminate with the return of Christ. This theory was all but destroyed after Word Wars I and II, and although the last 50 years of nuclear confrontation should have killed it, the new wave of Reconstructionism and Dominionists have tried to resuscitate it. It has never been popular among those who take Bible prophecy literally.

words of the Lord Jesus Christ Himself in Luke 18:8, "Nevertheless, when the Son of Man cometh, shall he find faith on the earth?" They argue that Jesus must be understood in the light of Isaiah and not vice versa.[1]

This brings me to the heart of what I want to say here. There is such a thing as allowing your theological presuppositions to so determine your hermeneutics (your approach to understanding the Bible) that the theological presuppositions become an authority superior to the Bible itself.

The first-century church had no helps or systems for understanding Scripture. Believers just read whatever portion of the Bible they had access to and accepted it. No wonder they were premillennialists, for that is the perspective that lines up with the plain meaning of Scripture.

Author Timothy Weber relates this charming story. Some students from a theological seminary were playing basketball one night in a local gymnasium. Late in the evening the janitor arrived and prepared to lock up the building. While waiting for the game to conclude, he sat down and began reading his Bible. He was still at it when the game ended and the players began filing out. One theological student noticed that the janitor was reading from the book of Revelation and asked him, quite smugly, if he understood what he was reading. "Sure do," the man replied. Somewhat taken aback by the janitor's confidence, the student, who had not quite mastered the prophetic panorama of Revelation yet, asked a second question. "Oh, yeah? What does it all mean?" "Simple," replied the janitor, "Jesus wins!"

That, in a nutshell, sums up the appeal of premillennialism for millions of people. Premillennialist eschatology provides the promise that eventually Jesus will win, even in a world that seems to be totally out of control. It guarantees that ultimately everything will make sense and will be fine. In a world like ours, that is no mean achievement.[2]

The Golden Rule of Interpretation

The best guide to Bible study is "the golden rule of biblical interpretation." To depart from this rule opens the student to all forms of confusion and sometimes even heresy.

When the plain sense of Scripture makes common sense, seek no other sense, but take every word at its primary, literal meaning unless the facts of the immediate context clearly indicate otherwise.

Anyone who follows the golden rule of interpretation will become a premillennialist. As a test of the validity of this golden rule, apply it to these readings from Revelation chapters 19 and 20 and draw your own conclusion:

> Then I saw heaven opened, and behold, a white horse. And He who sat on him was called Faithful and True, and in righteousness He judges and makes war. His eyes were like a flame of fire, and on His head were many crowns. He had a name written that no one knew except Himself. He was clothed with a robe dipped in blood, and His name is called The Word of God. And the armies in heaven, clothed in fine linen, white and clean, followed Him on white horses. Now out of His mouth goes a sharp sword, that with it He should strike the nations. And He Himself will rule them with a rod of iron. He Himself treads the winepress of the fierceness and wrath of Almighty God. And He has on His robe and on His thigh a name written: KING OF KINGS AND LORD OF LORDS (Revelation 19:11-16).

> And I saw the beast, the kings of the earth, and their armies, gathered together to make war against Him who sat on the horse and against His army....Then I saw an angel coming down from heaven, having the key to the bottomless pit and a great chain in his hand. He laid hold of the dragon, that serpent of old, who is the Devil and Satan, and bound him for a thousand years; and he cast him into the bottomless pit, and shut him up, and set a seal on him, so that he should deceive the nations no more till the thousand years were finished. But after these things he must be released for a little while.

> And I saw thrones, and they sat on them, and judgment was committed to them. And I saw the souls of those who had been beheaded for their witness to Jesus and for the word of God, who had not worshiped the beast or his image, and had not received his mark on

their foreheads or on their hands. And they lived and reigned with Christ for a thousand years. But the rest of the dead did not live again until the thousand years were finished. This is the first resurrection. Over such the second death has no power, but they shall...reign with Him a thousand years (Revelation 19:19–20:6).

The plain sense of these passages equals premillennialism. The study of prophetic passages is not difficult when we take the Bible literally whenever possible. If, however, a person begins to spiritualize or allegorize the text, he is hopelessly doomed to confusion and error. Taking the Bible literally makes even difficult passages more understandable.

On a flight from Salt Lake City to San Francisco I was seated next to a salesman who claimed he had never read a Bible. The closest he had been to church in his life was to drop his daughter off at a Congregational church every other week for Sunday school on his way to the golf course. I asked him if he would submit to an experiment, to which he agreed.

Many people say the Bible is a difficult book to understand, particularly the book of Revelation. Turning to Revelation 20:11-15, the description of the Great White Throne Judgment, I handed him my Bible with only a brief instruction: "This is a prophecy about a future event." I waited as he read. His joyful mood changed abruptly, and soon he exclaimed, "If that's true, I'd better get right with God." This man, responding to the plain sense of prophetic scripture, sufficiently understood God's warning and took precaution for that event by receiving Christ.

A Vital Distinction

The Church Is Not Israel!

When our Lord promised to found His church, Israel had been in existence almost 2,000 years. God created this special nation by performing a biological miracle on both Abraham and his wife Sarah, who was beyond childbearing age. This new ethnic people were first called *Hebrews*, then *Israelites*, and later *Jews.* God gave them the simple promise that if they would worship and obey Him, He would bless them. If they disobeyed and worshiped other gods, however, He would curse them.

The story of their disobedience is well known. Just over 600 years before Christ came into the world, God let them be taken captive by Babylon to teach them a lesson of dependence. Sadly, they did not profit by that experience or by the prophecies of Daniel, Isaiah, Jeremiah, and others. Instead, they were so disobedient that they failed to recognize their Messiah when He came; in fact, instead of accepting Him, they rejected and crucified Him. For that reason, Israel was put on prophetic "hold" and the church, which our Lord founded on the day of Pentecost, became the special focus of God's attention and has been for almost 2,000 years.

God is not finished with Israel, of course. Many unfulfilled promises of a kingdom of righteousness will be fulfilled during the Millennial kingdom when Christ, the legal heir of David, will rule the world as King of kings and Lord of lords. All the promises of greatness to the children of Israel will come to fruition at that time.

Some Christians attempt to make Israel and the church one and the same, suggesting that the church is now heir of all promises given to Israel. Reconstructionists, kingdom-now believers, some postmillennialists, and others look forward to Israel/the church bringing in righteousness and heralding the return of Christ to the kingdom, which they or their descendants hope to institute. To reach this conclusion, they must disregard the plain teaching of the Word of God by spiritualizing and allegorizing prophetic passages well beyond their literal meaning. It is interesting to analyze the writings of those who apply to the church the promises God gave to Israel, for they only claim the promises of blessing. Somehow they omit the promises of cursing, which Israel experienced when she disobeyed.

The Church Is a Separate Entity

Almost one year prior to His crucifixion, our Lord predicted that He would build His church on Himself. She was born on the day of Pentecost when the Holy Spirit filled believers and became the earthly manifestation of God, as was the temple in the Old Testament.

The church, or *ekklesia* ("called out ones"), is not a building made with hands. It is composed of those who became temples of the Holy Spirit when converted. This is a principle that those who have never taken the Bible literally still do not understand. Huge buildings or great denominations do not prove God's presence or blessing. God manifests Himself today through those Spirit-filled believers who do His will. The church is not Israel, nor is Israel the church. Those who await the promises of Israel to be filled in the church will wait in vain. Consider these unique and distinctive differences between the two living organisms:

1. *They have different originators.*

The Lord God brought Israel into being in a unique manner not only in the selection of Abraham and Sarah, but also in the choosing of their son Isaac's wife to preserve their ethnic identity.

Christ Himself, however, founded His church, as He promised in Matthew 16:13-20, and sent the Holy Spirit to indwell it.

2. *They have different foundations.*

Jesus Christ is the living foundation of the church (1 Corinthians 3:11). He had not yet been born on earth at the time of Israel's foundation. Actually, the church could not be established until after Christ died, was buried, rose again, and ascended into heaven. As Paul explained in Ephesians 2:20, Christ Himself is the "chief cornerstone."

Israel was not founded on the finished work of Christ on the cross but on God's promises to her, which are still in force and have yet to be fulfilled.

3. *They have different purposes.*

Israel was never given the Great Commission. She was to be the torchbearer of God's faithfulness to a nation that worshiped Him and would consequently enjoy His blessings. Israel came close as a nation to fulfilling that promise during the first part of Solomon's reign. For most of her history, however, Israel was a testimony to God's judgment upon sinners, yet she was ever His special nation.

The church, by contrast, is seen as the lampstand which, according to our Lord's promise, "the gates of Hades shall not prevail against" (Matthew 16:18). The church was given the promise and presence of the Holy Spirit with which to fulfill Christ's great commission (Matthew 28:19-20). Starting with

3,000 additions on the day of Pentecost and 5,000 more shortly thereafter, it has grown until today there could be an estimated 500 million believers worldwide—plus the multiplied millions that have been won to Christ all through the past 2,000 years of the church age.

The church is not perfect, and she has erred in her teaching ministry from time to time as the devil has led her astray; but whenever she has applied the Bible literally, the blessings of God and growth have followed. No passage of Scripture indicates that the whole world will receive Christ under the teachings of the church. Instead, there are "seasons of refreshing" from time to time when many come to faith in Him (see Acts 3:19).

4. *Their prophetic futures are different.*

The promises of God to Israel revolve around the restoration of the kingdom. After the Reformation, as people began to read the Bible again and take it literally, Christians started to look for the restoration of the Jews into the land of Israel according to Ezekiel 36–37 and other passages. They even founded societies for missions to the Jews in the early days of the premillennial revivals around 1740.

By contrast, the church does not look for an earthly kingdom. Whereas Israel seeks nationhood, and rightly so, the church is awaiting the coming of her Lord to take her to the Father's house as He promised. Israel plans to rebuild her temple in Jerusalem, but the church has no use for an earthly temple. As the Bride of Christ she is anticipating the Marriage Supper of the Lamb in heaven, which will give her a unique relationship to our Savior. Israel, the wife of God, was a cast-off wife because of her whoredoms (see Isaiah 54:5-8). She will, however, reside in the earthly Jerusalem, and a new heart will be implanted within her during the Millennium.

It is a sobering fact that Israel can expect to endure the Tribulation, a time period called "the time of Jacob's trouble" (Jeremiah 30:7). After the church is raptured, that time of trouble will begin. The layout of the book of Revelation reveals it. The church is not needed during the Tribulation, for the commission to reach the world for Christ will be extended to the Jews during that time. Why? Because the church won't be here.

Three Classes of People

The apostle Paul considered himself a Christian apostle to the Gentiles, yet he was an Israelite. It is not strange, then, that he should clearly lay out for us a threefold classification of people when he said, "Give no offense, either to the *Jews* or to the *Greeks* [Gentiles] or to the *church of God*" (1 Corinthians 10:32, emphasis added). The world even today is made up of those three kinds of people. Failure to comprehend that fact will hinder anyone's understanding of prophecy.

Jews: the descendants of Abraham through Isaac. They started out as Hebrews, became the 12 tribes of Israel, and near the close of the Old Testament and during the days of the New Testament until the present have been called Jews.

Gentiles: all the peoples of the world who are non-Jews. In the New Testament, a Gentile designates any lost member of the human race who is not a Jew.

The Church of God: the Lord's church is composed of individuals, whether Jew or Gentile, who have been born again by faith in the sacrifice of Christ for sin and His consequent resurrection.

A well-intentioned but ill-advised chorus used to be sung in our Sunday schools: "Every promise in the Book is mine, every chapter, every verse, every line. All are blessings of His love divine. Every promise in the Book is mine." That chorus was wrong because not every promise, every verse, and every chapter is ours. Much of the Bible is directed to Israel—past, present, and future. Some passages relate to the Gentiles, and many promises in the Book were addressed to the church. But "rightly dividing the Word of truth" (2 Timothy 2:15) means we apply only the promises of God that are ours; otherwise we will envision ourselves in two places at the same time.

A mid-Trib author friend of mine frequently tries to convince me of his position. Recently he mailed me a copy of a new book and asked what I thought. Because this book merged Israel and the church, I showed him that applying the promises intended for Israel to the church violated 1 Corinthians 10:32 and other passages. So far he has not responded. People with a system of interpretation other than taking the words literally unless the text clearly indicates otherwise usually don't want to be confronted with the Scriptures. They could well say the old adage, "Don't confuse me with the facts [Scripture]; my mind is made up." Such people do not want to be confronted with passages that are in conflict with their theological system.

Reviewing the Essentials

As a general rule, whenever you hear someone preach about Bible prophecy, be sure he uses the two essential keys to understanding Scripture: 1) Interpret the Bible literally (even the prophetic passages of Scripture) unless the context provides good reason to do otherwise. And 2) ask, Does he draw a distinction between Israel and the church?

The Handwritten Account by Margaret MacDonald of Her Vision

As recorded in Robert Norton's
The Restoration of Apostles and Prophets; In the Catholic Apostolic Church (1861)

It was first the awful state of the land that was pressed upon me. I saw the blindness and infatuation of the people to be very great. I felt the cry of Liberty just to be the hiss of the serpent, to drown them in perdition. It was just "no God."

I repeated the words, Now there is distress of nations, with perplexity, the seas and the waves roaring, men's hearts failing them for fear—now look out for the sign of the Son of man. Here I was made to stop and cry out, O it is not known what the sign of the Son of man is; the people of God think they are waiting, but they know not what it is. I felt this needed to be revealed, and that there was great burst upon me with a glorious light.

I saw it was just the Lord Himself descending from Heaven with a shout, just the glorified man, even Jesus; but that all must, as Stephen was, be filled with the Holy Ghost, that they might look up, and see the brightness of the Father's glory. I saw the error to be, that men think that it will be something seen by the natural, the eye of God in His people. Many passages were revealed, in a light in which I had not before seen them.

I repeated, "Now is the kingdom of Heaven like unto ten virgins, who went forth to meet the Bridegroom, five wise and five foolish; they that were foolish took their lamps, but took no oil with them, but they that were wise took oil in their vessels with their lamps." "But be ye not unwise, but understanding what the will of the Lord is; and be not drunk with wine wherein is excess, but be filled with the Spirit." This was the oil the wise virgins took in their vessels. This is the light to be kept burning— the light of God—that we may discern that which cometh not with observation to the natural eye. Only those who have the light of God within them will see the sign of His appearance.

No need to follow them who say, see here, or see there, for His day shall be as the lighting to those in whom the living Christ is. 'Tis Christ in us that will lift us up—He is the light—'tis only those that are alive in Him that will be caught up to meet Him in the air. I saw that we must be in the Spirit, that we might see spiritual things. John was in the Spirit, when he saw a throne set in Heaven.—But I saw that the glory of the ministration of the Spirit had not been know [sic].

I repeated frequently, but the spiritual temple must and shall be reared, and the fullness of Christ be poured into his body, and then shall we be caught up to meet Him. Oh, none will be counted worthy of this calling but His body, which is the church, and which must be a candlestick all of gold.

I often said, Oh, the glorious inbreaking of God which is now about to burst on this earth; Oh, the Glorious temple which is now about to be reared, the bride adorned for her husband; and Oh, what a holy, holy bride she must be, to be prepared for such a glorious bridegroom.

I said, Now shall the people of God have to do with realities— now shall it be known what it is for man to be glorified. I felt that the revelation of Jesus Christ had yet to be opened up—it is not knowledge about God that it contains, but it is an entering into God—I saw that there was a glorious breaking in God to be. I felt as Elijah, surrounded with chariots of fire. I saw as it were the spiritual temple reared, and the Head Stone brought forth with shoutings of grace, grace, unto it. It was a glorious light about the brightness of the sun, that shone round about me.

I felt that those who were filled with the Spirit could see spiritual things, and feel walking in the midst of them, while those who had not the Spirit could see nothing—so that two shall be in one bed, the one taken and other left, because the one has the light of God within while the other cannot see the Kingdom of Heaven.

I saw the people of God in an awfully dangerous situation, surrounded by nets and entanglements, about to be tried, and many about to be deceived and fall. Now will the wicked be revealed, with all power and signs and lying wonders, so that if it were possible the very elect will be deceived. This is the fiery trial which is to try us. It will be for the purging and purifying of the real members of the body of Jesus; but Oh, it will be a fiery trial. Every soul will be shaken to the very center. The enemy will try to shake in everything we have believed—but the trial of real faith will be found to honor and praise and glory. Nothing but what is of God will stand. The stony-ground hearers will be made manifest—the love of many will wax cold.

I frequently said that night, and often since, now shall the awful sight of a false Christ be seen on this earth, and nothing but the living Christ in us can detect this awful deceivableness of unrighteousness he will work—he will have a counterpart for every work of the Spirit. The Spirit must and will be poured out on the church, that she may be purified and filled with God—and just in proportion as the Spirit of God works, so will he—when our Lord anoints men with power, so will he. This is particularly the nature of the trial, through which those are to pass who will be counted worthy to stand before the Son of man.

There will be outward trial too, but 'tis principally temptation. It is brought on by the outpouring of the Spirit, and will just increase in proportions as the Spirit is poured out. The trial of the church is from Antichrist. It is by being filled with the Spirit that we shall be kept.

I frequently said, Oh be filled with the Spirit—have the light of God in you, that you may detect Satan—be full of eyes with—be clay in the hands of the potter—submit to be filled, filled with God. This will build the temple. It is not by might nor by power, but by My Spirit, saith the Lord. This will fit us to enter into the Marriage Supper of the Lamb. I saw it to be the will of God that all should be filled.

But what hindered the real life of God from being received by His people, was their turning from Jesus, who is the way to the Father. They were not entering in by the door. For He is faithful who hath said, by Me if any man enter in he shall find pasture. They were passing the cross, through which every drop of the Spirit of God flows to us. All power that comes not through the blood of Christ is not of God. When I say, they are looking from the cross, I feel that there is much in it—they turn from the blood of the Lamb by which we overcome, and in which our robes are washed and made white.

There are low views of God's holiness and a ceasing to condemn sin in the flesh, and a looking for Him who humbled Himself, and made Himself of no reputation. Oh! It is needed, much needed at present, a leading back to the cross.

I saw that night, and often since, that there will be an outpouring of the Spirit on the body, such as has not been, a baptism of fire, that all the dross may be put away. Oh, there must and will be such an indwelling of the living God as has not been—the servants of God sealed in their foreheads, great conformity to Jesus—just the bride made comely, by his comeliness put on her. This is what we are at present made to pray much for, that speedily we may all be made ready to meet our Lord in the air— and it will be. Jesus wants His bride. His desire is toward us. He that shall come, will come, and will not tarry. Amen and Amen. Even so, come Lord Jesus.

Bibliography

Bray, John L. *The Origin of the Pre-Tribulation Rapture Teaching*. Lakeland, FL: J.L. Bray Ministries, 1982.

Combs, James. *Baptist Bible Tribune*, October 24, 1990.

Elmore, Floyd Saunders. "A Critical Examination of the Doctrine of the Two Peoples of God in John Nelson Darby," 1991.

Ertle, Theodore W. Book review of *The Pre-Wrath Rapture of the Church* in *The Baptist Bulletin*, December 1990.

Froom, LeRoy Edwin. *The Prophetic Faith of Our Fathers*. Washington, D.C.: Review and Herald, 1946.

Harrison, Norman. *The End: Rethinking the Revelation, The Rapture: Pre-Mid or Post-Trib?* Grand Rapids, MI: Zondervan Publishing House, 1984.

Huebner, R.A. *Precious Truths Revived and Defended Through J.N. Darby*. Morganville, NJ: Present Truth Publishers, 1991.

Hunt, Dave. "'Pre-Wrath' or 'Pre-Trib' Rapture?" *The Omega Letter*, January 1991.

Ice, Thomas. "A Short History of Dispensationalism," Part II, *Dispensational Distinctives*, vol. 1, no. 2, March/April 1991.

———. "A Short History of Dispensationalism," Part III, *Dispensational Distinctives*, vol. 1, no. 3, May/June 1991.

———. "New, Improved Postmillennialism," *Biblical Perspectives*, vol. 1, no. 2, March/April 1988.

———. "The Origin of the Pre-Trib Rapture," Part I, *Biblical Perspectives*, vol. 2, no. 1, January/February 1989.

———. "The Origin of the Pre-Trib Rapture," Part II, *Biblical Perspectives*, vol. 2, no. 2, March/April 1989.

———. "Why the Doctrine of the Pretribulational Rapture Did Not Begin with Margaret MacDonald," *Bibliotheca Sacra*, April/June 1990.

Ironside, H.A. *A Historical Sketch of the Brethren Movement*. Neptune, NJ: Loizeaux Brothers, 1985.

———. *Addresses on the First and Second Epistles of Thessalonians*. New York: Loizeaux Brothers, 1947.

Karleen, Paul. *The Pre-Wrath Rapture of the Church—Is It Biblical?* Langhorne, PA: BF Press, 1991.

————. "Evaluating the Pre-Wrath Rapture of the Church," *Voice* magazine, January/February 1991 (published by Grandville Printing, Grandville, Michigan, and is the official organ of Independent Fundamental Churches of America).

LaHaye, Tim. *The Beginning of the End.* Wheaton, IL: Tyndale House Publishers, Inc., 1991.

————. *How to Study Bible Prophecy for Yourself.* Eugene, OR: Harvest House Publishers, 1990.

————. *Revelation Unveiled.* Grand Rapids, MI: Zondervan Publishing House, 1999.

Lindsey, Hal. *The Rapture.* New York: Bantam Books, 1983.

Ludwigson, R. *Simplified Classroom Notes on Prophecy.* Wheaton, IL: Litho, 1951.

Mayhue, Richard. *Snatched Before the Storm! A Case for Pretribulationism.* Winona Lake, IN: BMH Books, 1980.

Pierce, Robert. *The Rapture Cult.* Signal Mountain, TN: Signal Point Press, n.d.

Rosenthal, Marvin. *The Pre-Wrath Rapture of the Church.* Nashville: Thomas Nelson Publishers, 1990.

Ryrie, Charles. *The Basis of the Premillennial Faith.* New York: Loizeaux Brothers, 1953.

Sandeen, Ernest. *The Roots of Fundamentalism, British and American Millenarianism* 1800–1930. Chicago: University of Chicago Press, 1970.

Silver, Jesse. *The Lord's Return, Seen in History and in Scripture As Pre-Millennial and Imminent.* New York: Fleming H. Revell Company, 1914.

Stanton, Gerald. *Kept from the Hour.* Miami Springs, FL: Schoettle Publishing Co., Inc., 1991.

Stedman, Ray. Personal correspondence, July 18, 1991.

Sumner, Robert. "Did Dr. Ironside Change His Position?" *The Biblical Evangelist*, May 13, 1983.

Walvoord, John. *The Blessed Hope and the Tribulation.* Grand Rapids, MI: Zondervan Publishing House, 1976.

————. *The Millennial Kingdom.* Grand Rapids, MI: Zondervan Publishing House, 1959.

————. *The Rapture Question.* Grand Rapids, MI: Zondervan Publishing House, 1979.

Weber, Timothy. *Living in the Shadow of the Second Coming.* Chicago: University of Chicago Press, 1987.

Notes

Chapter Two—Translated—Snatched—Raptured!

1. Charles Ryrie, *The Basis of the Premillennial Faith* (New York: Loizeaux Brothers, 1953), 29.

2. "Then Martha, as soon as she heard that Jesus was coming, went and met Him, but Mary was sitting in the house. Then Martha said to Jesus, 'Lord, if You had been here, my brother would not have died. But even now I know that whatever You ask of God, God will give You.' Jesus said to her, 'Your brother will rise again.' Martha said to Him, 'I know that he will rise again in the resurrection at the last day.' Jesus said to her, 'I am the resurrection and the life. He who believes in Me, though he may die, he shall live. And whoever lives and believes in Me shall never die. Do you believe this?' She said to Him, 'Yes, Lord, I believe that You are the Christ, the Son of God, who is to come into the world' " (John 11:20-27).

3. Grant Jeffrey, *Apocalypse* (Toronto, ON: Frontier Research Publications, 1992), 85-94.

Chapter Three—Kept from the Hour

1. Editor, *Our Hope Magazine* (August 1950), 86. (For a more complete study of this, see Appendix A.)

2. Dr. Gerald B. Stanton, *Kept from the Hour* (Miami Springs, FL: Schoettle Publishing Co., Inc., 1991), 44-45.

3. Those wishing further confirmation, see Stanton, *Kept from the Hour*, 70-91.

Chapter Four—The Great Tribulation

1. For further study, see Tim LaHaye, *Revelation Unveiled* (Grand Rapids, MI: Zondervan Publishing House, 1999) and *How to Study Bible Prophecy for Yourself* (Eugene, OR: Harvest House Publishers, 1990).

Chapter Five—Blessed or Blasted Hope?

1. Tim LaHaye, *The Beginning of the End* (Wheaton, IL: Tyndale House Publishers, Inc., 1991).

Chapter Six—Who Says It's Obscure?

1. We do not have space to consider all seven churches. For that, please see Tim LaHaye, *Revelation Unveiled* (Grand Rapids, MI: Zondervan Publishing House, 1999).

Chapter Seven—The Glorious Appearing

1. For other Old Testament references to Christ's coming with His saints to set up His kingdom, see Psalm 72, Isaiah 24, Isaiah 40:4-10, and Daniel 2:44-45.

2. For additional New Testament teachings on the subject, read Matthew 13:38-43,47-50; Matthew 24:25; Mark 13; Luke 12:35-36; Luke 17; Luke 18:1-8; Luke 19:12-27; and Luke 21.

Chapter Eight—What Are the Options?

1. Hal Lindsey, *The Rapture* (New York: Bantam Books, 1983), 30.

Chapter Nine—The Case Against a Mid-Tribulation Rapture

1. Norman B. Harrison, *The End—Rethinking the Revelation: The Rapture: Pre-, Mid-, or Post-Tribulation?* (Minneapolis, MN: The Harrison Service, 1941), 31.

2. Dr. Gerald B. Stanton, *Kept from the Hour* (Miami Springs, FL: Schoettle Publishing Co., Inc., 1991), 117.

3. Ibid., 188.

4. Dr. John F. Walvoord, *The Rapture Question* (Grand Rapids, MI: Zondervan Publishing House, 1979), 123.

5. Stanton, 197-98.

Chapter Ten—The Case Against a Post-Tribulation Rapture

1. Dr. John F. Walvoord, *The Blessed Hope and the Tribulation, A Historical and Biblical Study of Posttribulationism* (Grand Rapids, MI: Zondervan Publishing House, 1976), 12-13.

2. Ibid., 13-14.

3. Ibid., 17.

4. Dr. John F. Walvoord, *The Rapture Question* (Grand Rapids, MI: Zondervan Publishing House, 1979), 131-32.

5. For further details, see *The Blessed Hope and the Tribulation* and *The Rapture Question*, both by John F. Walvoord, and *Kept from the Hour* by Dr. Gerald B. Stanton.

6. Richard L. Mayhue, *Snatched Before the Storm! A Case for Pretribulationism* (Winona Lake, IN: BMH Books, 1980), 13.

7. Dr. Gerald B. Stanton, *Kept from the Hour* (Miami Springs, FL: Schoettle Publishing Co., Inc., 1991), 250.

8. Ibid., 161.

9. Ibid., 163-64.

Chapter Eleven—The Pre-Tribulation Rapture: Believe It!

1. Dr. John F. Walvoord, *The Blessed Hope and the Tribulation: A Historical and Biblical Study of Posttribulationism* (Grand Rapids, MI: Zondervan Publishing House, 1976), 167.

2. Ibid., 164.

3. Ibid., 166.

4. Ibid., 159.

5. Ibid., 160.

6. Richard L. Mayhue, *Snatched Before the Storm! A Case for Pretribulationism* (Winona Lake, IN: BMH Books, 1980), 13-14.

7. Ibid., 165.

8. Dr. Robert Sumner, "Did Dr. Ironside Change His Position?" *The Biblical Evangelist* (May 13, 1983), 11.

Chapter Twelve—Target Number One

1. Floyd Saunders Elmore, "A Critical Examination of the Doctrine of the Two Peoples of God in John Nelson Darby," dissertation presented to the faculty of the Department of Systematic Theology, Dallas Theological Seminary, May 1990 (Ann Arbor, MI: UMI, 1991), 1.

2. Dr. H.A. Ironside, *A Historical Sketch of the Brethren Movement* (Neptune, NJ: Loizeaux Brothers, 1985), 98.

3. Ibid., 81.

4. Elmore, 12.

5. Ibid., 13.

6. Ibid., 13. Taken from Darby's *Letters*, 2:310.

7. Thomas D. Ice, "A Short History of Dispensationalism, Part II," *Dispensational Distinctives*, vol. 1, no. 2 (March/April 1991).

8. R.A. Huebner, *Precious Truths Revived and Defended Through J.N. Darby* (Morganville, NJ: Present Truth Publishers, 1991), 19, quoting J.N. Darby's *Letters of J.N. Darby* (new ed., 3 vols.), 3:298.

9. Ibid., 76.

10. Thomas D. Ice, "The Origin of the Pre-Trib Rapture, Part I" *Biblical Perspectives*, (January/February 1989), 6.

11. Huebner, 77.

12. R.A. Huebner, *The Truth of the Pre-Tribulation Rapture Recovered* (Morganville, NJ: Present Truth Publishers, 1982), 35.

13. Ice, 2-3.

14. Ice, 3.

15. Huebner, *Precious Truths Revived and Defended*.

16. Thomas D. Ice, "The Origin of the Pre-Trib Rapture, Part II," *Biblical Perspectives*, (March/April 1989), 5-6.

17. Ibid.

18. Huebner, *Precious Truths Revived and Defended*, 95.

19. St. Victorinus, Bishop of Petau, "The Writings of Tertullianus," trans. R.E. Wallis, *Commentary on the Apocalypse of the Blessed John*, vol. III, published by T. Clark, 1870, 428.

Chapter Thirteen—A Case Study in Slander

1. John L. Bray, *The Origin of the Pre-Tribulation Rapture Teaching* (Lakeland, FL: John L. Bray Ministry, Inc., 1982), 25. (John L. Bray Ministry, Inc., P.O. Box 90129, Lakeland, Florida 33804).

2. Dr. Robert Sumner, editor, *The Biblical Evangelist* (May 13, 1983), 1, 9.

3. Dr. Ray C. Stedman, personal correspondence, July 18, 1991.

4. Sumner, 10-11.

5. Ibid., 11.

6. Dr. H.A. Ironside, *Addresses on the First and Second Epistles of Thessalonians* (New York: Loizeaux Brothers, 1947), 53-54.

7. Sumner, 9.

8. Ibid.

Chapter Fourteen—MacPherson's Vendetta

1. Dr. Gerald B. Stanton, *Kept from the Hour* (Miami Springs, FL: Schoettle Publishing Co., Inc., 1991), 326-28.

2. Ibid., 328-29.

3. Ibid., 329.

4. Ibid., 331.

5. Dr. John F. Walvoord, *The Rapture Question* (Grand Rapids, MI: Zondervan Publishing House, 1979), 152.

6. Ibid., 153-54.

7. Dr. John F. Walvoord, *The Blessed Hope and the Tribulation* (Grand Rapids, MI: Zondervan Publishing House, 1976), 47.

8. Walvoord, *The Rapture Question*, 154-55.

9. Gary North, "Publisher's Foreword," in Greg L. Bahnsen and Kenneth L. Gentry, Jr., *House Divided: The Break-up of Dispensational Theology* (Tyler, TX: Institute for Christian Economics, 1989), p. XXXV.

10. Roy A. Huebner, *Precious Truths Revived and Defended Through J.N. Darby,* vol. 1 (Morganville, NJ: Present Truth Publishers, 1991), 163-64.

11. John L. Bray, *The Origin of the Pre-Tribulation Rapture Teachings* (Lakeland, FL: John L. Bray Ministry, 1982), 20-21.

12. Ibid., 23.

13. Ibid.

14. Dr. Thomas Ice, "Why the Doctrine of the Pretribulational Rapture Did Not Begin with Margaret MacDonald," *Bibliotheca Sacra,* vol. 47, num. 586 (April-June 1990), p. 156.

15. Ibid., p. 156, f.n. 7.

16. Dr. Thomas Ice, "The Origin of the Pretrib Rapture," Part I, *Biblical Perspectives,* vol. II, num. 1 (January-February 1989), p. 4-5.

Chapter Fifteen—The Pre-Wrath Rapture Myth

1. Marvin Rosenthal, *The Pre-Wrath Rapture of the Church* (Nashville: Thomas Nelson Publishers, 1990).

2. Ibid., 293.

3. Dr. Gerald B. Stanton, "A Critique of the Pre-Wrath Rapture Theory," *Biblical Perspectives,* vol. IV, nos. 1, 2 (January/February 1991).

4. Ibid., 6.

5. Dr. James O. Combs, "My Opinion of Marvin Rosenthal's Pre-Wrath Rapture," *Baptist Bible Tribune,* October 24, 1990, 14.

6. Dave Hunt, "'Pre-Wrath' or 'Pre-Trib' Rapture?" *The Omega-Letter* (January 1991), 17-18.

7. Dr. Paul Karleen, *The Pre-Wrath Rapture of the Church—Is It Biblical?* (Langhorne, PA: BF Press, 1991).

8. Dr. Paul Karleen, "Evaluating the Pre-Wrath Rapture of the Church," *Voice* magazine (January/February 1991), 9-10, 13. Published by Grandville Printing, Grandville, Michigan, this is the official organ of Independent Fundamental Churches of America.

9. Theodore W. Ertle, book review of Marvin Rosenthal's *The Pre-Wrath Rapture of the Church* (Nashville: Thomas Nelson Publishers, 1990) in *The Baptist Bulletin* (December 1990), 14.

10. Stanton, 1-3.

11. Ibid., 2-3.

12. Ibid., 7.

13. Ibid., 8.

14. Ibid. A more expanded review is found in Stanton's book *Kept from the Hour* on pages 374-400. It was originally published in *Bibliotheca Sacra* (January/March 1991), 90-111.

Chapter Sixteen—The Most Absurd Charge of All

1. A similar attack was launched by Joseph M. Caufield in 1984 in his book *The Incredible Scofield and His Book*. This was carefully answered by Dallas Seminary professor Dr. John D. Hannah in the July/September 1990 issue of *Bibliotheca Sacra*.

2. Robert L. Pierce, *The Rapture Cult* (Signal Mountain, TN: Signal Point Press, n.d.), 35.

3. Ibid.

4. Ibid.

5. Ibid.

6. Ibid., 38.

7. Ibid., 39.

8. Ibid., 41.

9. Ibid., 48.

10. Ibid.

11. Ibid.

12. Ibid., 49.

13. Ibid., 50-51.

14. Ibid., 49.

Chapter Seventeen—Why Do They Do It?

1. J.N. Darby, *The Hopes of the Church of God, In Connection with the Destiny of the Jews and the Nations,* lectures delivered Geneva, 1840 (London: G. Morris, n.d.), 24.

2. Dr. Robert Sumner, "Did Dr. Ironside Change His Position?" *The Biblical Evangelist* (May 13, 1983), 9.

3. Thomas D. Ice, "Did J.N. Darby Believe in the Pretrib Rapture by 1827?" *Dispensational Distinctives,* vol. 1, no. 6 (November/December 1991), 2.

4. Ibid.

Appendix B: Two Keys to Understanding Prophecy

1. *The Presbyterian Journal,* "Illegitimate Hermeneutics," no author given (September 6, 1978).

2. Timothy P. Weber, *Living in the Shadow of the Second Coming* (Chicago: The University of Chicago Press, 1987), 232-33.

Other Prophecy Books
by Tim LaHaye

Are We Living in the End Times? (Tyndale House)

Charting the End Times (coauthored with Thomas Ice, Harvest House)

Revelation Unveiled (Zondervan)

The Tim LaHaye Prophecy Study Bible (AMG Publishers)

Understanding Bible Prophecy for Yourself (Harvest House)

Prophetic Novels Coauthored
with Jerry B. Jenkins

The Left Behind® Series
Left Behind
Tribulation Force
Nicolae
Soul Harvest
Apollyon
Assassins
The Indwelling
The Mark
Desecration
(five additional books to come)

Left Behind: The Kids®

18 books as of September 2001,
with more to come